Clinical Manual of Psychiatry and Law

Clinical Manual of Psychiatry and Law

Robert I. Simon, M.D.

Clinical Professor of Psychiatry and
Director, Program in Psychiatry and Law,
Georgetown University School of Medicine, Washington, D.C.

Daniel W. Shuman, J.D.

M.D. Anderson Foundation Endowed Professorship in Health Law,
Professor of Law, Dedman School of Law,
Southern Methodist University, Dallas, Texas

American
Psychiatric
Publishing, Inc.

Washington, DC
London, England

Books published by American Psychiatric Publishing, Inc. (APPI), represent the views and opinions of the individual authors and do not necessarily represent the policies and opinions of APPI or the American Psychiatric Association.

To buy 25–99 copies of any APPI title, you are eligible for a 20% disco APPI Customer Service at appi@psych.org or 800-368-5777. To buy 1 copies, please e-mail us at bulksales@psych.org for a price quote.

Copyright © 2007 American Psychiatric Publishing, Inc.

WM
33
AA1
S5ca
2007

Manufactured in the United States of America on acid-free paper
11   10   09   08   07   5   4   3   2   1
First Edition

Typeset in Adobe's Formata and AGaramond.

American Psychiatric Publishing, Inc., 1000 Wilson Boulevard, Arlington, VA 22209-3901, www.appi.org

Library of Congress Cataloging-in-Publication Data
Simon, Robert I.
   Clinical manual of psychiatry and law / by Robert I. Simon, Daniel W. Shuman. — 1st ed.
      p. ; cm.
   Includes bibliographical references and index.
   ISBN 1-58562-249-4 (pbk. : alk. paper)
   1. Forensic psychiatry. I. Shuman, Daniel W. II. Title.
   [DNLM: 1. Psychiatry—legislation & jurisprudence—United States. 2. Liability, Legal—United States. 3. Patient Rights—United States. 4. Professional-Patient Relations—United States. WM 33 AA1 S5ca 2007]
   RA1151.S56 2007
   614'.15—dc22   2006024578

British Library Cataloguing in Publication Data
A CIP record is available from the British Library.

Contents

To our grandchildren,
Justin and Nicholas Simon
Jasper and Alistair Stockman-Simon
Maya and Ella Blecher

Acknowledgments

We want to thank Dr. Robert E. Hales for providing us the opportunity and encouragement to write the "Clinical Manual of Psychiatry and Law." No book can be written without the help of others. The editorial assistance of Ms. Julia Bozzolo; the legal research assistance by then third-year law student and now attorney-at-law, Ms. Britt Darwin; and the administrative assistance of Ms. Carol Westrick were invaluable to the production of this book. We thank them for their assistance.

Preface

Aworking knowledge of the law that regulates the practice of medicine and psychiatry in particular assists clinicians to provide good care to their patients and avoid unnecessary and counter-productive defensive practices. Clinicians cannot be expected to be as knowledgeable of the law as lawyers, but they do need to understand how the law and psychiatry interact in various common, clinical situations. This understanding should be a core competency for every clinician. To that end, a forensic psychiatrist and a professor of law with experience in psychiatry and law have teamed together to assist clinicians on how to partner clinical interventions with legal requirements applicable to patient care. In most instances, because the law derives its requirements from professional practice, good psychiatry and the law are complementary. Sometimes, however, the provision of good clinical care seems to be at cross purposes with legal requirements. This may be because psychiatrists misunderstand what the law requires of them and this is a matter which we hope this book will remedy. Other times, legal requirements may be at cross purposes with the provision of good clinical care. This may be because lawyers and judges misunderstand psychiatry—also a matter which we hope this book will remedy. Psychiatrists may be better able to address legal misunderstandings of psychiatry by understanding the legal process and what it seeks to accomplish.

Robert I. Simon, M.D.
Daniel W. Shuman, J.D.

Psychiatry and the Law

Overview of the Law

Although often overshadowed by pronouncements that frustrate psychiatrists and other mental health professionals, such as precipitate deinstitutionalization or limitations on treatment of seriously ill individuals, the law also plays an important protective role in the life of clinical psychiatrists. The law protects and enforces psychiatrists' rights to reimbursement for services rendered—for example, when psychiatrists and other physicians have claimed that managed care companies unfairly reduced their reimbursements, the law has provided a forum to be heard and to enforce preexisting agreements (Colliver 2005). The law also protects and enforces psychiatrists' rights to obtain and retain hospital staff privileges—for example, when psychiatrists and other physicians have claimed that their privileges have been denied or terminated in violation of antitrust law, the law has provided them a forum to be heard and to scrutinize the privilege requirements (Jefferson Parish Hosp. Dist. No. 2 v. Hyde 1984). The law protects the right of qualified psychiatrists to practice medicine—for example, when the state seeks to revoke a psychiatrist's or other physician's license to practice medicine, the law has required a substantial evidentiary showing (Nguyen v. State Dep't of Health 2001; Goldberg v. Department of Professional Regulation 2002).

Clinical psychiatrists, like other physicians, are the beneficiaries of a host of rights and privileges recognized in our legalistic society. Thinking about the law exclusively as a threat ignores the opportunities it provides to empower and protect psychiatrists, yet it is undeniable that a central legal focus of clinical psychiatrists is the risk of malpractice litigation.

A malpractice suit is a type of tort action. A *tort* is a civil wrong (a noncriminal or non-contract-related wrong) committed by an individual or entity (defendant) who has caused injury to a second individual (plaintiff) (Dobbs 2000; Keeton et al. 1984). A *tort claim* is a demand for an award of damages for the injuries that have occurred as the result of the defendant's tortious conduct. *Medical malpractice* is a tort committed as a result of negligence by physicians. (For additional legal definitions, see Appendix B, "Glossary of Legal Terms".)

Psychiatric malpractice is a growing area of tort law. This growth reflects both the progress made in psychiatric care and the psychological sophistication of the public and the judiciary. As society increases its use of psychiatric services, it manifests a greater willingness to hold psychiatrists accountable for the care they provide.

Malpractice Claims in the Managed Care Era

Malpractice claims are often brought when bad outcomes combine with bad feelings (Appelbaum and Gutheil 1991). A good doctor–patient relationship is an important protection against being sued. Ideally, managed care organizations (MCOs) are designed to provide quality medical care in a cost-effective manner. Good clinical care may be undermined, however, by negative incentives and other managed care cost-cutting policies that generate role conflicts for clinicians asked to be both patient advocates and guardians of society's resources (Pellegrino 1986). These competing tensions can jeopardize the doctor–patient relationship and lead to the provision of substandard care.

Managed care has transformed the relationship between psychiatrist and patient. Psychiatrists are now treating chronically, severely ill patients for shorter periods of time. Much less time is available to develop a therapeutic alliance with the patient. Split treatment, in which the psychiatrist prescribes medication while a nonmedical therapist conducts psychotherapy, is common. The psychiatrist usually shares the liability burden in a split-treatment situation if a malpractice claim is brought.

Other factors can heighten liability risks. Psychiatrists who have high-volume practices or who practice at a number of locations are at increased risk of being sued. The psychiatrist who sees more than 25 patients in a single day is at a disproportionately increased risk of being sued (American Psychiatric Association 1996). Although the psychiatrist with a high-volume practice has a greater chance of encountering a patient who will institute litigation in response to a bad outcome, increased liability exposure appears to be more a function of the decreased time spent with the patient than the nature of the patient. Supervision of other professionals also increases a psychiatrist's risk of being sued. Psychiatrists are increasingly providing primary care, managing patients with a variety of acute medical illnesses as well as chronic conditions such as hypertension or diabetes. Psychiatrists are also specializing in geriatric pharmacology, adolescent addiction medicine, pain management, treatment of dissociative identity disorder, and treatment of adult children of alcoholics (American Psychiatric Association 1996). Such specialization increases the risk of malpractice suits, particularly if psychiatrists practice outside their areas of training or expertise. The occasions for bad feelings and bad outcomes are many (e.g., poor communication, a perceived lack of caring or interest, unavailability during critical events, a perceived unresponsiveness to the patient's particular treatment needs) (Levinson 1994). All of these factors, combined with inept tort reform, have created a risky litigation environment for psychiatrists.

Patients requiring intensive care may not be treatable under the MCO restrictions of their health care coverage. These patients should be informed of the need for more treatment than is provided under their managed care plans. For example, a patient with borderline personality disorder may require ongoing treatment to prevent recurrent crises and depression. MCOs generally limit or deny payment for services but do not deny the actual services. It is the clinician who determines the patient's treatment needs. The psychiatrist may contract to treat the patient outside the plan (if permitted by the MCO) or make an appropriate referral.

Most MCOs and their peer reviewers are effectively immune from liability under state tort law (Stone 1995). The risk of state tort claims against managed care companies for the negligent performance of utilization review has been eliminated by the Employee Retirement Income Security Act of 1974 ([ERISA] 1991). ERISA preempts state laws and prohibits negligence claims in cases against employer-sponsored health plans. Recently, the U.S. Supreme Court resolved any lingering questions and held that ERISA preempts state law claims against MCOs for negligence in coverage decisions (Aetna Health, Inc. v. Davila 2004).

Managed care contracts that contain *hold harmless* and indemnification clauses are a source of potential trouble for psychiatrists and other mental health professionals. These clauses attempt to insulate MCOs from malpractice judgments against clinicians while also placing them in the position of acting as insurers for third-party payers. Clinicians should obtain legal counsel before signing any contract that contains such clauses.

Malpractice and Psychiatry: Incidence

There has been a steady rise in malpractice litigation against psychiatrists and other mental health professionals since the early 1970s. In 1975, the annual incidence of claims against psychiatrists was about 1 in 45, or approximately 2.2% (American Medical Association 1975). In the 1980s, a psychiatrist's chance of being sued in any single year was 1 in 25 (4%; Perr 1983). Thus the rate of occurrence nearly doubled. Through 1995, however, the incidence increased to approximately 1 in every 12 psychiatrists (American Psychiatric Association 1996). In some states, psychiatrists were sued at the rate of 1 in 6 every year. The rising incidence of malpractice claims against psychiatrists is expected to maintain its current pace. The creative expansion of legal theories of liability against psychiatrists on which relief may be granted will likely continue well into the twenty-first century.

The incidence of claims against psychiatrists still remains much lower than that of claims against other medical specialists. Although the potential for malpractice lawsuits remains high for psychiatrists who treat suicidal and violent patients, the success rate of plaintiffs in these and other malpractice actions is only 2–3 of every 10 litigated claims.

Malpractice Litigation: The Basics

Breach of Contract and Other Legal Actions

Before the more common legal claim of medical negligence against psychiatrists is discussed, it is important to mention that damage claims against psychiatrists may also result from a breach of contract or from an intentional tort.

A successful *breach of contract* claim can occur if a patient undertakes treatment based on an agreement in which the psychiatrist promises a result and fails to deliver. Liability in such cases is premised on the breach of a promise, not the quality of care provided, and can easily be obviated by avoiding promised cures.

In contrast with *negligence*, a voluntary act that is unreasonably risky, an *intentional tort* is a voluntary act that purposefully causes a harm or offense. Common examples of intentional torts include battery, assault, false imprisonment, and infliction of emotional distress. Another type of claim may be based on violations of a patient's civil rights pursuant to federal and state law (e.g., discriminatory treatment practices against institutionalized patients).

Medical Negligence

Negligence is conduct that causes harm through carelessness rather than by design or purpose. The fundamental failure underlying a malpractice action is that of medical negligence. Ordinary negligence in a medical malpractice claim is defined in most states as the failure to use the skill and learning that would ordinarily be used by a member of the defendant's profession in similar circumstances (Tendai v. Missouri State Bd. of Registration for the Healing Arts 2005). It occurs when the psychiatrist does or fails to do something he or she should have done (*omission*) or, conversely, when the psychiatrist does something he or she should not have done (*commission*) as dictated by customary professional practice.

There are four essential elements to a medical negligence claim, and although these criteria were originally created by the physician–patient relationship, they are nonetheless applicable to all professional relationships, including the psychiatrist–patient relationship (Dobbs 2000). First, the doctor must owe a legal duty to the patient. Second, the doctor must have failed to conform to the required standard created for those practicing in the particular area of medicine, resulting in what is commonly known as a breach of duty. Third, the injury must have resulted from the deviation to the required standard. Finally, there must be a reasonably close causal connection between the physician's conduct and the alleged harm (see Flores v. Center for Spinal Evaluation and Rehabilitation 1993).

Duty.   A *duty* is an obligation recognized by the law that requires a person to adhere to a certain standard of conduct to protect others from unreasonable risks (Gregory v. Kilbride 2002). In the psychiatric setting, a duty is created when the psychiatrist explicitly or implicitly accepts responsibility to treat a patient.

Standard of reasonable care.   The law holds physicians—including psychiatrists—to a standard of professional care when dealing with their patients. The standard of care most commonly applied in medical negligence cases is determined by comparing the degree of skill and learning customarily used by members of the profession in good standing in the same type of practice or specialty with the actions of the defendant psychiatrist (see Dodd v. Sparks Reg'l Med. Ctr. 2005). There is a trend, however, still representing a minority of states, that rejects the customary practice standard in favor of a "reasonable physician," which invites the courts to play a more active role in setting the standard of care (Peters 2000).

As in all malpractice cases, proof of the standard of care and of any alleged deviation usually must be established by expert testimony. In most states, the psychiatric expert is required to testify about what a qualified psychiatrist would have done in a similar situation. In cases where the alleged substandard conduct is so obvious (e.g., leaving a surgical instrument in the patient's chest), the courts have held that no expert testimony is required to prove that the conduct was negligent. With more than 450 types of therapy identified and innovation a common requisite to treating patients with difficult illnesses, courts have been restrained in finding a psychiatrist negligent simply because his or her treatment methods differ from those of mainstream psychiatrists. Policies and standards established by various national organizations such as the American Psychiatric Association, by the professional literature, and by the acceptance of the different methods of at least a respected minority of professionals may protect the innovative psychiatrist (Simon 1993). Reflecting professional norms of practice, courts have relied upon ethical precepts to establish the standard of care (Mazza v. Huffaker 1983). Finally, common sense goes a long way in distinguishing between an innovative treatment approach and a deviation in the requisite standard of care.

Causation.   When a psychiatrist deviates from a standard of care in the diagnosis and treatment of a patient and the patient alleges damage, a malpractice action will not succeed unless the damage was caused by the deviation from the standard of care. The law divides causation into two conjunctive categories (i.e., the plaintiff must satisfy both aspects of causation to prevail): cause-in-fact and proximate cause (legal cause). *Cause-in-fact* is commonly expressed by the "but for" rule and asks the question: but for the negligent conduct of the psychiatrist, would the patient have been injured? If the injury would have occurred without regard to the psychiatrist's substandard conduct, the "but for" rule is not satisfied and the malpractice claim should be dismissed.

In addition to the cause-in-fact requirement, the defendant's act or omission must also be the *proximate cause* of the injury. Proximate, or legal, cause exists when the nexus between the defendant's negligent conduct and the plaintiff's injuries is not too attenuated. The test for proximate cause is often expressed in terms of foreseeability. Thus the defendant psychiatrist is not necessarily responsible for all the consequences caused by his or her wrongful actions but rather only for those that could reasonably be anticipated or foreseen at the time of those actions. If the psychiatrist's actions are too remotely related to the patient's injury, then the psychiatrist's actions were not the proximate cause of the injury. For example, if a psychiatrist prescribed an unlimited amount of an antipsychotic drug for a patient, knowing that the particular patient had attempted to overdose on medication in the past, and the patient once again overdosed and died, then by prescribing the drug the psychiatrist's negligence was the proximate cause of death. On the other hand, if a neighbor stole the patient's prescription, overdosed, and died, then the psychiatrist's negligence is not the proximate cause of that death. Even though the patient would not have acquired the drugs but for the psychiatrist's wrongful act, the neighbor's intervening actions were not foreseeable. Proximate cause seeks a proportionate limit to the consequences of negligence for which the defendant is responsible.

Compensatory, Nominal, and Punitive Damages

If a patient is successful in establishing liability in a claim against a psychiatrist, the damages awarded should be commensurate with the injury sustained. The injury may be physical, psychological, or both. There are generally three types of damages: compensatory, nominal, and punitive. In a successful malpractice action, the plaintiff is entitled to an award of *compensatory damages*, which represent the amount of compensation needed to restore the plaintiff, as closely as possible, to his or her preaccident condition. In some extreme situations, *punitive damages* may be awarded. In a malpractice action, by statute or case law, punitive damages are allowable only when the defendant's conduct is shown to be willful or wanton (Owens-Illinois, Inc. v. Zenobia 1992). The purpose of punitive damages is to punish the wrongdoer rather than to compensate the victim. Mere negligence or gross negligence is insufficient to merit an award of punitive damages. *Nominal damages* are awarded when plaintiffs experience no actual harm or loss but only a technical injury to their legal rights, as in the case of a battery that causes no physical or emotional harm. Nominal damages are rare in malpractice suits.

Major Areas of Liability

Figure 1–1 illustrates the most common categories of allegation in malpractice claims against psychiatrists from 1999 through 2003, according to Professional Risk Management Services, Inc.

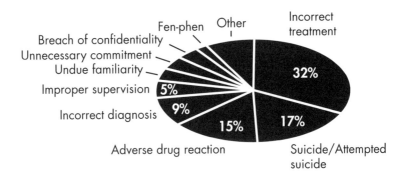

Figure 1–1.   Malpractice claims against psychiatrists: 1999–2003.
Source.   Professional Risk Management: "The Psychiatrists' Program: The American Psychiatric Association–Endorsed Psychiatrists' Liability Insurance Program." Washington, DC, 2004.

Defenses

Even though a plaintiff may establish the elements of a valid malpractice claim, he or she may nonetheless be denied recovery if the defendant psychiatrist successfully asserts an *affirmative defense* or a general defense that negates an essential element of the plaintiff's claim. The effect of an affirmative defense is that even if the plaintiff can prove that the defendant acted in the manner alleged, the plaintiff is not entitled to prevail for other affirmative reasons. For example, all civil claims are subject to a statute of limitations requiring that legal action be commenced within a prescribed period of time after the discovery or occurrence of the allegedly negligent act. If the claim is filed after the statute of limitations runs out and the defendant pleads and proves this affirmative defense, the suit is barred without regard to the wrongfulness of the defendant's conduct or the gravity of the harm it caused (King 1986). The time within which a lawsuit can be brought is governed by the laws of the state where the suit is being brought (Simon 1992).

Other general defenses may negate essential elements of the plaintiff's claim. For example, proof of the use of reasonable professional judgment negates the assertion that the defendant violated the standard of care (Centeno v. City of New York 1976). The credibility of this defense depends on the physician's compliance with the standard of care as documented by his or her own records. For example, in Centeno v. City of New York (1976), the court ruled that the decision to release a patient from the hospital and to place the patient on convalescent outpatient status prior to the patient's suicide based on the considered professional judgment of the attending physician was not a negligent act but was based on reasonable medical judgment.

Clinical Management of Legal Issues

Standard of Care in Managed Care Settings

Standard of care should be distinguished from *quality* of care. Psychiatrists are required to practice according to acceptable standards of care. The *standard of care* is a duty owed by psychiatrists to their patients. *Quality of care* refers to the adequacy of the total care the patient receives from psychiatrists, the treatment team, other mental health providers, reviewers, coordinators of care, and payers. Quality of care is also substantially influenced by patients' health care decisions and the allocation and availability of psychiatric services. The quality of care provided patients may fall below, equal, or even exceed the standard of care. For example, a short hospital stay might be sufficient to treat a patient who is transitorily suicidal, but a similar stay could represent substandard care for a patient with schizophrenia and command hallucinations dictating violence toward others. Short hospitalizations are not appropriate for every patient. Quality care for one patient is not quality care for all patients.

Conflict results when the quality of care that patients receive under managed care falls below the professional standard of care that psychiatrists are required to uphold. Psychiatrists must nonetheless provide competent diagnosis, treatment, and patient management. Although MCOs can establish quality-of-care policies and decide what level of care they will financially support, the standard of care is determined by how the average psychiatrist practices under the same or similar circumstances (Hoge 1996). Psychiatrists are understandably worried that courts will not take into account resource limitations imposed by managed care but will continue to apply the more expansive standards of care established under the traditional insurance system (Kuder and Kuntz 1996).

The standard of care in psychiatry has always been diverse and in flux. This is entirely appropriate, given that the causes of many mental illnesses are unknown and therapeutic innovation offers the hope of finding new and effective treatments (Simon 1993). Such a view is therapeutically ambitious and humanistic. On the other hand, MCO treatment policies are cost driven and therapeutically restrictive according to criteria of medical necessity. The meaning of the term *medically necessary* is elusive; it is a proprietary term that governs payment decisions under various private and public medical coverage systems (Simon 1998). Psychiatrists who are in doubt about the quality of care provided under managed care policies must look to the patient's best interests, uphold their professional and ethical responsibilities to patients, and accept the economic consequences if necessary (Abrams 1993). Most physicians support cost containment, efficiency, and accountability measures, provided that these measures do not interfere with the doctor–patient relationship and the provision of good clinical care (Simon 1987).

Clinical Risk Management

Clinical risk management is defined as the combining of professional expertise and knowledge of the patient with a clinically useful understanding of the legal issues governing psychiatric practice. Clinical risk management is patient centered, supporting the therapeutic alliance and treatment process (see Table 1–1). The purpose of clinical risk management is to provide optimal care for the patient and only secondarily to reduce the risk of legal liability. A clinically useful understanding of the legal requirements governing the practice of psychiatry is essential because it helps guard against unduly defensive practices that can keep the clinician from utilizing a full spectrum of effective treatments.

Some defensive practices are rooted in the best conservative traditions of medicine and are not necessarily reactions to litigation fears. The fundamental principle "first do no harm" is defensive, although it originates from the physician's basic concern for the patient's welfare. The use of careful documentation and appropriate consultation represents good clinical practice on behalf of the patient but also provides a shield against litigation. Unfortunately, the unduly defensive psychiatrist may put his or her own welfare first in the course of treating the patient. Clinical risk management is a means for practitioners to achieve greater freedom from destructive fears of litigation. The key is to know when and how to apply defensive measures and, at the very least, to be certain that patients are not harmed by such practices (Simon 1987).

Table 1–1. Basic elements of clinically based risk management

- Patient centered

- Clinically appropriate

- Supportive of treatment and the therapeutic alliance

- Working knowledge of legal regulation of psychiatry

- Clinical management of psychiatric-legal issues

- Wellness, not legal agenda

- "First do no harm" ethic

Source. Reprinted from Simon RI: *Assessing and Managing Suicide Risk: Guidelines for Clinically Based Risk Management.* Washington, DC, American Psychiatric Publishing, 2004, p. 19. Copyright 2004, American Psychiatric Publishing. Used with permission.

Positive and Negative Defensive Psychiatry

In general, *defensive psychiatry* refers to any act or omission that is performed not for the benefit of the patient but solely to avoid malpractice liability or to provide a legal defense against a malpractice claim. Defensive psychiatry comes in two forms—positive and negative—with some psychiatrists practicing both. *Positive* and *negative* do not refer to a value judgment but rather to acts of commission and omission. The positive defensive psychiatrist orders procedures and treatments to prevent or limit liability. These actions may or may not accord with good clinical practice. The negative defensive psychiatrist avoids procedures or treatments out of fear of being sued, even though the patient might benefit from these interventions. Defensive practices do not necessarily shield the psychiatrist against malpractice claims. On the contrary, substandard treatment may result. Thus the unduly defensive psychiatrist may have more litigation exposure.

Destructive Defensive Practices

Examples of defensive psychiatry gone astray are legion. For example, the patient with serious treatment-refractory depression that is unresponsive to drugs may be denied electroconvulsive therapy because of the clinician's unfounded fears of increased liability. The patient experiencing suicidal ruminations who could be treated safely as an outpatient but instead is hospitalized for purely defensive reasons is poorly served. The psychiatrist who prescribes homeopathic dosages of medication in the vain hope of helping the patient without risking any harm abrogates his or her professional and legal duty to provide good clinical care to the patient. The patient is unnecessarily exposed to side effects from the drug without the possibility of receiving any benefit. As a result, he or she may continue to suffer and remain impaired. In another example, duty-to-warn immunity statutes in some states permit psychiatrists to discharge this duty simply by warning an endangered third party and calling the police. Thus more clinically appropriate interventions such as starting or changing medications, scheduling more frequent appointments, or pursuing hospitalization may be overlooked by the clinician who reflexively seeks shelter from legal liability under these statutes.

Beyond Legal Requirements

Effective psychiatric treatment must address the tension between clinical practice and legal requirements. The clinician needs a clear working knowledge of the relevant legal requirements governing professional practice. Maintaining an adequate clinical record can be crucial in the defense of a malpractice suit. This bit of legal knowledge can go a long way toward easing the anxieties of therapists who fear being second-guessed by plaintiffs' experts in a court of law. Yet it is disconcerting to discover how often mental health professionals do not keep even minimally acceptable records.

Whenever a legal issue arises in clinical practice, every opportunity should be taken to turn it to therapeutic account for the patient (Roe and Ronen 2003; Wexler and Winik 1991). For example, the doctrine of informed consent is a legal requirement. However, disclosing information in a clinically supportive manner can also enhance the therapeutic alliance with the patient and turn a technical requirement into a therapeutic experience. Although often confusing in practice, good clinical care is good legal care (Winick 1991).

Psychiatrists have a professional and ethical obligation to provide care to their patients that transcends legal and regulatory standards. Legal standards are minimal by necessity. The role of tort law is to establish society's minimal expectations for reasonable behavior. Physicians, on the other hand, assume professional and ethical obligations to treat patients to the best of their abilities and according to the Hippocratic tradition. For example, the traditional rule of tort law states that a person has no duty to come to the aid of another in distress. A distinct exception to this rule has been created by a number of court decisions and some state statutes that impose a duty on therapists (usually psychiatrists and psychologists) to protect endangered persons from the violent acts of their patients. The psychiatrist, however, does not act in situations in which third parties are endangered by patients just from an obligation to meet the law's requirements. Before these legal duties were imposed, psychiatrists protected others who were endangered by their patients by various clinical means and, when all else failed, through involuntary treatment for violent patients. Similarly, most practitioners maintain a level of confidentiality that far exceeds the current requirements of state and federal statutes.

References

Abrams FR: The doctor with two heads: the patient versus the costs. N Engl J Med 328:975–976, 1993

American Medical Association: Malpractice in Focus. Chicago, IL, American Medical Association, 1975

American Psychiatric Association: Benefacts: a message from the APA-sponsored Professional Liability Insurance Program. Psychiatric News 31 (suppl 8):26, 1996

Appelbaum PS, Gutheil TG: Clinical Handbook of Psychiatry and the Law, 2nd Edition. Baltimore, MD, Williams & Wilkins, 1991, pp 173–174

Colliver V: WellPoint settles suit with doctors. San Francisco Chronicle, July 12, 2005, p D1

Dobbs D: The Law of Torts. St. Paul, MN, West Group, 2000

Hoge SK: APA resource document, 1: the professional responsibilities of psychiatrists in evolving health care systems. Bull Am Acad Psychiatry Law 24:393–406, 1996

Keeton WP (ed): Prosser and Keeton on the Law of Torts, 5th Edition. St. Paul, MN, West Publishing Co., 1984

King JF: The Law of Medical Malpractice in a Nutshell. St Paul, MN, West Publishing, 1986

Kuder AU, Kuntz MBF: Who decides what is medically necessary? in Controversies in Managed Mental Health Care. Edited by Lazarus A. Washington, DC, American Psychiatric Press, 1996, pp 159–177

Levinson W: Physician–patient communication: a key to malpractice prevention. JAMA 272:1619–1620, 1994

Pellegrino ED: Rationing health care: the ethics of medical gatekeeping. J Contemp Health Law Policy 2:23–45, 1986

Perr I: Psychiatric malpractice issues, in Legal Encroachment in Psychiatric Practice. Edited by Rachlin S. San Francisco, CA, Jossey-Bass, 1983, pp 47–59

Peters PG: The quiet demise of deference to custom: malpractice law at the millennium. Wash Lee Law Rev 57:163, 2000

Roe D, Ronen Y: Hospitalization as experienced by the psychiatric patient: a therapeutic jurisprudence perspective. Int J Law Psychiatry 26:317–332, 2003

Simon RI: A clinical philosophy for the (unduly) defensive psychiatrist. Psychiatr Ann 17:197–200, 1987

Simon RI: Clinical risk management of suicidal patients: assessing the unpredictable, in American Psychiatric Press Review of Clinical Psychiatry and the Law, Vol 3. Edited by Simon RI. Washington, DC, American Psychiatric Press, 1992, pp 3–63

Simon RI: Innovative psychiatric therapies and legal uncertainty: a survival guide for clinicians. Psychiatr Ann 23:473–479, 1993

Simon RI: Psychiatrists' duties in discharging sicker and potentially violent inpatients in the managed care era. Psychiatr Serv 49:62–67, 1998

Stone AA: Paradigms, pre-emption, and stages: understanding the transformation of American psychiatry by managed care. Int J Law Psychiatry 18:353–387, 1995

Wexler DB, Winick BJ: Essays in Therapeutic Jurisprudence. Durham, NC, Carolina Academic Press, 1991

Winick BJ: Competency to consent to voluntary hospitalization (a therapeutic jurisprudence analysis of Zinermon v. Burch). Int J Law Psychiatry 14:169–214, 1991

Legal References

Aetna Health, Inc. v Davila, 542 U.S. 200 (2004)

Centeno v City of New York, 48 A.D.2d 812, 369 N.Y.S.2d 710 (1975), aff'd 40 N.Y.2d 932, 389 N.Y.S.2d, 837, 358 N.E.2d 520 (1976)

Dodd v Sparks Reg'l Med. Ctr., S.W.3d (Ark. App., 2005)

Flores v Center for Spinal Evaluation and Rehabilitation, 865 S.W.2d 261 (Texas 1993)

Goldberg v Department of Professional Regulation, 771 N.E.2d 1075 (Ill. App. 2002)

Gregory v Kilbride, 565 S.E.2d 685 (N.C. App. 2002)

Jefferson Parish Hosp. Dist. No. 2 v Hyde, 466 U.S. 2 (1984)

Mazza v Huffaker, 300 S.E.2d 833 (N.C. App., 1983)

Nguyen v State Dep't of Health, 29 P.3d 689 (Wash. 2001)

Owens-Illinois, Inc., v Zenobia, 601 A.2d 633 (Md. 1992)

Tendai v Missouri State Bd. of Registration for the Healing Arts, 161 S.W.3d 358 (Mo. 2005)

Laws

70 Corpus Juris Segundum Physicians and Surgeons § 41 (1967)

Employee Retirement Income Security Act of 1974 (ERISA), 1991. 29 U.S.C.A. §§1001–1461 (1988 and Supp. 1991)

2

The Doctor–Patient Relationship

Overview of the Law

The establishment of the doctor–patient relationship is the legal predicate to the recognition of a professional duty of care owed to a patient. Because a medical malpractice claim demands proof that a doctor breached the duty he or she owed to a patient, the existence of a doctor–patient relationship and the duty of care it demands is a core issue in every malpractice claim. As a general rule, a psychiatrist in private practice is not required to accept anyone who seeks treatment and may choose whomever he or she wishes to treat (American Medical Association 1989; Gross v. Burt 2004). Similarly, psychiatrists have no legal obligation to provide emergency medical care to someone with whom they do not have a preexisting doctor–patient relationship, absent any contractual or statutory obligation (e.g., emergency department). Once a psychiatrist has agreed (explicitly or implicitly) to accept a patient, however, tort law anticipates continuity of care until the relationship is appropriately terminated.

The Legal Foundation for the Doctor–Patient Relationship

The legal foundation for recognizing the existence of a doctor–patient relationship is based on the agreement of the parties. Rather than impose duties that articulate when doctors *should* agree to treat patients, the law imposes duties when doctors *have* agreed to treat patients. The express or implied agreement to treat a patient creates a relationship with corresponding duties and rights for both parties (Oja v. Kin 1998). The doctor's duty of care is not predicated on the payment of a fee and arises even when care is provided gratuitously. It derives from the "agreement" by the physician to render services and the patient's reliance on that expectation.

The duty of care owed by the doctor to the patient as recognized under tort law does not demand that patients be cured but rather that the care not be negligent. Absent specific assurances by the doctor, initiating the professional relationship does not create any guarantee of specific results. Rather, initiation of the relationship implies a promise that the psychiatrist will exercise reasonable care according to the standards of the profession (Brown v. Koulizakis 1985).

When a psychiatrist is performing an evaluation for the benefit of a third party rather than treatment for the benefit of the patient, a doctor–patient relationship is generally not created. When the examination exclusively benefits a third party such as an employer (i.e., preemployment physical), insurance company (i.e., life insurance qualifying examination), or the courts (i.e., independent medical examination), usually no doctor–patient relationship and corresponding tort duty is found, because treatment or diagnosis in contemplation of treatment is not undertaken (State v. Supreme Court of Georgia 2005).

Psychiatrists who owe a duty of care to the patient and employ or supervise other professionals may be held vicariously liable for those other professionals' negligence, despite the absence of proof that the psychiatrist was negligent in care of the patient or in hiring, training, or supervising the employee (Lection v. Dyll 2001). Under the doctrine of *respondeat superior,* psychiatrists are vicariously liable, without regard to their own fault, for their employees' negligent acts in the scope of their employment. Whether the relationship is regarded as employer–employee, to which vicarious liability applies, or an independent contractor, to which vicarious liability does not apply, depends on the right or ability of the psychiatrist to control the other professional (e.g., supervisee or employee; Simons v. Northern P.R. Co.1933).

Fiduciary Role: Avoiding Conflict

One facet of the doctor–patient relationship policed by tort law is that of the *fiduciary* role the doctor is expected to play and the corresponding professional duties that arise (i.e., given the trust a patient places in his or her psychiatrist, a doctor owes duty of trust and candor). A psychiatrist is expected to act in good faith in his or her relations with a patient. This obligation is implicit within the consensual arrangement that gives rise to the relationship and inherent in all psychiatrist–patient relationships as an ethical and legal duty. Persons acting as a fiduciary are not permitted to use the professional relationship for their personal benefit. Thus, for example, psychiatrists must be particularly careful not to exploit transference for their personal gain. Double-agent role problems frequently arise when psychiatrists attempt to serve simultaneously the patient and an agency, institution, or society. These conflicts are examined in greater detail as they arise in the clinical management section of each chapter.

Termination and Abandonment

Once a professional relationship has been created, a psychiatrist is legally required to provide the patient treatment unless or until the relationship is properly terminated (Ricks v. Budge 1947). Improper termination constitutes the tort of abandonment and the risk of malpractice liability for consequential harm. Generally, the psychiatrist–patient relationship may be properly terminated in one of the following ways:

- Mutual agreement of psychiatrist and patient that the psychiatrist's services are no longer needed or useful
- A unilateral act of the patient that indicates a withdrawal from treatment
- A unilateral act of the psychiatrist that terminates treatment and provides a timely opportunity for the patient to obtain alternate care

A psychiatrist is not obligated to provide perpetual care for a patient. If there is no emergency or pending crisis (e.g., threatened suicide or danger to the public), generally a psychiatrist can lawfully terminate treatment by following certain procedures (Table 2–1).

Abandonment—tortiously failing to attend a patient absent the proper termination of the doctor–patient relationship—may be either overt or implied (e.g., failure to attend, monitor, or observe the patient). Many courts have widened the

Table 2–1.   Suggested guidelines for termination of patient treatment

1. Thoroughly discuss treatment termination with the patient.
2. Indicate the following in a letter of termination:
   a. Termination discussion (brief)
   b. Reason for termination
   c. Termination date
   d. Availability for emergencies only until date of termination
   e. Willingness to provide names of other appropriate therapists
   f. Willingness to provide medical records to subsequent therapist
   g. A statement of the need for additional treatment, if appropriate
3. Allow the patient reasonable time to find another therapist (length of time depends on availability of other therapists).
4. Provide the patient's records to the new therapist upon proper authorization by the patient.
5. If the patient requires further treatment, provide the names of other psychiatrists or refer the patient to a local or state psychiatric society for further assistance.
6. If the need for further treatment is recommended, a statement about the potential consequences of not obtaining further treatment should be provided.
7. Send the termination letter certified or restricted registered mail, return receipt requested.

concept of abandonment to include situations in which delay and inattention in providing care caused the patient injury, termed *constructive abandonment* (i.e., as though actual abandonment had occurred [Mains 1985]). For example, in Bolles v. Kinton (1928), the court stated that a physician cannot discharge a case by simply not attending the patient without sufficient notice. Others courts have found abandonment when psychiatrists make themselves inaccessible to patients, particularly if a crisis is occurring or foreseeable. The following have all been construed by the courts as negligent acts amounting to abandonment:

- Failure to provide patients with a way to contact the psychiatrist between sessions
- Failure to maintain reasonable contact with a hospitalized patient
- Failure to provide adequate clinical coverage when away from practice

Clinical Management of Legal Issues

Creation of the Doctor–Patient Relationship

A psychiatrist does not owe a professional duty of care to a person as a patient unless a psychiatrist–patient relationship exists. Once that relationship is established, however, duties attach, and the psychiatrist is liable for damages that are proximately caused by their breach (Roberts v. Sankey 2004). Whether a psychiatrist–patient relationship exists is a mixed question of law and fact. If the existence of a relationship is disputed, the court determines, as a preliminary matter, whether the patient entrusted care to the psychiatrist and whether the psychiatrist indicated acceptance of that care (Dehn v. Edgecombe 2005). Most often, a psychiatrist–patient relationship is established knowingly and voluntarily by both parties. Occasionally, however, a doctor–patient relationship is unwittingly created.

Although the law imposes no duty on physicians to accept a prospective patient, courts have been quick to recognize a doctor–patient relationship when the physician affirmatively undertakes to diagnose and or treat a person (Kelley v. Middle Tenn. Emergency Physicians, P.C. 2004). Several examples are instructive. Giving advice, making interpretations, or prescribing medication during the course of an independent medical evaluation may create a doctor–patient relationship (Newman and Newman 1989). A doctor–patient relationship may be created when a person is provided care over the telephone, if that person has the expectation that he or she is accepted for treatment. Courts will likely treat doctor–patient relationships created by e-mail as they have those created by phone, mail, or in person (Table 2–2).

Judicial decisions that hold therapists liable to third persons—not because they are patients, but because they allege that the therapist's negligent patient care resulted in harm to them—have increased. These claims have been made by persons about whom the patient made threats in therapy and who were later injured by the patient. The injured third party in these cases claims the threats were mishandled (Tarasoff v. Regents of the University of California 1976). Another class of third-party claims have been made by individuals who allege that, because of inappropriate therapies used by the psychiatrist, they were wrongfully remembered by the patient in therapy as having been the perpetrator of childhood sexual abuse (Appelbaum et al. 1997). The duty issue in these cases is separate from the duty issue that arises with participants in formal family or group therapy. The

Table 2–2. Actions by therapists that may create a doctor–patient relationship

- Online consultations
- Giving advice to prospective patients, friends, and neighbors
- Making psychological interpretations during an independent evaluation
- Writing a prescription or providing sample medications
- Supervising treatment by a nonmedical therapist
- Having a lengthy phone conversation with a prospective patient
- Treating an unseen person by mail
- Giving a prospective patient an appointment
- Telling walk-in prospective patients that they will be seen
- Acting as a substitute therapist
- Providing treatment during an evaluation

courts addressing these third-party claims do not focus on the requirements for the existence of a doctor–patient relationship but instead on whether the harm that may have been caused by the therapist's negligence is proximate or too remote to be attributed to any negligence in the care of the patient.

Unless they are a formal part of the patient's therapy, families are usually not considered parties to the case (Gutheil and Simon 1997). Family members who are brought into the patient's treatment in a brief, adjunctive role must be clearly informed that they are not being seen as patients. If therapy for other family members is indicated, they should be referred elsewhere for treatment.

Psychiatrists and other clinicians are often asked by friends, family members, neighbors, or colleagues for clinical advice or medications. These quasi-medical relationships are potentially fraught with serious problems (LaPuma and Priest 1992). Psychiatrists who wish to provide professional services in these situations must understand they may be creating a doctor–patient relationship with an attendant duty of care. As in the usual clinical situation, medical records should be maintained that document that the standard of care was met in evaluation, diagnosis, and indications for treatment.

Ordinarily, clinicians who perform preemployment, insurance, or workers' compensation examinations do so for the benefit of a third party, not the examinee, and accordingly a doctor–patient relationship does not arise for purposes of medical malpractice liability (Chiasera v. Employers Mut. Liability Ins. Co. 1979; Ervin v. American Guardian Life Assurance Co.1988; Violandri v. New York 1992). Independent of medical malpractice liability for negligence as a caregiver, psychiatrists may be liable for performing negligent examinations (McKinney v. Bellevue Hosp. 1992) or for defamation if untrue and damaging statements are made about the examinee (James v. Brown 1982). Therapists who examine litigants at the request of the court are typically immune from liability for negligence. Psychiatrists appointed by the court in civil commitment cases are generally protected from liability as well. When, however, the psychiatrist medically certifies his or her own patient, liability claims may not be barred by imposition of immunity for negligently initiated commitment. (This issue is examined further in Chapter 7, "Involuntary Hospitalization.")

"Curbside consultations," or informal advice given in response to a colleague's question, are not categorically excluded from the recognition of a duty of care enforceable in a medical malpractice claim because of their location, reimbursement, or informality. Rather, in the event of a malpractice claim, each consultation will be judged by the court on its own facts, applying the criteria generally applied for recognition of a doctor–patient relationship. Thus the law's expectations for consultations do not countenance a sliding competence scale for discounted opinions.

Patient Evaluation: The Right to Accept or Reject New Patients

When seeing a prospective patient for the first time, psychiatrists may want to conduct an evaluation before accepting the person as a patient. The clinician should inform the prospective patient that no treatment will be provided during the evaluation. In actual clinical practice, this may not always be possible. The psychiatrist usually does not know the extent of the prospective patient's disturbance prior to seeing him or her for the first time. Some individuals show floridly psychotic symptoms during the initial visit and may be a danger to themselves or others. The psychiatrist may decide to immediately intervene and forgo the initial evaluation period. The clinician's first duty is to the welfare of the patient.

The common law "no duty to rescue" rule is still very much good law. Not even health care professionals have a duty to come to the aid of a stranger who is helpless and in peril, but if that duty is undertaken there is an obligation to do so non-negligently (Shuman 1993). The application of this rule to a psychiatrist in private practice means that he or she is not required to accept a new patient, but if he or she does there is an obligation to provide competent care. Psychiatrists may feel helpless and trapped when confronted with a new patient who is in a crisis and requires immediate attention. Psychiatrists who do not want to accept the patient for treatment should attempt to find immediate, competent help. In some instances, this may require accompanying the patient to a hospital or an emergency department. Professional ethics and concern for the patient in crisis dictate that the patient be assisted in obtaining immediate care (Simon 1992).

Malpractice concerns can be an additional incentive to see prospective patients for an initial evaluation before accepting them for treatment. In split treatment or collaborative therapy, careful evaluation of the patient's suitability is necessary. Psychiatrists are increasingly vulnerable to lawsuits by patients seen within a short period of time, even less than 30 days. Eight out of every 10 persons who commit suicide have visited a physician within the 6 months prior to the attempt, and half (50%) have seen a physician within 1 month prior. The psychiatrist should perform a suicide risk assessment at the initial evaluation, even if the patient denies being suicidal.

Clinicians usually accept many more patients than they reject. Upon completion of the evaluation, a decision by both the psychiatrist and the patient can be made about whether to begin treatment. The psychiatrist should scrupulously avoid rendering advice, interpretations, or any other intervention that might be construed as treatment during the evaluation period.

Psychiatrists have no legal obligation to provide emergency medical care to a person who is not a patient (failure to provide emergency care to an existing patient may constitute abandonment). Nevertheless, the American Medical Association (1989) advises, "The physician should, however, respond to the best of his [or her] ability in cases of emergency where first aid treatment is essential" (p. 33). If a psychiatrist undertakes to render assistance to the person "at the wayside," Good Samaritan statutes provide a layer of protection for physicians providing gratuitous emergency medical care against damages arising out of any professional act or omission performed in "good faith" and not amounting to gross negligence (Estate of Heune ex. rel. Heune v. Edgecomb 2005). Good Samaritan laws typically include the physician who is not licensed in the state where the emergency care takes place (for a listing of Good Samaritan statutes, see Centner 2000).

Role Conflicts

The practice of psychiatry bristles with moral dilemmas. Role conflicts occur when mental health professionals have irreconcilable interests that interfere with their fiduciary responsibility to act solely in the best interest of the patient. These role conflicts are sometimes labeled as *double agentry,* which refers to a conflict between serving the patient and serving some external agency (The Hastings Center 1978). Role conflicts hold a high potential for interfering with the fiduciary duties psychiatrists owe their patients. For example, psychiatrists working in mental institutions must manage the conflict between serving their patients and advancing the goals of the institution and society. Following the emergence of *Tarasoff* in those states that recognize a psychotherapist's duty to protect third parties endangered by their patients, psychiatrists were explicitly called upon to balance the conflicting duty to protect patient confidentiality and to protect persons identified as at risk in a patient's confidential communications. Psychiatrists who work in prisons, in schools, or in the military regularly face potentially serious double-agent conflicts. Psychiatrists and other mental health professionals are expected to clinically manage conflicting pressures that inevitably arise from these different sectors without disrupting the doctor–patient relationship.

Therapists who sexually exploit their patients violate their fiduciary responsibilities. Such violation also may occur when patients who have been sexually abused are referred to a new therapist for much-needed treatment, and the new therapist, because of forensic interests or moral outrage, converts the treatment relationship into a forensic case. The therapist may encourage the patient to file a lawsuit and help initiate ethical and licensure proceedings against the former therapist. Therapists should not confound treatment with advocacy. The roles of treater and expert witness must be kept separate to avoid serious conflicts of interest (Strasburger et al. 1997). Advocacy should not be misrepresented to the patient as treatment. "Once a patient, always a patient" is a sound principle that allows patients to go about their lives free from the presence and influence of their therapists.

Supervisor–Supervisee Relationships and Liability

Under the doctrine of *respondeat superior* (vicarious liability), an institution and its staff (e.g., supervising psychiatrist) may be liable for the negligent acts and omissions of other mental health professional employees in the scope of their employment. Vicarious liability is imposed based on the negligence of the employee, not the employer.

A professional distinction exists in a psychiatrist's supervisory obligation for medical and nonmedical psychotherapists. The American Psychiatric Association's (1980) *Official Actions: Guidelines for Psychiatrists in Consultative, Supervisory, or Collaborative Relationships With Nonmedical Therapists* states that the psychiatrist who supervises a nonmedical therapist is responsible for the patient's diagnosis and treatment plan and ensuring that the treatment plan is properly administered with suitable adjustments for the patient's condition. The guidelines do not specify the frequency of supervisory contacts. While supervising nonmedical therapists, psychiatrists are responsible for the patients as though the patients are their own. The guidelines have not been updated to accord with the current systems of mental health care delivery.

Direct and Vicarious Liability

When a psychiatrist supervises a psychiatric resident or intern who is treating the psychiatrist's patient, the resident or intern may be considered a *borrowed servant*. As a result, the psychiatrist is vicariously responsible for negligence of the resident or intern that leads to harm (Frazier v. Hurd 1967). Interns and residents treating their own patients but supervised by a psychiatrist may incur liability directly for negligence, whereas the supervisor and the institution may incur vicarious liability. Residents are held to the same standard of care as attending psychiatrists when they represent themselves to the public as treaters of mental illness. Psychiatrists supervising other graduate psychiatrists may be viewed as independent contractors who would not likely be liable for acts of negligence of the supervised psychiatrist. Although not strictly consultative, the supervisory relationship with graduate psychiatrists appears to be closer to the consultative model, even though it occurs on a continuing basis.

The psychiatric treatment team concept has gained considerable popularity in the managed care era. The team usually contains a psychiatrist, nurses, social workers, and other mental health professionals. Team members may be held liable for the negligence of an individual team member. Psychiatrists also may be held liable under the doctrine of joint and several liabilities for the negligent acts of partners, even though they have not treated the patient (Fanelli v. Adler 1987). Finally, vicarious liability may be imposed on psychiatrists for the negligent acts of employees committed within the scope of their employment (Steinberg v. Dunseth 1994).

Collaborative Relationships: Split Treatment

In a collaborative relationship, responsibility for the patient's care is shared according to the qualifications and limitations of each discipline (American Psychiatric Association 1980). The responsibilities of each discipline do not diminish those of the other discipline. Split treatment is an example of a collaborative relationship. The shrinking of available mental health dollars and increases in administrative pressure from third-party payers, particularly managed care organizations (MCOs), are the driving forces behind the increasing utilization of split treatment in the clinical management of the severely mentally ill.

The psychiatrist–psychotherapist team must overcome some difficult hurdles to facilitate the collaboration (Meyer and Simon 1999a, 1999b). The patient's clinical illness cannot be easily placed into the domain of one clinician or the other. Because neither clinician can rightfully claim to be in charge of the other, there is no established clinical hierarchy. Often, there is neither a preexisting agreement by which clinicians convey information about the patient nor one about what information needs to be conveyed. Psychiatrists and their nonphysician mental health colleagues should reach an agreement about the respective clinical duties of each clinician and a plan for clinical interactions. The main liability dangers of collaborative treatment include the following:

- Failure to establish clear lines of communication and clinical responsibility in split-treatment situations, early and in writing, between the psychiatrist and the nonmedical therapist (e.g., coverage for emergencies, hospitalizations, absences).
- Insufficient clinical knowledge of the patient
- Failure to provide careful monitoring of the patient's clinical condition
- Failure to maintain ongoing communication with the nonmedical therapist regarding the patient's treatment

Patient Billing

Dubious Practices

Conflicting, self-serving interventions can occur over billing and fees. Most therapists explain their fees at the beginning of treatment so that patients can agree, disagree, or enter into negotiations for a mutually agreed-on fee. Role conflicts can arise over billing for times reserved or by discounting or inflating bills. *Discounting* of bills occurs when the patient has insurance but is unable to pay the full portion of the bill. The therapist may accept either no payment or a lower payment from the patient. When the psychiatrist accepts the insurance reimbursement as payment in full, the insurer is actually paying 100% of the bill. Insurance carriers consider this practice to be fraudulent because the participating psychiatrist is pocketing their "overpayment."

Psychiatrists who inflate bills to insurance carriers may also be vulnerable to charges of fraud and misrepresentation. *Inflating* of bills refers to charging the insurance carrier a higher fee than the therapist is actually charging the patient. When this happens, the difference is pocketed or applied to the patient's portion. Therapists are not agents of the insurance company, nor should they be agents of the patient against the carrier. Exaggerating the severity of a patient's mental disorder to obtain coverage under managed care is a related deceptive practice. A position of neutrality on insurance matters maintains the psychiatrist's integrity and preserves the treatment. Engaging in dubious fee practices undermines the credibility of the psychiatrist if she or he becomes entangled with the patient in litigation.

Psychiatrists are entitled to charge a reasonable fee for their services. Billing for missed appointments is appropriate if the patient is advised of this practice at the outset and freely consents. Charges for missed sessions should not be represented as treatment sessions to third-party payers. This practice could be interpreted as misrepresentation and fraud. Psychiatrists who receive direct payment from third-party payers are not paid for appointments that are reported as missed. Moreover, under provider contractual agreements, most MCOs and other third-party payers prohibit psychiatrists from billing the patient for any unauthorized services, including missed appointments. The ethical and prudent course is to note missed appointments on the billing form, even if the psychiatrist must take a financial loss. In some circumstances, a legitimate arrangement may be worked out with the patient to pay for missed appointments.

Nonpayment: Clinical Issues

In general, the psychiatrist has no legal duty to continue to treat patients who do not pay. The psychiatrist, however, must be careful not to abandon the patient. The patient who runs out of money during the course of extended therapy presents a difficult problem. Terminating the patient's treatment may be very destructive to the unique relationship that developed between psychiatrist and patient. The psychiatrist may decide to treat the patient for a token fee until the patient's financial situation improves, at which time a new fee can be negotiated. Allowing the patient to pay the money owed at a later date places the psychiatrist in the position of a creditor, a potentially conflicting role. Similarly, entering into a barter arrangement with a nonpaying patient should be avoided. Patients in need of treatment may not be able to objectively assess the value of their goods. When others assume financial responsibility for the patient, the therapist may wish to formalize the arrangement with a written agreement. As insurance benefits for psychiatric care continue to be cut back by MCOs and other third-party payers' cost-containment policies, treatment of patients needing further care may be improperly terminated.

Abandonment

Once the psychiatrist agrees to treat the patient, a psychiatrist–patient relationship is formed with the duty to provide treatment as long as is necessary. When the psychiatrist–patient relationship is unilaterally and prematurely terminated by the psychiatrist without reasonable notice, the psychiatrist may be liable for abandonment if care is still needed by the patient (see Grant v. Douglas Women's Clinic P.C. 2003). If an emergency exists, the psychiatrist should see the patient through the current crisis or make suitable arrangements for attendance of another qualified mental health professional (see Johnson v. Vaughn 1963). For patients in perpetual crisis, this is a daunting task. Similarly, terminating treatment of a chronically ill patient who is in serious psychiatric difficulty should be deferred until the immediate crisis is over or until the patient is well enough to be transferred or discharged.

Although the doctor–patient relationship may be terminated unilaterally by the patient, the following actions by a patient do not, in and of themselves, terminate the doctor–patient relationship:

- Nonpayment of a bill (However, there *are* limits: for example, in Surgical Consultants, P.C. v. Ball [1989], the court ruled that the doctor did not have to continue treatment when the patient failed to pay her bill after 11 sessions.)

- Noncooperation in treatment (However, the physician does not have to continue treatment when there is no hope of helping the patient through current therapy.)
- Unilateral consultation with another mental health professional
- Failure to keep an appointment

None of these actions by the patient, in and of themselves, constitutes unilateral termination of treatment. However, these issues should be taken up as treatment matters. If the patient stops coming for regularly scheduled appointments, does the therapist have a duty to contact the patient? The answer to this question depends on whether the patient's absence is a direct function of mental illness. The more severe the illness, the more the psychiatrist should assume responsibility for contacting the patient. When it is not clear whether the patient has terminated treatment, the psychiatrist should attempt to clarify the patient's intentions concerning further treatment. If a patient stops coming for treatment without further explanation, the psychiatrist should send a certified letter (return receipt requested) to ascertain whether treatment has been terminated by the patient.

When the doctor–patient relationship has not been properly terminated by the patient, by the psychiatrist, or by the mutual agreement of both, the negligent acts may be categorized as abandonment of the patient (see Table 2–3).

Table 2–3. Abandonment: improper termination

- Failure to stay abreast of the patient's condition
- Failure to admit the patient to a hospital when warranted
- Premature discharge of the patient from the hospital
- Failure to provide patients with a way to contact the psychiatrist between sessions
- Failure to maintain reasonable contact with a hospitalized patient
- Failure to provide adequate clinical coverage when away from practice
- Failure to maintain appropriate treatment boundaries (e.g., therapist–patient sex)
- Termination of a patient requiring treatment solely on the basis of the managed care organization's denial of benefits

Psychiatrists who request other psychiatrists to hospitalize their patients should stay in contact with the admitting psychiatrist and shift temporarily into a consultative role. Unless the patient is being permanently transferred to the care of the hospitalizing psychiatrist, the referring psychiatrist should continue to stay abreast of clinical developments with his or her patient. Communication between psychiatrists is essential to the patient's care.

Finally, abandonment may become an issue when therapists do not list a phone number in the telephone directory or with directory assistance. Being inaccessible to patients measurably increases their anxiety and causes some patients to go to extraordinary lengths to find their therapists. Ready availability of the psychiatrist appears to diminish patients' anxiety and results in fewer calls. In addition, if an emergency should arise, claims of abandonment are preempted when the psychiatrist can be easily contacted. Leaving a message on the answering service such as "If you have a true emergency, please go to your nearest emergency department" may be perceived by the patient as abandonment. In an emergency, patients want to speak to their psychiatrists. Waiting for hours to be seen in an emergency department may exacerbate the patient's illness and result in the patient leaving prematurely.

Coverage

When a psychiatrist obtains clinical coverage for absences from his or her practice, a clinician of similar experience and training should be found. Clinical information about patients who may be considered at risk for suicide or vulnerable to regression in the clinician's absence should be provided to the covering psychiatrist with the patient's permission. Patients need to be informed of the name of the psychiatrist providing coverage as well as the length of the treating psychiatrist's absence. A psychiatrist who obtains coverage is not generally liable for the covering psychiatrist's negligence unless the covering psychiatrist is acting as an agent of the psychiatrist or due diligence was not exercised in selecting the substitute covering psychiatrist. If a fixed stipend is paid to the covering psychiatrist from fees collected, an agent (employee) relationship is likely established. If the patient is billed and the proceeds are shared with the covering psychiatrist after expenses, then a partnership is created. To reduce legal entanglements, the covering psychiatrist should bill independently for services rendered.

Termination

The psychiatrist has the right to terminate a doctor–patient relationship if proper notice is given so that the patient may find a suitable substitute (see Brandt v. Grubin 1974).

Unilateral Terminations

A psychiatrist may seek to terminate a patient's treatment because of managed care limitations on insurance benefits. However, the liability exposure for terminating treatment of a patient in crisis because of managed care restrictions is high. As noted earlier, termination of treatment for the patient in crisis should be deferred until his or her situation is reasonably stabilized. Before termination, the psychiatrist should give the patient sufficient notice to make other treatment arrangements. The psychiatrist should also review with the patient the current diagnosis, the importance of continuing with prescribed treatments, and the need for additional treatment. A note in the patient's chart and a brief letter sent to the patient should summarize the psychiatrist's treatment recommendations. The psychiatrist may decide to continue to treat a patient after managed care benefits end. Managed care contracts should be checked for any clause that prohibits treatment of managed care patients under a private fee-for-service arrangement.

The patient has the right to leave treatment at any time and without notice. In some instances, the patient may terminate by simply not showing up for scheduled appointments. A patient who is mentally ill and poses a substantial danger to self or others may suddenly decide to terminate. In such instances, the psychiatrist's ethical and professional duties to care for the patient continue and require that the psychiatrist consider a variety of clinical interventions.

Some patients are genuinely difficult and demanding in their own right, presenting unique problems that some psychiatrists can handle better than others. The fit between psychiatrist and patient may not be workable. If treatment becomes stalemated or contentious, the patient should be referred elsewhere.

Professional and ethical duty demands that the psychiatrist not treat patients beyond the point of benefit. Patients can become mired in therapeutic stalemates extending for years. This situation tends to occur when an Axis I clinical syndrome is successfully treated, but the remaining Axis II personality disorder goes undiagnosed or is intractable to treatment. Even though the patient may strenuously resist, it is not abandonment if such a patient is referred to another therapist who may be able to treat the patient more effectively once the previous treatment is appropriately terminated.

Method of Termination

Termination and the treatment issues surrounding it should be openly discussed with the patient and a notation of the discussion placed in the patient's record. A certified letter notifying the patient of termination should be sent and a return receipt requested. If the terminated patient is seen again after the letter is issued and termination is still intended, the entire termination process must be reinstituted (Table 2–1).

How much time should the patient be given to find another therapist? The time allowed should be based on the severity of the patient's condition and the availability of alternative care. Patients who present with complex, severe mental illnesses may find it more difficult to find a psychiatrist willing or able to treat them. Sufficient notice also depends on the locality. The availability of psychiatrists in rural settings is often limited. The patient may need more time to find a psychiatrist than would be necessary in an urban area. The courts have used such normative words as *ample, sufficient,* and *reasonable* when referring to the time that should be given the patient to find a substitute.

Managed Care and the Discharge of Hospitalized Patients

Doctors—not hospitals or MCOs—are responsible for the discharge of patients (Simon 1997). Hospitalized psychiatric patients should not be summarily discharged because insurance coverage for recommended continued hospitalization is denied. Provisions for continuing adequate care should be made before the patient is discharged. Occasionally, a hospital will pressure a psychiatrist to discharge a patient whose insurance benefits have ended. If the patient presents a high risk of danger to self or others, both the psychiatrist and the hospital will be at increased risk of liability if the patient or a third party is harmed. Managed care considerations must not be permitted to override treatment and discharge decisions. The premature discharge of psychiatric inpatients that are at increased risk of committing violence toward themselves or others is expected to become an increasingly important area of litigation in the managed care era (Simon 1998).

MCO cost-containment policies often restrict physicians' therapeutic discretion even as the physicians' professional and legal responsibilities to patients continue unchanged. For example, hospital lengths of stay may be abbreviated, often inappropriately, for inpatients with serious psychiatric disorders. When managed care guidelines conflict with the psychiatrist's duty to provide appropriate clinical care, the psychiatrist should vigorously appeal managed care decisions that abridge necessary treatments. If advocacy efforts fail, patients should be informed of their right to appeal MCO denial of services that the psychiatrist has documented as medically necessary. Once a treatment plan is recommended to the patient, the psychiatrist has a duty to complete the treatment or arrange for a suitable treatment alternative (Siebert and Silver 1991). MCOs generally limit or deny *payment* for services but not the actual services themselves. The physician is responsible for decisions involving patient care and disposition (Wickline v. California 1986; Wilson v. Blue Cross of So. California et al. 1990).

References

American Medical Association: Current Opinions: The Council on Ethical and Judicial Affairs of the American Medical Association. Chicago, IL, American Medical Association, 1989

American Psychiatric Association: Official actions: guidelines for psychiatrists in consultative, supervisory, or collaborative relationships with nonmedical therapists. Am J Psychiatry 137:1489–1491, 1980

Appelbaum PS: General guidelines for psychiatrists who prescribe medication for patients treated by nonmedical therapists. Hosp Community Psychiatry 42:281–282, 1991

Appelbaum PS, Uyehara LA, Elin MR (eds): Trauma and Memory: Clinical and Legal Controversies. New York, Oxford University Press, 1997

Centner TJ: Tort liability for sports and recreational activities: expanding statutory immunity for protected classes and activities. J Legis 26:1–44, 2000

Gutheil TG, Simon RI: Clinically based risk management principles for recovered memory cases. Psychiatr Serv 48:1403–1407, 1997

LaPuma J, Priest ER: Is there a doctor in the house? An analysis of the practice of physicians treating their own families. JAMA 267:1810–1812, 1992

Mains J: Medical abandonment. Med Trial Tech Q 31:306–328, 1985

Meyer D, Simon RI: Split treatment: clarity between psychiatrists and psychotherapists, part I. Psychiatr Ann 29:241–245, 1999a

Meyer D, Simon RI: Split treatment: clarity between psychiatrists and psychotherapists, part II. Psychiatr Ann 29:327–332, 1999b

Newman A, Newman K: Physician's duty in independent medical evaluations. Leg Aspects Med Pract 17:8–9, 1989

Shuman DW: The duty of the state to rescue the vulnerable in the United States, in The Duty to Rescue: The Jurisprudence of Aid. Edited by Menlowe M, McCall Smith A. Brookfield, VT, Dartmouth Publishing, 1993, pp 131–158

Siebert SW, Silver SB: Managed health care and the evolution of psychiatric practice, in American Psychiatric Press Review of Clinical Psychiatry and the Law, Vol 2. Edited by Simon RI. Washington, DC, American Psychiatric Press, 1991, pp 259–270

Simon RI: Clinical Psychiatry and the Law, 2nd Edition. Washington, DC, American Psychiatric Press, 1992

Simon RI: Discharging sicker, potentially violent psychiatric inpatients in the managed care era: standard of care and risk management. Psychiatr Ann 27:726–733, 1997

Simon RI: Psychiatrists' duties in discharging sicker and potentially violent inpatients in the managed care era. Psychiatr Serv 49:62–67, 1998

Strasburger LH, Gutheil TG, Brodsky A: On wearing two hats: role conflict in serving as both psychotherapist and expert witness. Am J Psychiatry 154:448–456, 1997

The Hastings Center: In the Service of the State: The Psychiatrist as Double Agent (Special Supplement). Hastings-on-Hudson, NY, The Hastings Center, 1978

Legal References

Bolles v Kinton, 83 Colo. 147, 153, 263 P. 26, 28 (1928)

Brandt v Grubin, 131 NJ Super 182, 329 A.2d 82 (1974)

Brown v Koulizakis, 229 Va. 524, 331 S.E.2d 440 (1985)

Chiasera v Employers Mut. Liability Ins. Co., 101 Misc.2d 877, 422 N.Y.S.2d 341 (1979)

Dehn v Edgecombe, 865 A.2d 603 (Md., 2005)

Estate of Heune ex. rel. Heune v. Edgecomb, 823 N.E.2d 1123 (Ill. App., 2005)

Ervin v American Guardian Life Assurance Co., 545 A.2d 354 (Pa. Super. Ct., 1988)

Fanelli v Adler, 516 N.Y.S.2d 716, 131 A.D.2d 631 (N.Y.A.D. 2 Dept., 1987)

Frazier v Hurd, 149 N.W.2d 226 (Mich. App., 1967)

Grant v Douglas Women's Clinic P.C., 580 S.E.2d 532 (Ga. App., 2003)

Gross v Burt, 149 S.W.3d 213 (Tex. App., 2004)

James v Brown, 637 S.W.2d 914 (Tex., 1982)

Johnson v Vaughn, 370 S.W.2d 591 (Ky., 1963)

Kelley v Middle Tenn. Emergency Physicians, P.C., 133 S.W.3d 587 (Tenn., 2004)

Lection v Dyll, 65 S.W.3d 696, 704 (Tex. App. Dallas, 2001) review denied (Nov. 8, 2001)

McKinney v Bellevue Hosp. 584 N.Y.S.2d 538, 183 A.D.2d 563 (N. Y. A. D. 1 Dept., 1992)

Oja v Kin, 581 N.W.2d 739, 229 Mich.App. 184 (Mich. App., 1998)

Ricks v Budge, 64 P.2d 208 (Utah, 1947)

Roberts v Sankey, 813 N.E.2d 1195 (Ind. App., 2004)

Simons v Northern P.R. Co., 22 P.2d 609 (Mont., 1933)

State v Supreme Court of Georgia, 613 S.E.2d 647 (Ga., 2005)

Steinberg v Dunseth, 631 N.E.2d 809, 813 (Ill. App.), cert. denied, 642 N.E.2d 1304 (Ill. 1994)

Surgical Consultants, P.C. v Ball, 447 N.W.2d 676 (Iowa Ct. Appl., 1989)

Tarasoff v Regents of the University of California, 17 Cal.3d 425; 551 P.2d 334 (Cal. Rptr., 14 1976)

Violandri v New York, 184 A.D.2d 364, 584 N.Y.S.2d 842 (1992)

Wickline v California, 183 Cal. App.3d 1175, 228 Cal. Rptr. 661 (Cal. Ct. App., 1986)

Wilson v Blue Cross of So. California et al., 222 Cal. App.3d 660 (1990)

3

Confidentiality and Testimonial Privilege

Overview of the Law

Confidentiality and *privilege* have specialized and distinct legal meanings. *Confidentiality,* in the context of a psychiatrist–patient relationship, refers to the right of patients to have their communications with the psychiatrist not be disclosed to outside parties without authorization and the correlative duty of a psychiatrist to ensure that those communications are not disclosed. In general, issues of confidentiality arise outside of the courtroom—for example, in the dilemma of what information about a patient a psychiatrist may disclose as part of a case report in a scholarly journal, or in the dilemma of what may be said to police who are investigating a patient for a serious crime. Confidentiality is the privacy created, typically by state law, that governs the psychiatrist–patient relationship (United States v. Chase 2003). However, the psychiatrist's legal duty of confidentiality is not a limitation on the power of a court to compel a witness to disclose relevant evidence in a trial. That is the subject matter of testimonial privilege.

Testimonial privilege issues arise inside the courtroom. When it applies, privilege operates as a limitation on the power of the court to compel a psychiatrist to disclose communications between psychiatrist and patient cloaked by the privilege. Typically, modern privileges are contained in rules of evidence that have been created by court-appointed committees and authorized by the legislature. Some testimonial privileges are created by the legislature in the form of statutes. Occasionally, a court will recognize a privilege not enacted by statute or codified in the rules of evidence. For example, in Jaffee v. Redmond (1996), the U.S. Supreme Court recognized a psychotherapist–patient privilege in the federal courts even though the rules of evidence sanctioned by the court did not include such a privilege.

Confidentiality and Privilege: Clinical-Legal Foundation

The rules that recognize and safeguard patient confidences are derived from four general sources. Many states have explicitly recognized a duty of confidentiality in professional licensure laws or confidentiality statutes or explicitly recognize a psychiatrist–patient privilege by rule of evidence or statute. A second source is the incorporation in state licensing laws of the ethical codes of the various mental health professions containing a duty of confidentiality. Third is judicial recognition of a privilege under the always-evolving common law. Although the common law has never recognized a physician–patient privilege, in Jaffee v. Redmond (1996), the U.S. Supreme Court ruled that confidential communications between psychotherapist and patient are privileged and therefore protected from compelled disclosure in federal trials. That decision does not apply in state court cases, however, where most psychotherapist–patient privilege issues arise. Fourth, beyond common law evolution of privileges, some courts have found protection against compelled disclosure of psychiatrist–patient communications to be constitutionally compelled as an aspect of the right of privacy. Although there is no explicit constitutional right of privacy, numerous U.S. Supreme Court decisions, including Roe v. Wade (1973) and Griswold v. Connecticut (1965), have found such a right drawing from several constitutional guarantees.

Confidentiality

The duty of confidentiality contemplates that a patient who consults with a psychiatrist for treatment is entitled to expect that a psychiatrist will not reveal any information disclosed by the patient in confidence to anyone unless it is necessary for treatment of the patient (e.g., consultation with a colleague about the best drug regimen), the patient consents to disclosure or waives confidentiality (e.g., patient asks to have records sent to his or her divorce attorney to assess merits of child custody claim), or an exception to confidentiality applies (e.g., duty to report child abuse). Implicit in this description is that this duty of confidentiality will not arise when the purpose of the consultation is not treatment but instead a forensic assessment that is intended to be shared with lawyers, judges, and/or jurors. Whether such consultation fits within attorney–client confidentiality is another matter. This absence of confidentiality, as well as any limitation on the maintenance of confidentiality in a therapeutic relationship, should be explained to patients at the beginning of an evaluation or treatment. Psychiatrists should have a working familiarity with the relevant statutes, rules, and case law in their states that govern confidentiality and disclosure (Corcoran and Winslade 1994; see Table 3–1).

Confidentiality After Death

Although the patient's direct interest in confidentiality may cease after his or her death, the interests of other patients who may fear embarrassing disclosures after their deaths remain. Unless there is a specific court decision or statute providing for the release of patient records after death (see Tex. R. Evid. 510[c][1] and Tex. Health & Safety C. § 611.003[a], stating that the representative of the patient may receive the information), the duty to maintain confidentiality that existed in life follows the patient in death. Family and friends who were not privy to confidential information before the patient's death are not automatically privy to that information because the patient is no longer alive (American Psychiatric Association 2001).

When a deceased patient's family requests the medical record, written authority from the executor or administrator of the patient's estate should be obtained before releasing it. When the estate has been settled, and an executor or administrator no longer exists, a court order should be required to release the records. Consultation with an attorney is advisable when ethical obligations to preserve confidentiality and legal requirements for disclosure appear to conflict.

When a psychiatrist is permitted to reveal confidential information after the patient's death, the minimum information for the task at hand should be

Table 3–1.   Examples of statutory disclosure requirements

- Physical evidence or suspicion of child abuse
- Initiation of involuntary hospitalization
- "Duty to warn" endangered third parties or law enforcement agencies
- Commission of a treasonous act
- Intention to commit a future crime
- HIV infection (some states require that the patient's name be reported)

provided. For example, details of the patient's therapy are rarely, if ever, required. Relevancy is the guiding rule. The controversy raised by the disclosures of the treating psychiatrist following the death of a major American poet, Anne Sexton, underscores many of the complex legal and ethical issues surrounding after-death release of confidential information (Goldstein 1992).

The American Psychiatric Association's (1987) *Guidelines on Confidentiality* are explicit concerning disclosure of information by a psychiatrist after the death of a patient.

> Psychiatrists should remember that their ethical and legal responsibilities regarding confidentiality continue after their patients' deaths. In cases in which the release of information would be injurious to the deceased patient's interests or reputation, care must be exercised to limit the released data to that which is necessary for the purpose stated in the request for information. (p. 1523)

Comments about third parties are rarely necessary for the purposes of record keeping (i.e., facilitating ongoing treatment, future availability for other physicians, research, or legal purposes). The risk of liability is unnecessarily increased when words contained in a medical record independently reflect on and defame those still living.

Exceptions to Confidentiality

AIDS/HIV Reporting

All states require that AIDS cases be reported to public health authorities. Some states also require reporting of the patient's name. A number of states require the reporting of cases or names of individuals who test positive for HIV. Confidentiality and disclosure issues with HIV-positive individuals are discussed in an official American Psychiatric Association policy statement (American Psychiatric Association 1993).

Revelation of Criminal or Other Wrongdoing

The law does not generally require a psychiatrist to report past criminal offenses disclosed by a patient (or otherwise provide patient information to the police; Slovenko 1998), and there is good reason for psychiatrists not to do so. Apart from the harm such a breach of confidentiality would cause in the relationship, certain psychiatric patients confess to crimes that they have not committed. Unless the therapist has corroboration that the patient has recently committed a heinous crime that may be repeated or that the patient may be a serial killer, the mere revealing of the crime should be handled initially as a treatment issue. If a patient confesses to having committed a serious crime in the past, the therapist's response should be that the revelation is dealt with as a treatment issue. The psychiatrist is not a law enforcement agent and should not confuse treatment with forensic roles. If the conflict for the patient is whether to go to the authorities, the optimal approach would be to attempt to resolve this issue in therapy.

Future crimes are another matter. In some states, therapists may be required to reveal a patient's intent to commit some future crime (e.g., a threat on the life of the President) if "disclosure is the only means of averting harm…when the disclosure was made" (United States v. Glass 1998, p. 1359; see also United States v. Chase 2000 and United States v. Hayes 2000).

Certain types of offense are singled out for special treatment because of the vulnerability of the victims of these crimes. Suspected child abuse overrides our concern with confidentiality. All states, including the District of Columbia and other federal jurisdictions, require health care providers and other mandated reporters to report child abuse. Child abuse laws generally require reporting of any physical injuries suspected of being inflicted on a child by other than accidental means or in any situation in which a child is believed to have been injured by abuse or neglect (Kaplan 1996). The typical statutory language requires reporting if there is reason to believe or reason to suspect child abuse (e.g., § 210.115 R.S. Mo. [2005], stating "reasonable cause to suspect"). Child abuse reporting laws apply to physical abuse, sexual abuse, emotional maltreatment, and physical neglect. In addition, in some states the duty to take reasonable precautions to prevent impending harm to identifiable victims has been imposed by courts adopting a *Tarasoff*-type duty to protect endangered third persons through disclosure to law enforcement or a warning to the victim (Tarasoff v. Regents of the University of California 1976).

Limitations on confidentiality created by mandatory reporting, particularly the duty to warn and protect endangered third parties or to inform the police, should be disclosed to patients who are making threats against identifiable persons or who were threatening or violent to others just prior to evaluation. *Jaffee* reminds therapists that, in addition to the more common disclosures that may arise in treatment, a discussion should also occur about ethically and legally mandated disclosures (Corcoran and Winslade 1994).

If a psychiatrist concludes that a warning should be issued to the police or an endangered third party, there is a difference of opinion whether the confidentiality of the communication that gave rise to the warning is lost. For example, the warning of endangered third parties has resulted in psychiatrists being compelled to testify to otherwise confidential communications in criminal cases (Leong et al. 1992). However, in United States v. Glass (1998), a federal court of appeals reasoned that "compliance with the professional duty to protect does not imply a duty to testify against a patient in criminal proceedings or in civil proceedings other than directly related to the patient's involuntary hospitalization, and such testimony is privileged and inadmissible if a patient properly asserts the psychotherapist/patient privilege" (p. 1360; see also United States v. Hayes 2000).

Health Insurance Portability and Accountability Act

In 1996, Congress passed the Health Insurance Portability and Accountability Act of 1996 (HIPAA [P.L. 104-191, 110 Stat.1936]). HIPAA includes a federal privacy rule aimed at protecting patients' health care information. HIPAA statutes preempt state statutes regarding safeguarding of confidentiality in situations in which the two statutes differ, unless the state statute is more stringent than the HIPAA guidelines. The statute that protects the patient's confidentiality more prevails (see 45 Code of Federal Regulations pts 160 and 164). In cases in which the patient has not executed a release, HIPAA requires a court order, subpoena, or formal discovery request with an adequate protective order. Under HIPAA regulations, disclosure of protected health information in the course of any judicial or administrative proceeding is allowed with written authorization of the patient, a subpoena to the physician, or through a court order (see 45 Code of Federal Regulations §§ 164.508; § 164.510; § 164.512[e] [2003]). The protective order must prohibit the use of protected health information for any purpose other than the litigation to obtain patient records.

Psychotherapy notes are accorded a greater level of protection under HIPAA. Psychotherapy notes are distinguished from the rest of the individual's medical record, and a separate authorization for disclosure of psychotherapy notes is required (see 45 Code of Federal Regulations § 164.512[e][1]).

Before protected health information can be disclosed in response to a subpoena, signed individual authorization or assurance from the requesting party that attempts have been made to notify the party whose health records are sought or to obtain a protective order prohibiting disclosure for any purpose outside the litigation is required (see 45 Code of Federal Regulations § 164.512[e][1]).

Waiver of Confidentiality

The confidentiality of psychiatrist–patient communications is not absolute. It may be waived by the patient as long as appropriate safeguards are observed to determine that the patient has the capacity to make the decision and that the decision is voluntary and informed. Indeed, statutes in several states provide patients with the right of access to their records and an implicit right to share those records with persons of their own choosing. Therapeutic discretion to withhold information from the patient exists in most states when the psychiatrist establishes that disclosure would be detrimental to the patient (see Mantica v. New York State Dept. of Health 1999). Psychiatrists should satisfy themselves that the patient waiving confidentiality understands the kind of information requested and the nature of the information in the record. If the patient lacks the mental capacity to make a rational choice, a substitute decision-maker should be consulted.

A patient's express waiver of confidentiality authorizing the disclosure of records should be documented in writing and kept as a permanent record. Blanket consent forms tend to be too general. Instead, consent should be given for a specific release of information. A sample consent form that preserves patient self-determination is shown in Figure 3–1. A valid, informed

Date:

I hereby authorize Dr. _____ to release the circled information for
the following purposes:

_____

_____
[Specify any limitations.]

• Psychiatric and medical history, including diagnoses
• Records of outpatient treatment
• Records of psychiatric hospitalization and treatment
• Limited psychiatric information as follows:

I understand that I have a right to inspect and copy any information authorized for release
by me. I also have the right to revoke consent at any time. This is a ❑ one-time consent or
❑ continuing consent [please check one]. I have been apprised of the possible problems of
waiving the privilege of privacy. Please send this information to the following individual and
address:

Name: _____

Signature: _____

Address: _____

_____

_____

Figure 3–1.   Authorization for release of medical information.

authorization for the release of information protects a psychiatrist ethically
and legally. State law and mental health confidentiality statutes generally
specify the requirements for a valid authorization.

Patients regularly waive confidentiality in a variety of situations. Patients
waive confidentiality to make benefit claims to insurance companies and to
managed care organizations (MCOs). Subjects of psychiatric examinations by
a psychiatrist retained by the defendant in civil disability and injury claims
waive confidentiality (Fed.R.Civ. P.35) as a condition of the examination (itself a condition of making the claim).

Confidentiality is also waived in various therapeutic contexts. For example, a limited waiver of confidentiality ordinarily exists when a patient participates in group therapy. A participant may be entitled to expect that the other participants would not make disclosures to third parties. In at least several states, group members cannot be compelled to testify to communications made during group therapy (C.B. v. Sabalos 2000; State v. Andring 1984). Still, the process of group therapy is based on a more expansive sharing of the patient's communications with the therapist.

Testimonial Privilege

Testimonial privileges are a recognition by the state of the importance of protecting information provided by a patient to a psychotherapist (see N.J. Stat. § 45:14B-28 [2005]). Their justification is that the need to protect the therapeutic relationship from outside intrusion outweighs the necessity for evidence to ensure an accurate outcome in court. The recognition of a psychiatrist–, physician–, or psychotherapist–patient testimonial privilege to further the goals of that relationship limits the authority of the courts to obtain relevant testimonial evidence for the resolution of a disputed claim in a trial at which life, liberty, or property may hang in the balance. Accordingly, courts are typically loathe to recognize privileges and quick to find exceptions or waiver of privileges.

If the jurisdiction in which the trial occurs recognizes a relevant testimonial privilege, for it to apply, typically there must be a confidential communication between a patient—one who seeks treatment or diagnosis in contemplation of treatment (i.e., the psychiatrist–patient privilege does not apply to forensic evaluations or preemployment examinations)—and a qualified professional as defined by the privilege (e.g., physician, psychiatrist, or psychologist). The information that is usually privileged includes not only the patient's direct communications but also information gained through examination and treatment as well as the physician's diagnosis and conclusions. The scope of information cloaked by the privilege varies among states as a function of their support or hostility to the privilege.

Only confidential communications of a professional nature are protected by the privilege (Table 3–2). Thus nonessential third parties present during the communication between the therapist and the patient may destroy the privilege or may be compelled to testify and are not barred by privilege. Al-

Table 3–2. Testimonial privileges: psychotherapist–patient communications

- General physician–patient
- Psychiatrist–patient
- Psychologist–patient
- Psychotherapist–patient

though many testimonial privileges apply in both criminal and civil proceedings, some are explicitly inapplicable in criminal matters, given the concern with accuracy in criminal proceedings where life and liberty hang in the balance (Tex. R. Evid. 510).

Waiver of the Privilege

Although the privilege may benefit the psychiatrist as well as the patient, the patient—not the psychiatrist—is the holder of the privilege. Only the patient may decide whether to assert the privilege and prohibit the psychiatrist from giving or being compelled to give evidence about confidential patient communications. If, however, the patient is not present when the privileged information is sought from the psychiatrist (e.g., before a grand jury) and has not informed the psychiatrist of his or her preference, the psychiatrist should presume that the patient wishes to invoke the privilege and refuse to provide evidence of privileged communications unless informed to the contrary by the patient or until ordered to do so by a judge who has ruled on the applicability of the privilege.

A competent, adult privilege holder may waive the testimonial privilege and authorize a psychiatrist to give evidence of confidential communications. If the patient has been adjudicated incompetent, the legal guardian possesses the authority to waive the privilege. Parents or guardians have the authority to waive the privilege for a minor child, although older adolescents may possess the right under certain circumstances.

Testimonial Privilege Exceptions

Psychotherapist–patient privileges are not absolute—all have some exceptions. Although the exceptions vary, the most common are included in Table 3–3.

Table 3–3.   Testimonial privilege: common exceptions

- Child abuse reporting
- Involuntary hospitalization and sexually violent predator commitments (civil commitment proceedings)
- Court-ordered evaluations
- Cases in which a patient places his or her mental state in question as a claim or defense (patient–litigant exception)
- Criminal proceedings
- Child custody disputes
- Child abuse proceedings

The last exception listed, known as the patient-litigant exception, is commonly raised in will contests, workers' compensation cases, child custody disputes, personal injury lawsuits, and medical malpractice cases. It applies when the patient-litigant relies on his or her mental or emotional state or condition to support a claim (e.g., personal injury claim) or defense (e.g., insanity defense).

Liability

An unauthorized or unwarranted breach of confidentiality can cause a patient or litigant great harm. The policy of the law is to encourage patients to trust the confidentiality of the physician–patient relationship; therefore, a psychiatrist can be held liable for breaching confidentiality. Serving as the basis for a tort or breach of contract claim may place the breach of confidentiality before the court as the basis for damages.

Minors

The general rule is that a duty of confidentiality follows the legal ability to consent to treatment. Mental health confidentiality statutes usually provide a definition of minors. The parents or guardians of a minor are the child's legal decision makers. Thus, in general, parents of a minor have a right to know about the course of treatment to which they consented as well as the diagnosis and prognosis. Confidential information, however, must be revealed cautiously so that damage is not done to the treatment or to the child's relationship with caregivers.

One married parent's consent is generally sufficient for therapists to release medical records or testify about treatment of a child. If the child's parents are divorced, the custodial parent generally has the right to consent to nonemergency care as well as to disclosures regarding that care. When there is disagreement between the parents about who has the capacity to consent to treatment or disclosure, the therapist should seek guidance, through counsel, from the applicable statutes and case law, divorce decree, and/or the courts.

In states where minors are legally able to consent to specific treatment without a finding that they are emancipated or mature, they are able to authorize the disclosure of medical information. Otherwise, minors generally lack the capacity to give a valid authorization to release records or testimony about treatment. Exceptions exist, of course. In most states, a minor may be found mature if he or she has sufficient intelligence and maturity to understand and appreciate risks and benefits of a treatment and give consent to treatment without parental approval. Specific categories of minors (e.g., married minors or minors serving in the armed services) are regarded as enjoying the status of emancipated minor and may consent to medical care as well as the disclosure of medical records. Consent of a parent generally is not required in a genuine emergency.

Regardless of whether a minor patient has the legal capacity to consent to treatment or disclosure of treatment records, every effort should be made to preserve confidentiality for the sake of the treatment. The conflicting interests of the minor's independent right to confidentiality and the parents' need to have information for making reasonable treatment decisions are always present. In *The Principles of Medical Ethics With Annotations Especially Applicable to Psychiatry* (American Psychiatric Association 2001), recognition is given to these conflicting interests: "careful judgment must be exercised by the psychiatrist in order to include, when appropriate, the parents or guardian in the treatment of a minor. At the same time, the psychiatrist must assure the minor proper confidentiality" (p. 8, Section 4, Annotation 7). Whenever information about an adolescent is to be released to a third party, the psychiatrist should obtain the written authorizations of both the parents and the patient.

Economic reality rather than legal theory may determine the right to control the release of confidential information. Therapists or hospitals are often unwilling to treat a minor patient without the consent and signature of a financially responsible person. When the parent receives an itemized bill or statement from a therapist or an insurance provider explanation, privacy can no longer be maintained. Parents are entitled to inquire about the professional services provided to their child for which they are being billed. If parents do not consent to nonemergency treatment of a minor, they are not responsible for payment of care. Some state statutes make this explicit (Simon 1997).

Subpoenas

A *subpoena* is a court order, typically issued in the name of the clerk of the court, commanding a person to appear at specified time and location to give evidence in a judicial proceeding. There are two basic types of subpoenas: the *subpoena duces tecum* requires the psychiatrist to bring medical records, and the *subpoena ad testificandum* requires the attendance of the psychiatrist, usually for testimony. Although the violation of a court order may be punished as contempt of court, the receipt of the subpoena does not automatically require the immediate disclosure of confidential communications. The subpoena does not address or purport to resolve issues of privilege and confidentiality, but for the court to do so these matters must be appropriately raised in a timely manner. When no written patient consent accompanies the subpoena, the psychiatrist should ascertain from the patient or the patient's attorney whether consent is forthcoming. Typically the claim of privilege or confidentiality is made by the attorney for the patient in a motion to quash the subpoena or a motion for a protective order. For this to occur, the psychiatrist must immediately notify the patient of the subpoena so the patient can notify counsel. A psychiatrist who receives a subpoena should continue to regard all information obtained during the course of therapy as confidential and privileged until receipt of a court order denying application of the privilege or a written consent from a competent patient.

Attempting to avoid being served a subpoena is both unrealistic and unethical (Simon 1992). Psychiatrists who believe that certain disclosures would be unethical and damaging to the patient may decide to resist disclosure within the full limits of the law. If this fails, psychiatrists may still refuse to divulge information as a matter of conscience. In this situation, however, psychiatrists risk a contempt-of-court citation and its legal consequences, including a fine or imprisonment (Caesar v. Mountanos 1977; Lifschutz 1970).

Record Keeping

Documentation is an essential part of patient care. It encourages the practitioner to sharpen clinical focus and clarify the decision-making process. The record becomes an active clinical tool, not just a paper document. The clinician treats the patient, not the chart (Simon 2004). Careful documentation, as a risk management tool, also supports good clinical care.

Clinically, keeping a record during the course of the patient's treatment serves a number of purposes. Review of prior sessions allows the treater to assess the patient's treatment response and clinical course. If the patient interrupts or terminates treatment but later decides to resume therapy, the prior record will prove helpful in refreshing the therapist's memory. Accurate record keeping may help resolve disputes over billing for professional services. Additionally, pressure for record keeping is increasing because of the need to maintain quality for accreditation, for financial reimbursement, and for legal purposes. The growing use of electronic recording and transmission of personal medical information by fax, Internet, and computers raises major concerns about the maintenance of confidentiality. Indeed, HIPAA's purpose is to improve "the efficiency and effectiveness of the health care system, by encouraging the development of a health information system through the establishment of standards and requirements for the electronic transmission of certain health information" (Health Insurance Portability and Accountability Act of 1996, P.L. 104-191, sec. 261).

Generally, in the absence of corroborating records, an assertion in court that certain actions were taken is a question for the fact finders who must consider the issue of proof. When an adequate record exists, the possibility of proving that an action (e.g., treatment or procedure) was taken is significantly enhanced. In essence, good medical records are comprehensive, contemporaneous, concise, careful, and complete.

The record should document major management and treatment decisions (see Table 3–4). Usually, no useful purpose is served by noting the patient's or the therapist's fantasies, derogatory opinions toward others, or any other information not directly relevant to documenting treatment decisions. Treatment process notes documenting intimate details may be necessary for supervision of student psychotherapists and psychoanalysts. A consistent policy of destroying treatment process records should be considered. The destruction of records

Table 3–4.   Major management and treatment decisions to be documented

- Medications and amounts
- Medication instructions
- Benefits, risks, and side effects of medications
- Risk-benefit assessments
- Informed consent
- Waivers of confidentiality
- Adherence to treatment
- Significant phone conversations
- Reasoning supporting treatment interventions and noninterventions

can be certified and the certificate kept permanently. However, special care must be taken for records of events that may result in litigation. Altering a record with the intent to impair its availability in a judicial proceeding is a crime (18 U.S.C. § 1512[c]).

Many states allow patients access to their records. The psychiatric record, however, can become an iatrogenic factor in exacerbating a patient's condition, especially if it contains damaging or frightening information. The physical record maintained by the psychiatrist is the property of the psychiatrist. The information contained in the record belongs to the patient. The original record should never be relinquished to the patient. Only a copy of the record should be provided. It is prudent for the psychiatrist to be present when patients inspect their records in order to answer questions and to ensure that no changes are made in the record.

Some clinicians may keep two separate sets of records: one set for diagnosis, prognosis, and treatment decisions and the other for speculations of the psychiatrist and the fantasies and intimate details of the patient's life. Although Illinois and the District of Columbia appear to permit dual records, such a distinction is unlikely to provide insulation from discovery. See, for example, D.C. Code § 7-1201.03:

> If a mental health professional makes personal notes regarding a client, such personal notes shall not be maintained as a part of the client's record of mental

health information…and shall not be disclosed except to the degree that the personal notes or the information contained therein are needed in litigation brought by the client against the mental health professional on the grounds of professional malpractice or disclosure in violation of this section.

Concealing records is a violation of the law. Instead, the psychiatrist should exercise caution when writing in the patient's record, entering only information that is pertinent to the diagnosis and treatment plan of the patient. Medical records should never be altered, particularly in anticipation of or following notice of a lawsuit. The courts have recognized a duty to preserve evidence material to a potential civil action as a tort, in and of itself, referred to as *spoliation of evidence* (Boyd v. Travelers Ins. 1995). If the psychiatrist needs to make additional notations in the record, the notes should occur in proper sequence and be accurately dated.

State laws and administrative regulations in a number of states require that a patient record be kept. Some state regulations and statutes specify the number of years that medical and hospital records must be held (e.g., in 22 Tex. Admin. Code Sec.165.1, records must be kept 7 years from the anniversary of the last treatment). In the absence of such requirements, records should be kept until the relevant statute of limitations (i.e., the time period in which a claim must be asserted or lost) has lapsed. Statutes of limitations usually require that a medical malpractice claim be brought within 2–3 years from the time of the last treatment or from the time of discovery of the injury caused by the treatment (Tex. Civ. Prac & Rem. Code § 74.251 [2005]). The running of the statute of limitations is typically tolled (halted) during any period of the claimant's minority and/or mental incapacity. Some statutes spell out the nature, content, and style of record keeping to be maintained, who may receive records, and under what conditions. Psychiatrists need to be aware of these requirements and conduct their record keeping accordingly.

Professional organizations do not provide specific guidelines for record keeping. The American Psychiatric Association, however, has published resource documents that provide guidance on maintaining confidentiality in the era of information technology (American Psychiatric Association 1996a, 1996b). State licensing and certification laws may contain record-keeping requirements. Violation of these legal requirements may lead to suspension or loss of the practitioner's license. No time limit exists for ethical charges made by patients with professional organizations. Licensing authorities are not constrained by the same time limitations established for instituting legal claims. Patients may bring ethics complaints after civil and criminal statutes of limitation have expired. Although some states impose 6-year record-keeping requirements, this is a cogent reason to consider keeping patient records indefinitely.

Managing Clinical-Legal Issues

Delinquent Bills

There is no ethical principle that forbids therapists from using collection agencies or the courts to collect bills from patients. Nonetheless, ethical and legal obligations to protect the patient's confidentiality continue even though the patient breaches the treatment contract by not paying the bill. Patients may not want therapists to reveal their status as patients and may sue for breach of confidentiality when disclosure of such information is made to a collection agency or in a court proceeding.

Whenever possible, therapists should try to recover fees by means other than collection agencies or the courts. If the patient is unresponsive, the therapist may decide to bring suit or employ a collection agency. The patient should be informed that such actions will take place if the bill is not paid within a specified period of time. When using a collection agency or suing, the therapist is ethically and legally obligated to reveal only essential information that is necessary for the purpose of fee collection. Essential information includes the patient's name and the amount owed. Itemized bills should be general, indicating "office visits" rather than the type of therapy. Any applicable statutes should be consulted regarding the procedure for collection and any limits placed on the type of patient information that can be legally disclosed (see D.C. Code § 7-1203.04 [2005] disclosures for collection of fees). Therapists may not harass patients by threatening criminal prosecution, disclosing false information to ruin their credit reputation, contacting the debtor's employer before obtaining a judgment, making unjustified disclosures of information about the debt, using abusive language, or other tactics. Similarly, they should not hire anyone who resorts to these types of tactics. Therapists must not withhold services that they are legally required to provide in order to put pressure on patients for payment.

Writing About Patients

Education, research, or entertainment does not excuse a breach of confidentiality. Psychiatrists are obliged to disguise their clinical data, even to the detriment of its scientific, educative, or entertainment value, to safeguard the privacy of their patients (Slovenko 1983). Although there is some debate about whether it is ever appropriate to publish a case report without the patient's consent, at minimum if a patient's identity cannot be adequately disguised, consent of the patient is certainly required for publication. When the psychiatrist does not obtain the patient's consent and the patient's identity is recognized, the psychiatrist may be subject to legal liability (Roe v. Doe 1975).

Although consent obtained prospectively may suffice (i.e., before beginning treatment or before the writing is created), to be fully informed, the patient should be provided the opportunity to review the book, article, or other product. In addition, consultation with another psychiatrist should be considered in order to evaluate the patient's capacity to consent if there may be any doubt about this issue.

Confidentiality in Managed Care Settings

The psychiatrist should obtain consent from the patient or an appropriate substitute decision-maker before providing information to the MCO. The subscriber's consent should not be automatically relied upon. Even if the patient has signed the insurer's blanket authorization form, the subscriber's consent may be insufficient if she or he no longer possesses decision-making capacity. If the patient is not the subscriber, then a file signature may not have been obtained, and no prior consent exists to release information to the MCO. Unknown callers who state they are utilization reviewers requesting information about a patient should be independently verified. The caller's name and telephone number should be obtained and that person's employment and position with the MCO checked.

A conservative approach that provides just enough information for utilization review purposes is sufficient (American Psychiatric Association 1996a, 1996b). Violent fantasies and impulses, whether directed at oneself or others, represent highly personal, sensitive information that must be handled with professional tact and discretion. The temptation to exploit such information by emphasizing (if not exaggerating) it may arise as the only way of obtaining necessary care for the patient. If insurance benefits are denied, the psychiatrist cannot readily discharge a patient who is diagnosed as severely psychiatrically ill.

References

American Psychiatric Association: AIDS Policy: position statement on confidentiality, disclosure, and protection of others. Am J Psychiatry 150:852, 1993

American Psychiatric Association: Resource Document on Computerized Records: A Guide to Security. Washington, DC, American Psychiatric Association, 1996a

American Psychiatric Association: Resource Document on Preserving Patient Confidentiality in the Era of Information Technology. Washington, DC, American Psychiatric Association, 1996b

American Psychiatric Association: The Principles of Medical Ethics With Annotations Especially Applicable to Psychiatry. Washington, DC, American Psychiatric Association, 2001, p 8, Section 4, Annotation 7

American Psychiatric Association Committee on Confidentiality: Guidelines on confidentiality. Am J Psychiatry 144:1522–1526, 1987

Corcoran K, Winslade WJ: Eavesdropping on the 50-minute hour: managed mental health care and confidentiality. Behav Sci Law 12:351–365, 1994

Goldstein RL: Psychiatric poetic license? Postmortem disclosures of confidential information in the Anne Sexton case. Psychiatr Ann 22:341–348, 1992

Kaplan SJ: Physical abuse of children and adolescents, in Family Violence: A Clinical and Legal Guide. Edited by Kaplan SJ. Washington, DC, American Psychiatric Press, 1996, pp 1–35

Leong GB, Eth S, Silva JA: The psychotherapist as witness for the prosecution: the criminalization of Tarasoff. Am J Psychiatry 149:1011–1051, 1992

Melton GB, Petrila J, Poythress NG, et al: Psychological Evaluations for the Courts, 2nd Edition. New York, Guilford, 1997

Simon RI: Clinical Psychiatry and the Law, 2nd Edition. Washington, DC, American Psychiatric Press, 1992

Simon RI: Discharging sicker, potentially violent psychiatric inpatients in the managed care era: standard of care and risk management. Psychiatr Ann 27:726–733, 1997

Simon RI: Assessing and Managing Suicide Risk: Guidelines for Clinically Based Risk Management. Washington, DC, American Psychiatric Publishing, 2004

Slovenko R: The hazards of writing or disclosing information in psychiatry. Behav Sci Law 1:109–127, 1983

Slovenko R: Psychotherapy and Confidentiality: Testimonial Privileged Communication, Breach of Confidentiality, and Reporting Duties. Springfield, IL, Charles C. Thomas, 1998

Legal References

Boyd v Travelers Ins. Co., 652 N.E.2d 267, 166 Ill.2d 188 (Ill., 1995)

Caesar v Mountanos, 542 F.2d 1064 (9th Cir., 1976), cert denied, 430 U.S. 954 (1977)

C.B. v Sabalos, 7 P.3d 124 (Ariz. App., 2000)

Griswold v Connecticut, 381 U.S. 479 (1965)

Jaffee v Redmond, 518 U.S. 1, 116 S.Ct. 1923, 135 L.Ed.2d 337 (1996)

Lifschutz, 2 Cal.3d 415, 467 P.2d 557, 85 Cal Rpt. 829 (1970)

Mantica v New York State Dept. of Health, 94 N.Y.2d 58, 699 N.Y.S.2d 1 (1999)

Roe v Doe, 420 U.S. 307 (1975)

Roe v Wade, 410 U.S. 113 (1973)

State v Andring, 342 N.W.2d 128 (Minn., 1984)

Tarasoff v Regents of the University of California, 17 Cal.3d 425; 551 P.2d 334 (Cal. Rptr., 14 1976)

United States v Chase, 340 F.3d 978 (9th Cir., 2003)

United States v Glass, 133 F.3d 1356 (10th Cir., 1998)

United States v Hayes, 227 F.3d 578 (6th Cir., 2000)

Laws

18 U.S.C. § 1512(c)

22 Tex. Admin. Code Sec. 165.1

45 Code of Federal Regulations pts 160 and 164

210.115 R.S. Mo. 2005

D.C. Code § 7-1201.03

D.C. Code § 7-1203.04 (2005)

Fed.R.Civ. P.35

Health Insurance Portability and Accountability Act of 1996 (HIPAA), Public Law 104-191, 110 Stat.1936 (1996).

N.J. Stat. § 45:14B-28 (2005)

Tex. Civ. Prac & Rem. Code § 74.251 (2005)

Tex. Health & Safety Code § 611.003(a)

Tex. R. Evid. 510

Tex. R. Evid. 510(c)(1)

4

Informed Consent and the Right to Refuse Treatment

Overview of the Law

Informed consent is a judicial construct designed to reflect our deeply held belief in the importance of individual autonomy. In the context of medical care, an application of this principle of autonomy—the right of competent adults to determine what shall be done with their own bodies—has defined the contours of the physician–patient relationship. Violation of these contours through failure to obtain patient consent before providing a particular medical procedure or treatment has been treated as medical malpractice. Recognizing that meaningful consent to medical care must be informed about risks, benefits, and alternatives, the case law has evolved to require consent to be informed in order to be valid in most circumstances.

There are three conjunctive components of an informed consent: 1) competency (intelligent); 2) information (knowing); and 3) voluntariness. The case law often refers to informed consent as requiring that the patient's decision be knowing, intelligent, and voluntary (Long v. Jaszczak 2004). We use *competency* in lieu of *intelligent* and *information* in lieu of *knowing* as more familiar and more useful constructs for clinical psychiatrists, without intending to change the required substance. Unlike some legal requirements that are played out primarily in the courts, informed consent begins with clinicians. Clinicians provide the first level of screening in identifying whether the patient's health care decision-making capacity reveals the potential to evaluate relevant information and communicate a competent or intelligent choice. To ensure an informed or knowing choice, the clinician must ensure that the patient has been told about the information relevant to that choice—the risks, benefits, and prognosis both with and without treatment—and about alternative treatments and their risks and benefits. Finally, to ensure a voluntary choice, the clinician must ensure that the patient's choice is not the result of threats or coercion.

Competency

Only competent persons may give a valid informed consent. Absent evidence to the contrary (e.g., guardianship order, loss of cognitive capacity), however, adults are presumed to be legally competent to provide informed consent. Legal standards for competence to consent to treatment are determined by state law and are typically very narrowly defined by cognitive capacity. The standards do not turn on specific psychiatric diagnostic categories. Clinical conditions that produce affective incompetence or denial of illness are not usually recognized by the law unless they significantly diminish a patient's cognitive capacity. Patients with mental disorders may understand information provided about their condition but lack insight and be unable to appreciate the information's significance. Incapacity to make health care decisions does not prevent treatment, it merely requires the clinician to obtain substitute consent, although the patient's refusal to consent to treatment cannot be equated with incompetency.

In In the Guardianship of John Roe (1992), the Massachusetts Supreme Judicial Court recognized that the denial of illness can be a factor in concluding that a patient is incompetent to make treatment decisions. Moreover, patients with mood disorders may feel too good (omnipotent) or too bad (hopeless) to make a rational choice about taking recommended medications. Schizophrenic patients often fear that a drug will do serious harm. They lack a balanced consideration of both the risks and the benefits of a proposed medication. One study, which used three different assessment instruments to measure subjects' competency to make treatment decisions, found that patients with schizophrenia or major depression demonstrated poorer understanding of treatment disclosures, poorer reasoning in decision making regarding treatment, and a greater likelihood of failing to appreciate the severity of their illness or the potential treatment benefits than did comparison subjects (Grisso and Appelbaum 1995).

Competency is not a scientifically determinable state—it is situation specific. Although there are no hard and fast definitions, legally germane to determining competency is the patient's ability to understand the particular treatment option being proposed; evaluate the relevant risks, benefits, and alternatives; make a treatment choice; and communicate that choice.

A review of case law and scholarly literature reveals four basic standards for determining competency in health care decision making (Appelbaum et al. 1987). Table 4–1 lists these standards, in order of levels of mental capacity they require. Many courts prefer the first two standards. However, an informed consent reflecting the patient's autonomy, personal needs, and values requires the application of rational decision making to the risks and benefits of appropriate treatment options provided by the clinician.

A valid consent can be either *express* or *implied* from the patient's actions. It is legally prudent to memorialize the consent in writing. Although some states require written consent for certain procedures (e.g., abortion, see Fl. Stat. Ann. § 390.0111 [2005]; surgery, see Alaska Admin. Code tit. 7, § 12.120 [c] [2005]), there is no general requirement that psychiatric treatment consent be written to be valid (see Ha. Rev. Stat. § 334E-1 [2005]).

The competency issue is particularly sensitive when dealing with minors or persons with mental disabilities who lack the requisite mental capacity to consent. In both cases, the law generally recognizes that an authorized representative or guardian (e.g., a parent) may consent for the patient. In the case of minors, however, some states permit children as young as age 12 years who are victims of abuse or at risk of serious harm to consent to outpatient mental health care (Cal. Fam.Code § 6924 [2005]).

Information

The standard for the knowledge that must be disclosed in order for the patient to make an informed decision varies from state to state. Traditionally, the duty to disclose has been measured by a professional standard: either what a reason-

Table 4–1.   Standards of competency for health care decision making

- Communication of choice
- Understanding of relevant information provided
- Appreciation of available options and consequences
- Rational decision making

able physician would disclose under the circumstances or the customary disclosure practices of physicians in a particular community. The landmark case of Canterbury v. Spence (1972) established a patient-oriented standard. This standard focused on the "material" information a reasonable person in the patient's position would want to know in order to make an informed decision. Most courts apply this objective standard, and some have expanded "material risks" to include information regarding the consequences of not consenting to the treatment or procedure (Truman v. Thomas 1980).

A *material risk* is defined as one that a physician knows (or should know) would be considered significant by a reasonable person in the patient's position. Even in patient-oriented jurisdictions, there is no duty to disclose every possible risk. The issue of how much information a patient must be provided in order to constitute a valid consent is normally resolved by requiring a doctor to convey all appropriate information in terms that the "average patient" would want and be able to understand (see Table 4–2).

Voluntariness

For consent to be considered voluntary, it must be given freely by the patient and without the presence of any form of coercion, fraud, or duress impinging on the patient's decision-making process. In evaluating whether consent is voluntary, the courts typically examine all of the relevant circumstances, including the psychiatrist's role in the process and the patient's mental state.

Exceptions

There are two basic exceptions to the requirement of informed consent. First, in situations in which immediate treatment is necessary to save a life or prevent serious harm and it is impossible to obtain either the patient's consent or that

Table 4–2.   Informed consent: reasonable information to be disclosed

Although there exists no consistently accepted set of information to be disclosed for any given medical or psychiatric situation, as a rule of thumb, five areas of information are generally provided:

1. Diagnosis: Description of the condition or problem

2. Treatment: Nature and purpose of the proposed treatment

3. Consequences: Risks and benefits of the proposed treatment

4. Alternatives: Viable alternatives to the proposed treatment, including risks and benefits

5. Prognosis: Projected outcome with and without treatment

of someone authorized to provide consent for the patient, the law presumes that the consent would have been granted. Two criteria must be met when applying this exception. First, the emergency must be serious and "imminent," and second, the patient's condition—and not the surrounding circumstances (e.g., adverse environmental conditions)—determines the existence of an emergency.

The second exception, therapeutic privilege, is more difficult to apply. Courts differ in their standards for invoking therapeutic privilege. Under therapeutic privilege, informed consent is not required if a complete disclosure of all possible risks and alternatives would likely be injurious to the patient's health. Failure to obtain informed consent from a patient before administering medication because the psychiatrist fears that the patient will refuse the medication is not an appropriate exercise of therapeutic privilege. Therapeutic privilege should not be used as a means of circumventing the requirement to obtain a patient's informed consent for recommended treatment or procedures but rather to avoid interjecting trauma unnecessarily through the consent process.

Waiver

A physician need not disclose risks of treatment when the patient has competently, knowingly, and voluntarily waived the right to be informed (e.g., when the patient does not want to be informed of drug side effects). Waiver is not an exception to the requirement of informed consent. Waiver of the right to be informed releases the doctor from the responsibility to provide a full disclosure because the patient has chosen to make a decision on limited information or some other construct or with no information.

Absent waiver or exception, a psychiatrist who treats a patient without first obtaining informed consent is subject to a liability claim. Treatment without the patient's consent or treatment against a patient's wishes may constitute *battery* (an intentional tort), an impermissible touching. Treatment commenced with an inadequate consent may constitute medical negligence—unreasonable failure to comply with the standard of care to disclose information to the patient before beginning treatment.

The law of informed consent consists largely of judge-made common law of torts that governs relations between health care providers and their patients. The right to refuse treatment rests on constitutional and statutory provisions designed to protect patients' autonomy from health care providers who use the power of the state to confine people against their will. The topics of informed consent and the right to refuse treatment are closely related because both deal with aspects of personal autonomy. Unlike the informed consent that usually originates at the beginning of voluntary treatment between a physician and a patient, the right to refuse treatment normally does not arise until the patient is already receiving some degree of treatment from a clinician or health care institution on an involuntary basis.

Right to Refuse Treatment

Although not absolute, most jurisdictions recognize that an institutionalized mentally disabled person has a right to refuse treatment. Buttressed by constitutionally derived rights to "privacy" and freedom from cruel and unusual punishment, the common law tort of battery, and the doctrine of informed consent, the courts have generally concluded that the state's interests in the confinement of persons with mental disabilities do not, without additional findings, permit the state to compel treatment. The right to refuse treatment often runs directly counter to the dictates of clinical judgment (i.e., to treat and protect) and the state's correlative *parens patriae* and police power concerns. Attempting to balance these interests, the courts vary considerably regarding the parameters of this right and the procedures to be followed.

Two landmark cases illustrate this point. In Rennie v. Klein (1983), the U.S. Third Circuit Court of Appeals recognized a qualified right to refuse neuroleptic medications for involuntarily hospitalized patients in state institutions. The court concluded, however, that this right may be curtailed "whenever, in the exercise of professional judgment, such an action is deemed necessary to prevent the patient from endangering himself or others." In Rogers v. Okin (1984) (later Mills v. Rogers 1984), the U.S. First Circuit Court of Appeals recognized a right to refuse antipsychotic medication, absent an emergency (e.g., serious threat of extreme violence or personal injury), for committed patients who were not adjudicated incompetent. Incompetent persons have a similar right to refuse treatment, but it must be exercised through a "substituted judgment treatment plan" that has been reviewed and approved by the court. These two decisions are often viewed as legal bookends to the right to refuse treatment. The *Rennie* case became the model for legal decisions that adopted a treatment-driven rationale for the right to refuse treatment. *Rogers* became the basis for rights-driven approaches taken by other courts in litigating the right to refuse treatment.

Numerous state and federal decisions have also tackled aspects of this issue. Nearly all states recognize an involuntarily hospitalized patient's right to refuse medication in the absence of an emergency. Case law determinations of what constitutes an emergency for these purposes range from a risk of "imminent" harm to self or others to a deterioration in the patient's mental condition if treatment is halted. Until either more states enact legislation or the U.S. Supreme Court squarely rules on this issue, jurisdictions will continue to vary regarding the substance of the right to refuse treatment and the procedures by which this right can be implemented.

Clinical Management of Legal Issues

Informed Consent

The legal doctrine of informed consent is consistent with the provision of good clinical care. Informed consent allows patients to become partners in treatment determinations that accord with their own needs and values. In the past, physicians operated under the medical principle of *primum non nocere*— "first do no harm." Today, psychiatrists are required to practice within the legal model of informed consent and its concerns with patient autonomy. Most psychiatrists find increased patient autonomy desirable in fostering development of the therapeutic alliance that is so essential to treatment. Patient independence is the goal of most psychiatric treatments.

Competency

Competence can be a confusing term because it may be used to mean legal competence, or it may have a broad variety of subjective clinical definitions. Mishkin (1989) recommended distinguishing the terms *incompetence* and *incapacity*. *Incompetence* refers to an adjudication of status by a court, and *incapacity* indicates a functional inability determined by a clinician. An operational definition of *competence* is the mental capacity to make a decision in accordance with the patient's goals, concerns, and values. Clinicians use various terms, such as *decision-making capacity, medical-psychological capacity, clinical competence,* or *functional capacity* in defining the mental capacity to consent to treatment.

The criteria used to define or measure legal competency are heavily weighted in favor of cognitive functioning. Cognitive functioning may be reasonably intact but unusable if behavioral control is under the influence of a mood disorder. Thus it is arguable that patients with such conditions are affectively incompetent. For instance, a severely depressed patient may fully understand the nature of his or her disorder but may nonetheless reject treatment because of pervasive feelings of hopelessness, helplessness, and worthlessness. Manic patients tend to emphasize the risks of medications while denying their mental illness.

Clinical Evaluation

When clinicians evaluate a patient's competency, they do so from a clinical perspective. No matter what test of competency is used, the following may influence the evaluation of competency. A number of factors influence the evaluation of competency (Table 4–3).

The mental capacity to give consent is typically influenced by a number of psychological and physical factors. The determination of health care decision-making capacity in psychiatric practice is not a single event but a continuous process.

Competency is a here-and-now, contextual matter. The competence of a patient is determined in reference to a particular issue at a particular time. Rarely is a patient so incompetent as to be unable to express a preference about medical care. Even patients adjudicated incompetent by a court may retain some capacity to express a preference about medical care decisions. Moreover, the law's standards for competence require only *minimal* mental capacity

Table 4–3. Factors influencing the evaluation of patient competency

- Clinician–patient interaction
- Third-party information (e.g., family, spouse, partner, other)
- Accuracy of the historical data provided by the patient
- Accuracy of current information provided to the patient
- Patient's mental state
- Setting and circumstances where the consent is obtained

to understand the nature of a particular choice. At a minimum, in assessing decision-making capacity, the patient should be able to understand the particular treatment choice proposed, to make a treatment choice, and to be able to communicate that decision. When this decision-making capacity is lacking, medical decision making is frequently referred to a substitute decision-maker. When a patient demonstrates this decision-making capacity, a decision by that patient that seems irrational is not by itself a basis for a determination of incompetence. Legal advice may be needed if the competency issue cannot be resolved by additional medical and psychiatric consultation.

Minors

Traditionally, minors have been considered by the law to lack the competence to make treatment decisions. Normally, to treat a minor, a mental health professional must obtain the consent of the parent or legal guardian. There are, however, exceptions to this rule. An exception is permitted for emergencies; this exception is an extension of that provided for adults. In some states, an exception is allowed that permits treatment in the case of incest or abuse or if the delay in obtaining parental consent would, in the physician's judgment, endanger the health of the minor. An exception also exists for the emancipated minor who is no longer under parental control. Marriage or military service emancipates a minor. Age, residence, financial independence, property ownership, pregnancy, and parenthood also will be considered by the court in determining a minor's appropriate status.

The mature-minor exception allows a physician to treat a minor based on the patient's consent if the minor demonstrates sufficient capacity to appreciate the nature, extent, and consequences of medical treatment. For example, in Cardwell v. Bechtol (1987), the court held that the mature-minor exception applied "when the child is close to maturity and knowingly gives an informed consent." In *Cardwell*, the minor was only 5 months short of the legal age for consent, and the court found that she could make a mature decision to receive back treatment. Although not every state has adopted the mature-minor exception, there are no reported decisions in which physicians were held liable for treating consenting minors over age 15 years.

In cases involving divorced parents, decision-making authority regarding health matters, education, and religious training of minor children belongs to the custodial parent except by agreement or in the case of an emergency. Under appropriate circumstances, psychiatrists may obtain a history from the noncustodial parent and, if full evaluation seems indicated, provide an affidavit or testify for the noncustodial parent who is requesting the court to order or permit such an evaluation. The law uses the word *parent* in the context of consent to a child's treatment or evaluation to mean the parent who has been awarded custody under a divorce decree (Gary v. Gary 1982).

Because minors are not, in general, competent to consent to their own medical care, they may not voluntarily hospitalize themselves. Addressing the constitutionality of a statutory admission procedure that permitted hospitalization of a minor upon a parent's application without judicial oversight, the U.S. Supreme Court in Parham v. J.R. (1979) found that the federal due-process clause does not require a formal or quasi-formal commitment hearing. The court held, however, that due process does require that a neutral fact finder make an inquiry to determine whether the state's statutory requirements for a child's admission have been satisfied. The inquiry can be conducted by a staff physician as fact finder if the physician independently evaluates the child's mental and emotional condition and need for treatment. This physician or fact finder must also have the authority to refuse admittance to any child not satisfying the medical standards for admission. Moreover, once a child is admitted, his or her continuing need for commitment must be reviewed with the same procedure.

Physician Standards for Disclosure

As already mentioned, the psychiatrist is not required to inform the patient of every conceivable risk of treatment or diagnosis. As the risk of harm and magnitude of harm increases, the danger becomes greater, and the procedure becomes more intrusive, the obligation to inform the patient is more likely to be recognized. When less harmful but equally effective alternative treatments are available, the duty to disclose alternative treatments is heightened accordingly. For instance, if an antipsychotic medication is prescribed for a nonpsychotic patient with anxiety symptoms when a benzodiazepine would be equally effective, the increased risk of serious side effects from the antipsychotic medication as well as the availability of potentially less risky treatments will require disclosure.

Selective serotonin reuptake inhibitors are first-line treatment for major depression. In the past, heated controversy existed on the issue of psychotherapy versus medication for major depression (Klerman 1990; Stone 1990). Today, patients should be informed of the availability of a wide variety of antidepressant drugs in combination with psychotherapies that have proven to be effective treatments. The type of information generally disclosed is outlined in Table 4–2. Typical risks include the probability of death, problems of recuperation, potential for disability, and the chances of disfigurement. For example, tardive dyskinesia could result in disfigurement. Patients also should be given an adequate opportunity to have all of their questions answered.

Exceptions to Disclosure

As noted, the most common exceptions to disclosure are emergency and therapeutic privilege.

Emergency

The law implies consent in an acute, life-threatening crisis requiring immediate medical attention and treatment. The law assumes that every rational person under these circumstances would consent to treatment. Often, clear definitions of psychiatric emergencies do not exist in state law. Clinicians should document the circumstances of the emergency at the time or as soon thereafter as is practicable and address the requirements of any relevant case law or statutes.

Therapeutic Privilege

Therapeutic privilege allows a physician to withhold full disclosure of risks in cases when such disclosure might have a serious, detrimental effect on the patient's physical and psychological health. Some psychiatrists misunderstand therapeutic privilege to apply if the information provided may cause the patient to reject treatment. This is incorrect. Therapeutic privilege should not be used to circumvent the legal requirement to obtain patient consent. Clinically, therapeutic privilege should be invoked only after it is clear that disclosure could cause the patient to become so alarmed and distraught that significant disruption of the patient's decision-making abilities or serious clinical regression would likely occur. Although the doctrine of therapeutic privilege has been recognized by a number of courts and is codified in some statutes, not all courts have accepted it (Barcai v. Betwee 2002).

Waiver

Waiver is not an exception to informed consent; rather, it is the result of a competent patient's decision to forgo application of informed consent. On occasion, a patient may request not to be informed about the risks of or alternatives to a treatment or procedure. When patients voluntarily and knowingly make this request (i.e., they realize they have a right to this information and are competent), the request may be honored and the information disclosure requirement for consent is deemed waived. A record should be made of the patient's waiver in the medical chart as well as a notation that the implications of such a waiver were discussed as a treatment issue.

Maintaining a Clinical Perspective

The psychiatrist is primarily responsible for discussing treatment with the patient and obtaining consent. Sending a nurse or other mental health personnel to obtain consent is usually insufficient in itself. The psychiatrist should be available to answer questions by the patient about the proposed treatment. The information needs to be presented in a manner that is intelligible to the patient. False assurances of no risk should be avoided in favor of supportive, hopeful statements about treatment. Risks should be explained to next of kin when exceptions are made to informing the patient directly. Finally, although not generally legally required, clear documentation of the consent process undertaken with the patient is the hallmark of good practice.

Informed Consent and the Psychotic Patient

Psychiatrists must obtain consent for all patients before beginning treatment. Furthermore, consent should be viewed as a continuing educational process rather than a single ritualistic act in the service of defensive psychiatry. Even though a patient is psychotic, the psychiatrist is not relieved from obtaining consent for treatment or as an ongoing requirement. Because psychosis does not necessarily equate with an inability to consent, some patients with psychosis are capable of giving a valid consent to treatment. If psychosis has affected a patient's decision-making capacity, substitute consent is required. Clinicians must guard against a bias in favor of treatment that assumes that if the patient consents to treatment, the consent is competently given. For patients lacking the capacity to consent, informed consent should be obtained from a substitute decision-maker.

Some patients may initially refuse treatment recommendations as a way of dealing with feelings of helplessness or for other important psychological reasons. Nonetheless, the vast majority of patients accept treatment recommendations after first refusing (Simon 1992). It needs to be established that the consent to treatment is competently given. Consideration should be given to renewing consent more frequently for patients (both inpatients and outpatients) taking high dosages of antipsychotic or other medications.

Some acutely psychotic patients may require a delay in starting drug therapy until the therapeutic alliance has had time to develop. Initially, these patients may not be able to provide a valid consent if disclosure of side effects seriously frightens them or when such disclosure contributes to further regression. Furthermore, acutely disturbed patients may not be able to understand the information provided or to weigh risks and benefits of a proposed treatment or procedure. Nonetheless, the law requires that informed consent be obtained from the first day of treatment. Problems with patient competence may be addressed by the use of substitute decision-makers, who can be close relatives in some jurisdictions. A number of states, however, do not permit consent to treatment by next of kin for patients with mental disorders. Moreover, a number of jurisdictions require an adjudication of incompetence and the appointment of a guardian to provide substitute consent. In some states, only the substituted consent of a judge is valid. Substitute consent by treatment review panels and other administrative bodies may also be available (Zito et al. 1984).

Situations in which nonconsenting patients with psychosis represent an acute threat of harm to themselves or others may be treated as an emergency exception to informed consent. A patient who has been incapacitated may quickly regain and maintain capacity shortly after hospitalization, even without medication. As soon as the patient regains sufficient mental capacity to give a valid consent to treatment, it should be obtained directly from the patient. Patients who do not indicate a choice by either accepting or refusing treatment should have their competency assessed on other reasonable criteria (e.g., compliance with ward routine, relationships with staff). A thorny problem is presented by patients who do not voice an acceptance or refusal of treatment but give non-verbal assent by following instructions for hospitalization and treatment. These patients may lack the mental capacity to consent to treatment and should be monitored on a continuing basis for their capacity to provide a valid consent.

In some states, involuntarily hospitalized patients with psychosis who remain incompetent and refuse treatment but represent no danger to themselves or others may not be treated unless they are first adjudicated incompetent and a surrogate decision-maker is appointed. In an increasing number of states, nonjudicial administrative procedures that meet due-process requirements are being used in determining the need for involuntary medication (Grisso and Appelbaum 1995).

Under managed care, hospital stays have been greatly reduced, often to less than a week of inpatient care. Only the most disturbed patients who are suicidal, homicidal, or both are admitted. Sufficient time does not usually exist for the psychiatrist and staff to develop a therapeutic alliance with patients who have severe mental disorders. Consequently, these patients may continue to refuse treatment, requiring involuntary hospitalization and transfer to a state institutional facility.

Incompetent Patients: Consent Options

A number of consent options are available for patients lacking the mental capacity to provide or withhold consent to treatment (see Table 4–4).

Proxy consent by next of kin is becoming less available as an option. Relying on the consent of next of kin in treating a patient who is believed to be incompetent may increase the risk of liability. If, for example, it is later discovered that the patient was incompetent and that the relative had no authority to consent, the psychiatrist may be held liable for conducting an unauthorized treatment. Moreover, proxy consent by next of kin for treatment of a mental disorder is not available in a number of jurisdictions where the consent must be obtained by a judicial decree.

Table 4–4.   Common consent and review options for patients lacking mental capacity for health care decisions

- Proxy consent of next of kin[a]
- Adjudication of incompetence; appointment of a guardian
- Institutional administrators or committees
- Treatment review panels
- Substituted consent of the court
- Advance directives (living will, durable power of attorney, or in some cases, health care proxy)

[a]Where it exists, it may be excluded for treatment of mental disorders.

Substitute Decision-Makers

The courts are reluctant to impose liability on the psychiatrist who acts in good faith and uses reasonable medical judgment in making a medical determination of health care decision-making capacity, particularly if the treatment is needed and the incapacity of the patient is clear. The risk of a lawsuit, however, can be reduced by adhering to statutory procedures for the determination of incompetency and obtaining substituted consent. When a psychiatrist is in doubt regarding a patient's capacity to make a treatment decision, peer as well as legal consultation may be necessary.

When patients lack the mental capacity to give or withhold consent for treatment, substitute consent from a decision-maker must be sought. When the psychiatrist suspects patient incompetence and proxy consent is not permitted, a judicial determination of incompetency and permission to treat may be required, either through a court order for treatment or a declaration of incompetence and the appointment of a guardian who will provide treatment consent. In most states, involuntarily hospitalized patients who are thought to lack the mental capacity to refuse treatment cannot be treated against their will without an adjudication of incompetence and the substituted consent of the court. Involuntary hospitalization does not automatically equate with incompetence to consent to or refuse treatment.

Consent by Third Parties

The statutes of every state define procedures by which a judicial determination of competency and the establishment of guardianship can be made. A petition may be filed with the appropriate court for a declaration of incompetency and guardianship. Typically, when available, a family member or relative is appointed guardian. Although some courts will appoint a general guardian to make all decisions, limited guardianship often is provided for the purpose of consent to treatment. Unless proxy consent by a relative is provided by statute or judicial opinion, good-faith consents by next of kin should not be relied on in the treatment of a psychiatric patient who is believed to be incompetent (Klein et al. 1994).

An increasing number of alternatives exist for addressing the problem of persons who may be in need of psychiatric care but lack the capacity to consent and do not meet the requirements for involuntary hospitalization. A *durable power of attorney* permits a person while competent to authorize another person to make decisions on his or her behalf if he or she should become incompetent. Because durable power of attorney does not specifically focus on health care, there is some concern about its application in the medical setting as well as whether it complies with the requirements of competence when executed and gives the person the right to revoke it when competent. In order to rectify these uncertainties, a number of states have passed health care proxy laws. The *health care proxy* is a legal instrument akin to the durable power of attorney but specifically created for health care decision making (Task Force on Life and the Law 1991). The law still requires that the person executing the document be competent at the time of its execution and that the document permit its author to revoke it while competent. Living-will laws permit individuals to explicitly state their wishes concerning life-sustaining treatment. Efforts to fashion a psychiatric living will as an alternative to involuntary treatment have been attempted. The legal sufficiency of such a document remains untested and presents the same questions about competence at its execution and the right of the person to revoke it.

Consent Refusal and Patient Management

Despite time and resource restrictions in managed care settings, every effort should be made to develop a working alliance with a nonconsenting patient. Legal alternatives to obtaining consent from the patient should not be used unless required by an emergency, by the failure of clinical interventions, or by law.

Initially, the patient's refusal is a treatment issue. Concerns expressed by patients based on previous experience with adverse drug effects or observations of other patients undergoing unpleasant or frightening side effects are common. A number of factors play a major psychological role in drug refusal (see Table 4–5). The act of taking medications may break down denial, confirming the patient's worst fears about being mentally ill. Psychological support is critical to the patient's continued adherence to treatment recommendations.

Voluntary Hospitalization

Most state statutes have attempted to encourage voluntary admission in the hope of aiding treatment. Individuals who voluntarily admit themselves are presumed to understand the conditions of admission as a matter of law.

Patients are generally required by hospitals to sign consent forms for admission. Patients should be informed whether the voluntary admission is pure or conditional. *Pure*, or *informal*, voluntary admission permits the patient to leave the hospital at any time. Absent meeting the requirements of an emergency detention provision in the state's involuntary commitment law, only moral suasion may be used to encourage the patient to stay. *Conditional* voluntary admission contains a provision that permits detaining the patient for a specified period of time after the patient has given written notice of intention to leave. This provision is used when the patient appears to be a danger to self or others.

In the U.S. Supreme Court case Zinermon v. Burch (1990), a mentally ill patient who lacked the capacity to give informed consent for treatment was permitted to go forward with a civil rights action against state officials after he was committed to a state hospital using voluntary commitment procedures. The court held that Florida must have some system of procedures to screen all voluntary patients for competency and exclude incompetent persons from the voluntary admission process. This decision is observed more its breach. Although it was anticipated that *Zinermon* would force states to focus on competency screening of voluntary admissions, the statutes in most states have not been revised to require compliance with *Zinermon* competency screening for voluntary hospitalization. The American Psychiatric Association task force report *Consent to Voluntary Hospitalization* (American Psychiatric Association 1993) provides helpful guidelines for obtaining appropriate consent from patients who are voluntarily hospitalized. The task force report makes the basic assumptions that 1) preservation of voluntary admission whenever possible is preferable to admitting large numbers of involuntary patients and 2) the primary safeguards for

Table 4–5. Psychological factors influencing drug refusal

- Transference and countertransference issues
- Fears about taking medications
- Prior adverse reactions to medications
- Hospital staff conflicts
- Influence of family and friends
- Nonadherence as a power struggle
- Primary and secondary gain from disabling symptoms
- Denial of mental illness

patients who are voluntarily hospitalized are clinical, not legal. In practice, the distinction between voluntary and involuntary admission is not as clear as stated in statutory law. Patients often are induced or pressured into accepting voluntary admissions. If voluntary admission were to be maintained as truly voluntary, involuntary admissions would likely increase.

Consent Forms

Although an occasional statute may specify that a written consent form be used, no such legal requirement usually exists. The advantages of a written disclosure form signed by the patient are that 1) the patient cannot later claim that adequate information was not provided and 2) the signed form provides concurrent documentary evidence of what was disclosed and that the consent process took place.

When a consent form is used, it should be included as part of the informing process. The form should be considered a memorandum of agreement between the clinician and the patient without adding new information. Thus the form may be presented after negotiations are complete and the patient has consented to treatment. The consent form is used to document the existing consent rather than to obtain it and is intended to protect the institution and the psychiatrist, not the patient.

The greatest disadvantage of written consent forms is that a particular treatment hazard or side effect may be omitted. Consent forms are "all or nothing" concerning the information provided. The best means of protecting oneself against an unjustified claim of lack of informed consent is to write a note in the patient's record. Consent forms may be perceived as adversarial, especially by suspicious or paranoid patients. In psychiatric practice, the treating clinician should obtain the patient's consent for treatment. The obtaining of consent should not be delegated to nurses or other personnel. The reasoning for invoking an exception to obtaining consent should be clearly explained.

Informed Consent in Managed Care Settings

As part of the psychiatrist's continuing legal and professional duty to the patient (or the patient's substitute decision-maker) to obtain informed consent, full disclosure should be made of all treatment options, even those not covered under the terms of a managed care plan (Simon 1998). Patients should also be informed about grievance and appeals processes if insurance coverage for recommended treatments is denied. "Gag rules" under managed-care contractual provisions are often illegal (Picinic 1997). Gag rules limit information about treatment options furnished by physicians to patients or prohibit physicians from revealing restriction of benefits or provider financial incentives. Managed care contracts that contain limitations on full disclosure to patients should not be signed.

Anticipated limitations on inpatient treatment imposed by managed care should be discussed with the patient early in the admission process so that alternative treatment plans can be considered and hasty decisions avoided. Disclosures about treatment limitations need to be made in a clinically supportive manner, particularly with potentially violent patients. Patients can become quite disturbed when psychiatrists speak to them about limitations of coverage. The patient may perceive the psychiatrist as working for the insurance company, thus adversely affecting the doctor–patient relationship. (Consent to provide information to managed care organizations is discussed in Chapter 3, "Confidentiality and Testimonial Privilege").

References

American Psychiatric Association: Task Force Report 34: Consent to Voluntary Hospitalization. Washington, DC, American Psychiatric Association, 1993

Appelbaum PS, Lidz CW, Meisel A: Informed consent: legal theory and clinical practice. New York, Oxford University Press, 1987, pp 84–87

Grisso T, Appelbaum PS: Comparison of standards for assessing patients' capacities to make treatment decisions. Am J Psychiatry 152:1033–1037, 1995

Klein JI, Onek JN, Macbeth JE: Legal and Risk Management Issues in the Private Practice of Psychiatry. Washington, DC, American Psychiatric Press, 1994

Klerman GL: The psychiatric patient's right to effective treatment: implications of Osheroff v Chestnut Lodge. Am J Psychiatry 147:409–418, 1990

Mishkin B: Determining the capacity for making health care decisions. Adv Psychosom Med 19:151–166, 1989

Picinic NJ: Physicians, bound and gagged: federal attempts to combat managed care's use of gag clauses. Seton Hall Legis J 21:567–620, 1997

Simon RI: Clinical Psychiatry and the Law, 2nd Edition. Washington, DC, American Psychiatric Press, 1992

Simon RI: Psychiatrists' duties in discharging sicker and potentially violent inpatients in the managed care era. Psychiatr Serv 49:62–67, 1998

Stone AA: Law, science, and psychiatric malpractice: a response to Klerman's indictment of psychoanalytic psychiatry. Am J Psychiatry 147:419–427, 1990

Task Force on Life and the Law: The Health Care Proxy Law: A Guidebook for Health Care Professionals. Albany, NY, New York State Department of Health, 1991

Zito JM, Lentz SL, Routt WW, et al: The treatment review panel: a solution to treatment refusal? Bull Am Acad Psychiatry Law 12:349–358, 1984

Legal References

Barcai v Betwee, 50 P.3d 946 (Haw., 2002)

Canterbury v Spence, 464 F.2d 772 (D.C. Cir., 1972), cert denied, 409 U.S. 1064 (1972)

Cardwell v Bechtol, 724 S.W.2d 739 (Tenn., 1987)

Charters v U.S., 829 F.2d 479 (4th Cir., 1987), on rehearing 863 Fed 302; cert denied 494 U.S. 1016 (1990)

Gary v Gary, 631 S.W.2d 781 (Tex. Ct. App., 1982)

In the Guardianship of John Roe, 583 N.E.2d 1282 (Mass., 1992)

Long v Jaszczak, 688 N.W.2d 173 (N.D., 2004)

Mills v Rogers, 478 F.Supp. 1342 (D. Mass., 1979), aff'd in part, rev'd in part, 634 F.2d 650 (1st Cir., 1980), vacated and remanded sub nom, 457 U.S. 291 (1982), on remand 738 F.2d 1 (1st Cir., 1984)

Parham v J.R., 442 U.S. 584 (1979)

Rennie v Klein, 462 F.Supp. 1131 (D. N.J., 1978), suppl., 476 F.Supp. 1294 (D. N.J., 1979), modified, 653 F.2d 836 (3d Cir., 1981), vacated and remanded, 458 U.S. 1119 (1982), on remand, 720 F.2d 266 (3d Cir., 1983)

Rogers v Okin, 738 F.2d 1, 14-15 (1st Cir., 1984)

Truman v Thomas, 27 Cal.3d 285, 611 P.2d 902, 165 Cal.Rptr 308 (1980)

Zinermon v Burch, 494 U.S. 113 (1990)

Laws

Alaska Admin. Code tit. 7, § 12.120 (c) (2005)

Cal. Fam.Code § 6924 (2005)

Fl. Stat. Ann. § 390.0111 (2005)

Ha. Rev. Stat. § 334E-1 (2005)

5

Psychiatric Treatment

Tort Liability

Overview of the Law

A patient, or the administrator of the estate of a deceased patient, who has a good-faith basis to believe that a psychiatrist's negligence harmed the patient, is entitled to institute a medical malpractice claim for compensatory damages. This risk of litigation that psychiatrists face is an inherent cost of our decision to maintain open courts to provide the citizenry with an alternative to less-civilized methods for resolving disputes. For psychiatrists, the risk of malpractice litigation is also affected by the disorders of many of the patients they treat. There is nothing a clinical psychiatrist can do to reduce that risk of a lawsuit to zero, short of not seeing patients.

For those who choose to continue to see patients, there are several important responses to this risk. First, it is critically important to maintain adequate professional liability insurance. Even in cases in which the psychiatrist's conduct is ultimately judged to meet relevant standards and the claim dismissed, the costs of defending the lawsuit, the bulk of which are not recoverable, may be substantial. Although professional liability insurance does not reimburse income lost as a consequence of malpractice litigation, it does include the legal costs of defending against a malpractice claim. Second, in general, the best clinical practice is also the best risk management. Clinical psychiatrists may quibble about the outcome of certain individual cases, but a review of reported psychiatric malpractice decisions upholding a judgment for the plaintiff would likely yield professional consensus that the defendant's conduct amounted to substandard care. Third, for those instances in which there is a gap between good clinical practice and good risk management, understanding what the law requires for a malpractice claimant to prevail informs clinical psychiatrists how treatment issues may be best approached.

Tort law requires that a medical malpractice claimant prove that the allegedly errant physician breached a duty owed to the claimant and that this breach was the proximate cause of harm suffered by the patient. In cases brought by a person who was then a patient of the psychiatrist there is typically little question that a duty was owed to the patient. Often such cases are not brought, however, because of the difficulty of proving that but for the psychiatrist's negligence, things would have turned out very differently (for the better). In those cases that are brought, a major issue is often the question of breach of duty. Negligence law judges this breach of duty by asking whether the defendant behaved as society expects a reasonable person to behave under the circumstances. In the case of medical malpractice, the law does not expect that all patients will be cured or even that physicians will never err. What we ordinarily expect of the reasonable physician is compliance with the standard of care established by the relevant professional community. The physician's conduct is contrasted with that of the average or prudent physician in a similar situation, accounting for specialty and often geographic variables. Many states, such as California, have legislated these standards:

> In any civil action to recover damages resulting from personal injury or wrongful death…in which it is alleged that such injury or death resulted from the negligence of a health care provider…the claimant shall have the burden of proving by the preponderance of the evidence that the alleged actions of the health care provider represented a breach of the prevailing professional standard of care for that health care provider. The prevailing professional standard of care for a given health care provider shall be that level of care, skill and treatment which, in light of all relevant surrounding circumstances, is recognized as acceptable and appropriate by reasonably prudent similar health care providers. (Cal. Gen. Stat. Ann. § 52-184c [2006])

This chapter addresses that standard of care for clinical psychiatrists in the use of three modes of therapy: psychopharmacology, electroconvulsive therapy (ECT), and psychotherapy.

Psychopharmacology

Standard of Care

Typically, when treating a patient with medication, the exercise of reasonable care requires a thorough clinical evaluation of the patient, including all appropriate laboratory tests, a review of present and past medication use and drug allergies, and a complete background history. The psychiatrist also has a duty to advise the patient about the use of medication and to provide sufficient information that an informed consent may be obtained. If a physical examination is indicated, it can be performed by the psychiatrist or the patient may be referred. Depending on the type of treatment and the nature of the patient, it may be prudent to refer the patient for a physical examination to avoid potential troublesome transference and countertransference developments. Some psychiatrists routinely obtain vital signs of patients who are taking medications.

Medication and Liability

The law recognizes that psychiatric treatment is inexact and therefore does not demand that treatment invariably be successful, only that it be reasonable according to prevailing professional standards. In administering psychotropic medication, certain treatment procedures are generally considered standard, and unless an emergency situation arises, they should generally be followed (see Table 5–1).

Table 5–1.   Standard drug treatment procedures

- A complete clinical history
- Disclosure of sufficient information to obtain informed consent for procedures and treatments
- Documentation of all treatment decisions, particularly when a medication is changed, adjusted, or reinstated
- Appropriate supervision of a patient's clinical course
- Monitoring the patient's reaction to the medication

When typical antipsychotic medications (neuroleptics) are prescribed, the patient's potential for developing tardive dyskinesia (TD) is a major concern. Several large judgments have been rendered against psychiatrists for failure to obtain informed consent from or to properly monitor the clinical course of a patient on neuroleptic medication who subsequently developed TD (American Cyanamid v. Frankson 1987; Barclay v. Campbell 1986; Clites v. State 1982). Psychiatrists administering psychotropic medication should become familiar with the TD management guidelines promulgated by the American Psychiatric Association (APA; see Table 5–2).

These guidelines remain pertinent in the era of atypical antipsychotics, even though current research indicates a significantly lower incidence of TD with these newer agents (Glazer 2000). No official guideline, however, can substitute for sound clinical judgment in the treatment and management of patients.

Electroconvulsive Therapy

ECT continues to be used by psychiatrists in treating mainly major depressive disorder. The APA Task Force on ECT has made specific, nonbinding recommendations for its use and administration (American Psychiatric Association 2000). Legislative and judicial decisions regarding ECT include numerous indications and contraindications for its use. Provisions often are made for consultation and review, medical procedures required before and during treatment, regulation of the frequency of treatment, and specific record-keeping requirements (Newell 2005; Winslade et al. 1984). Furthermore, the Joint Commission on Accreditation of Healthcare Organizations (JCAHO) considers ECT to be a special treatment procedure and requires hospitals to have written policies concerning its use (Joint Commission on Accreditation of Healthcare Organizations 1999). Violation of statutory regulations or JCAHO and hospital policies governing ECT may be compelling evidence of the breach of relevant professional standards.

Malpractice liability arising from the use of ECT has generally been confined to five situations: 1) conducting an inadequate pretreatment examination; 2) being negligent in administration of premedication; 3) being negligent in administration of ECT, resulting in fractures or other injuries; 4) failing to provide adequate posttreatment supervision; and 5) obtaining inadequate or no informed consent for ECT (this creates the greatest potential for liability, by far).

Table 5–2. Recommendations for prevention and management of tardive dyskinesia

1. Review indications for antipsychotic drugs; consider alternative treatments when available.

2. Educate the patient and his or her family regarding benefits and risks. Obtain informed consent for treatment and document it in the medical record.

3. Document objective evidence of the benefit from antipsychotic treatment and review it periodically (at least every 3–6 months) to determine ongoing need and benefit.

4. Utilize the minimum effective dosage for long-term treatment.

5. Exercise particular caution with children, the elderly, and patients with affective disorders.

6. Examine the patient regularly for early signs of dyskinesia and, if present, document them in the medical record.

7. If tardive dyskinesia is suspected, also consider alternative causes of the dyskinesia.

8. If presumptive tardive dyskinesia is present, reevaluate the indications for continued antipsychotic treatment and obtain informed consent from the patient regarding continuing or discontinuing neuroleptic treatment. Consider obtaining a consultation.

9. Many cases of tardive dyskinesia will improve and even remit with antipsychotic discontinuation or dosage reduction. If treatment for tardive dyskinesia is indicated, utilize more benign agents first (e.g., benzodiazepines and tocopherol) but keep abreast of new treatment developments.

10. If tardive dyskinesia is severe or disabling, consider obtaining a second opinion.

Source. Reprinted from American Psychiatric Association: *Tardive Dyskinesia: A Task Force Report of the American Psychiatric Association.* Washington, DC, American Psychiatric Association, 1992, pp. 250–251. Copyright 1992, American Psychiatric Association. Used with permission.

Psychotherapy

Psychotherapy is understood by the law to be inexact, evolving, and based on principles difficult to quantify and measure. Currently more than 450 schools of psychotherapy exist. This belies assertions that that there is a single therapy that constitutes the gold standard, let alone an assertion that any recognized psychotherapy, if done right, would result in a "cure." Consequently, malpractice actions for negligent psychotherapy are infrequent and typically unsuccessful (Simon 1991a). As a rule, the choice of a particular therapeutic practice or technique need only be considered "reasonable" as judged by an ordinary therapist. This standard is very broad and vague. However, that should not be interpreted to imply that insofar as the law is concerned, psychiatrists can do no wrong in psychotherapy. Certain actions (such as sexually exploiting the patient's transference) have been regarded as clearly on the wrong side of this fuzzy line for reasonable psychotherapy and are therefore subject to legal action. Other wrongdoing in the conduct of psychotherapy, such as breach of confidentiality, abandonment, and negligent termination, has also been held to violate the standard of care.

A number of malpractice lawsuits are brought against therapists for treatment-boundary violations under legal theories of negligent psychotherapy and abandonment. Reasonably clear boundaries for the conduct of psychotherapy exist that are accepted by most competent therapists from a wide variety of theoretical orientations (Greenberg and Shuman 1997; Simon 1992b). Although a number of boundary violations may eventually evolve into therapist–patient sex, many other such violations do not. Nonetheless, patients may also be psychologically harmed by boundary violations that do not lead to therapist–patient sex (Simon 1991b). Boundary violations may precede exploitation of the patient for money or a social relationship. Unchecked boundary violations usually produce serious errors in diagnosis and treatment. Boundary violations that harm the patient are invariably associated with other negligent treatment.

Clinical Management of Legal Issues

Prescribing Medication

Unapproved Uses

Prescribing an approved medication for an unapproved use does not violate federal law. However, the reasonableness of prescribing or failing to prescribe an approved medication for an unapproved use may be at the core of a medical malpractice claim (Henry 1999). When a psychiatrist prescribes a drug for a use that is not approved by the U.S. Food and Drug Administration (FDA)—for example, an atypical antipsychotic for a patient's anxiety disorder, lithium for violence, medroxyprogesterone acetate for paraphilias, a tricyclic and monoamine oxidase inhibitor or other drug combination for refractory depression—the decision should be based on a firm scientific rationale and research. The psychiatrist should have accessible texts or peer-reviewed journal articles to support the decision to prescribe the drug or drugs for that unapproved use. For instance, the psychiatric literature recommends the prescribing of a variety of drugs in patients with rapid-cycling bipolar disorder that do not have FDA approval for that use (Simon 1997). Off-label prescribing of medications is at the discretion of the physician once a drug has been approved (see Femrite v. Abbott Northwestern Hosp. 1997; United States v. Evers 1978). The psychiatrist is not restricted by FDA-approved indications and labeling.

The standard for informed consent requires heightened disclosure when a drug is prescribed for an unapproved use. The patient (or guardian) should be informed that he or she will be taking a drug for a use that has not been approved by the FDA and warned of all reasonably foreseeable risks. The nature of the disclosure should be recorded in the patient's chart. Once a drug is marketed, its use is the responsibility of physicians, and its prescription requires an exercise of their discretion.

A number of medications used by psychiatrists to treat various psychiatric disorders in children do not have FDA approval to be used as psychopharmacological agents. There is a scant scientific knowledge base in the psychiatric literature and few data available from controlled clinical trials to support off-label prescribing for children. Until more studies become available, clinicians have found a number of these drugs to be useful in treating children by following clinical hunches, by using trial and error, or through just plain serendipity. Recently, however, the FDA has issued a black box warning about the potential increased risk of suicide in child and adolescent patients prescribed antidepressants. As of this writing, research has not settled the issue of whether antidepressants cause or precipitate suicide in children and adolescents. Psychiatrists should not be deterred from prescribing antidepressants to children and adolescents, provided that the diagnosis and indications are clear, that the dosage of medication is appropriate, and that the patient's follow-up is careful. A study by G.E. Simon et al. (2006) of about 60,000 enrollees in an insurance plan found that the risk of suicide decreased by 60% during the first month of antidepressant treatment and declined in the following 5 months. Suicide risk was highest during the month before treatment was initiated.

Unapproved Drugs

The prescription of an unapproved drug is a criminal offense. The introduction or delivery into interstate commerce of an unapproved drug is prohibited by 21 U.S.C. § 355. In a world wired by the World Wide Web and with countries that strike different risk-benefit balances in their approach to new drug approvals, this prohibition on unapproved drugs has become a live issue for the FDA and clinical psychiatrists. For example, a few years ago this issue arose prominently with regard to clomipramine, which had been approved for use in the treatment of obsessive-compulsive disorder (OCD) in Canada and other countries before it was officially approved in the United States. The psychiatric literature supported the treatment of OCD with clomipramine. Its side-effect profile was similar to that of other tricyclic antidepressants.

Generally, the FDA's policy is not to prosecute physicians who prescribe legitimate drugs approved in other jurisdictions. In limited circumstances, access to unapproved drugs may be available under regulations established under the authority of the FDA (King 1998). The risk of malpractice is increased, however, if a patient is harmed by a drug that is not approved as effective and safe by the FDA.

Physicians' Desk Reference or Drug Insert

The *Physicians' Desk Reference* (PDR) is published privately by a commercial firm. The publisher compiles, organizes, and distributes product descriptions prepared by the manufacturers' medical department and consultants. The FDA requires that products that have official package inserts be reported in the PDR in the identical language appearing on the circular.

A drug's package insert lists almost all of the side effects ever reported in drug trials, even if not shown to have been produced by the drug under consideration (i.e., side effects found in similar drugs are also reported). The side effects reported in the package insert may not be weighted according to the probability of occurrence in the course of clinical usage. The legal significance of the package insert or PDR listing varies with each jurisdiction.

Courts generally follow the reasoning in Ramon v. Farr (1989), which held that drug inserts do not by themselves set the standard of care. Rather, such inserts are only one factor to be considered among others, such as the scientific literature, approvals in other countries, expert testimony, and other pertinent factors. The existence of a substantial scientific literature that justifies the clinician's treatment is more persuasive than FDA approval. Although the PDR is frequently used by lawyers in court, it would be a serious error for clinicians to regard the PDR as a primary standard-of-care reference that constrains their clinical judgment. Psychiatrists are responsible for making informed decisions, taking into account their own clinical training and experience and the relevant psychiatric literature. The PDR is not a comprehensive clinical text. Patient care may be compromised if psychiatrists rely on the PDR rather than the professional literature and the usual community standards of practice as their main source of clinical guidance. The PDR should be considered as only one of several sources of information that a psychiatrist may rely on for making medication decisions.

Inappropriate Administration of Psychotropic Medications

Inappropriate administration of medication includes the following: 1) failure to perform or obtain an adequate physical examination when indicated, and 2) failure to obtain a medical history before prescribing psychoactive medication.

Psychiatrists must familiarize themselves with their patients' medical history and physical condition before prescribing medications. A history of allergic reactions to medications must be noted. Psychiatrists are required to search out medical causes of psychological illness, either by their own examination or by referral to competent specialists.

The use of polypharmacy, or multiple medications, has often been disparaged by some clinicians as a "shotgun" approach to treatment that significantly increases the possibility of serious side effects. Nevertheless, certain patients may benefit from rational psychopharmacology in situations in which diagnostic clarity exists and response to single-drug regimens has been poor.

An attempt to impose social control on mentally ill patients through "chemical straitjackets" is particularly inappropriate if the objectionable behavior is not directly the result of a psychiatric disorder. For example, an antipsychotic medication may be lifesaving for a severely agitated elderly patient with congestive heart failure, dementia, and psychosis. Antipsychotic medications should not be used to suppress objectionable behavior that is a lifelong aspect of the patient's personality rather than symptomatic of a treatable psychiatric disorder. In addition, psychoactive drugs should not be used as punishment. Although chemical "restraints" raise issues concerning deprivation of civil rights, malpractice actions are more likely.

The enactment of statutory regulations establishing medication-prescribing guidelines will influence the standard of care in providing drug therapy. For example, the Omnibus Budget Reconciliation Act of 1987, implemented October 1, 1990, regulates the use of psychotropic drugs in long-term health care facilities receiving funds from Medicare and Medicaid (Hendrickson 1990). The Health Care Financing Administration (now the Center for Medicare Services) guidelines for antipsychotic drugs include documentation of the psychiatric diagnosis or specific condition requiring antipsychotic use, prohibition of as-needed antipsychotic use, and gradual dosage reductions of antipsychotic drugs combined with attempts at behavioral programming and environmental modification (Health Care Financing Administration 1989).

Exceeding Recommended Dosages

Some psychiatric patients may require the administration of psychoactive medications that exceed dosage guidelines. The reasons for such a decision must be clearly documented in the patient's record. The patient should be informed that drug guidelines are being exceeded. If very high levels of medication are required, the patient may need to be hospitalized until a safer maintenance level of the medication can be achieved.

Exceeding recommended dosages is not necessarily negligent. Some patients require high dosages of medication to achieve a therapeutic effect. The prescription of high dosages of an antipsychotic for a chronically schizophrenic patient would likely produce significant toxicity if given to a nonpsychotic patient. Generally, medication dosage is a function of the patient's psychiatric condition and the level of medication required to bring about improvement or remission while the physician carefully monitors the patient. Undertreating invariably proves ineffective, while possibly subjecting the patient to serious medication side effects. Paradoxically, the liability exposure of the clinician is increased. Again, careful documentation of treatment rationale is the clinician's best friend if litigation should arise.

A psychiatrist covering for another psychiatrist should prescribe only enough medication to hold the patient over until the treating psychiatrist's return. Typically only a brief history, including diagnosis and treatment, is provided, either orally or in writing, to the covering psychiatrist. Therefore, renewal of medications over the telephone must be done with great care. In some instances, renewal of medications may require seeing the patient.

Monitoring Side Effects

Psychiatrists have a duty to use reasonable care in prescribing, dispensing, and administering medication. Monitoring the patient and warning of side effects fall within this duty. As part of the working alliance with patients, the psychiatrist provides information about the possible side effects of medication and encourages the patient to report troubling side effects. Open communication about potential problems with medications enhances the therapeutic process through the establishment of trust and reduces the problem of noncompliance.

Patients must be warned about driving or working around dangerous machinery if the medications that they are taking produce drowsiness or slow reflexes (Taylor v. Smith 2004). Similarly, patients must be warned of the dangers of mixing alcohol with psychoactive drugs. Drug-induced memory impairment, especially with benzodiazepines, may result in amnesia that can be psychologically and socially disabling.

Monitoring the patient's clinical condition rather than placing exclusive reliance on laboratory test results is imperative. For example, patients undergoing lithium therapy have developed signs and symptoms of toxicity even when lithium levels are in the therapeutic range (Lewis 1983).

Prescribing for Unseen Patients

Psychiatrists who work in clinics may be asked to prescribe medications for patients seen only by nonmedical therapists. Reports received from a nonmedical therapist about an unseen patient are usually not a sufficient basis for prescribing medication. Nonmedical therapists are not trained in psychopharmacology. Psychiatrists who prescribe medication are responsible for such treatment, even though another provider is primarily responsible for the overall care of the patient. In split-treatment arrangements, psychiatrists remain highly vulnerable to malpractice actions stemming from improper supervision of patients who develop serious or fatal reactions to medications (Simon 2004).

In large hospitals or institutions, psychiatrists may not be able to see all of their patients. They may be asked to write a prescription covering a period of many months for drugs that are dispensed by nurses or mental health aides. The psychiatrist should see the patient before writing a renewable prescription. The number of renewals should be specified. Open-ended prescription renewals is a questionable practice and an invitation for liability if the patient is injured. If the patient cannot be seen or the number of renewals cannot be specified, the reasons should be carefully documented. Psychiatrists sometimes authorize a prescription for persons unknown and unseen who live at some distance where medical services are not readily available. Prescribing for unseen patients may be construed as creating a doctor–patient relationship if an untoward reaction to the medication becomes the basis of a lawsuit.

No stock answer exists for how frequently a psychiatrist should see a patient. Generally, psychiatrists should schedule return visits with a frequency that accords with the patient's clinical needs. The longer the time between visits, the greater the risk of adverse drug reactions and clinical developments in the patient's condition. Patients who are being treated should not be allowed to go unsupervised.

The psychological issues surrounding patient compliance and noncompliance with prescribed medications are complex and need to be explored by the psychiatrist with the patient. Patient nonadherence to prescribed medications is well known to be high. For this reason, medications should be dispensed in the context of a therapeutic relationship in which the many psychological meanings associated with the taking of medication can be explored (Simon 1992a).

Generic Drugs

Generic drugs that contain the same active ingredients as established brand-name drugs may not possess the same clinical efficacy because of differential absorption, distribution, and elimination rates in the human body. In patients prescribed generic drugs, a lack of symptom improvement may be due to the generic drug's lack of therapeutic efficacy. Whether generic or brand-name, the well-selected drug that achieves maximal therapeutic efficacy in the shortest time will likely be cost saving in the long run.

The psychiatrist is responsible for selecting the appropriate medication for the patient. Only when the psychiatrist signs the "generic substitution permissible" line may the pharmacist substitute a less-expensive drug with the same active ingredients. In a number of states, drug product selection laws stipulate that the prescriber must expressly indicate "do not substitute" in some manner when declining generic substitution. To pursue a consistent prescribing and monitoring policy, the psychiatrist should be aware of the legal issues surrounding generic drugs (Simon 1992a).

Finally, prescriptions must be written legibly. Illegible prescriptions are a major source of drug-dispensing errors. If the psychiatrist's handwriting tends to be unreadable, the prescription should be printed legibly. In addition, the amount should be written out so that the number of doses cannot be changed by drug-abusing patients. The directions for taking the medication generally should be specific rather than written "sig: as directed." Abbreviations should be avoided.

Tardive Dyskinesia

Much TD litigation has been in the context of equity (e.g., injunction, or mandatory relief, such as in the case of Rennie v. Klein [1978]) rather than malpractice cases. Nevertheless, a significant number of malpractice lawsuits have been brought against psychiatrists by patients who developed TD. The allegations of negligence regarding treatment with typical antipsychotics (neuroleptics) have included improper dosages, excessive length of treatment, failure to monitor, inappropriate indications, and failure to obtain informed consent (warning of the risk of TD) (Simon 1990). Findings of relatively low incidence of TD with the newer atypical antipsychotics await more research to establish the long-term safety of these medications. Patients prescribed atypical antipsychotics should be informed of TD as a possible side effect, although current research indicates a low incidence.

The greater the seriousness of the risk of any treatment, the greater the clinician's obligation to disclose relatively remote risks. If alternative treatments are available that present a lesser risk or a greater probability of success, the need to disclose increases. For example, if an antipsychotic is prescribed when a benzodiazepine or other medication might be equally effective (such as in the treatment of an anxiety disorder), then detailed disclosure of the risks of neuroleptic treatment is necessary.

Because the incidence of TD is quite low within the first 6 months of antipsychotic treatment, some clinicians believe that it is not a material risk at the start of treatment and need not be disclosed (Schatzberg and Cole 1991). Nevertheless, plaintiffs' attorneys have pointed out in court that all psychiatrists have been on notice concerning TD since 1973. At that time, psychiatrists were first informed of TD through the FDA's *Drug Bulletin,* a publication sent to all physicians who have a drug prescription number. Furthermore, informed consent is required by law from the first day of treatment unless an emergency exists or therapeutic privilege can be legitimately asserted.

When TD occurs several years after initiation of antipsychotic treatment, the absence of an initial informed consent may cause serious legal problems. For example, many patients with chronic mental illness may be transient. They may be taking antipsychotics that were prescribed by a number of previous physicians. Furthermore, these patients may not be able to provide the current psychiatrist with an accurate medication history. A delay in obtaining informed consent from such patients extends the period of continuous antipsychotic drug intake without a valid consent. The patient may develop TD while under the treatment of a subsequent psychiatrist who is merely continuing or adjusting the antipsychotic medication. Providing and recording full disclosure to patients is, with certain exceptions, the best policy medically, ethically, and legally.

The level of detail and complexity of information about TD, as with all disclosures to patients, should be tailored to the patient's mental capacity to understand the information. The acceptance of treatment by an incompetent patient is often not questioned because it accords with the psychiatrist's therapeutic intent. Consent options for patients who lack health care decision-making capacity are discussed in Chapter 4 of this volume, "Informed Consent and the Right to Refuse Treatment." A patient with psychosis and TD may be able to give an informed consent for continued antipsychotic drug treatment. When restarting antipsychotic drugs with patients manifesting TD, informed-consent procedures should be started immediately. If the patient needs to continue antipsychotic therapy in the presence of TD, a confirming second opinion should be obtained.

Electroconvulsive Therapy

The APA Task Force on ECT recommended that policies and procedures should be developed to ensure proper informed consent. Informed consent should include how, when, and by whom the treatment will be administered as well as the nature and scope of information provided (American Psychiatric Association 2000; see Table 5–3). Policies and procedures should be consistent with JCAHO and hospital policies as well as local and state regulatory requirements, which vary substantially among the various jurisdictions.

Table 5–3. Recommended information to be provided to patients being considered for electroconvulsive therapy (ECT)

- Who is recommending ECT and for what reason

- A description of applicable treatment alternatives

- A description of the ECT procedure, including the times when treatments are given and the location where treatments will occur

- A discussion of the relative merits and risks of the different stimulus electrode placements and the specific choice that has been made for the patient

- The typical range for number of treatments to be administered as well as a statement that reconsent will be obtained if the number of treatments in the index course exceeds a set maximum number (for that facility)

- A statement that there is no guarantee that ECT will be effective

- A statement concerning the need for continuation treatment

- A description of the likelihood and severity (in general terms) of major risks associated with the procedure, including mortality, cardiopulmonary dysfunction, confusion, and acute and persistent memory impairment; in addition, delineation of the common minor side effects of ECT (e.g., headaches and musculoskeletal pain)

- A statement that consent for ECT also entails consent for appropriate emergency treatment in the event that this is clinically necessary during the time the patient is not fully conscious

- A description of any restrictions on patient behavior likely to be necessary before, during, or after ECT

- An offer to answer questions at any time regarding the recommended treatment and the name(s) of the individual(s) who can be contacted with such questions

- A statement that consent for ECT is voluntary and can be withdrawn at any time

Source. Reprinted from American Psychiatric Association: "Consent for Electroconvulsive Therapy," in *The Practice of Electroconvulsive Therapy: Recommendations for Treatment, Training, and Privileging,* 2nd Edition (A Task Force Report of the American Psychiatric Association). Washington, DC, American Psychiatric Association, 2000, p. 107. Copyright 2000, American Psychiatric Association. Used with permission.

Some states limit the administration of ECT to competent patients who give informed consent or incompetent patients subject to a court order for such treatment. No emergency implied consent exception to these requirements exists in these states (Simon 1992a), which have prioritized autonomy over the therapeutic benefits that ECT provides.

Psychotherapy

Very few therapists warn patients of the risks of a proposed method of psychotherapy, although the potential benefits may be extolled. Nevertheless, untoward transference reactions, regressive dependency states, and worsening clinical conditions occur with some regularity in psychotherapy. Prolonged nontherapeutic stalemates are relatively common. To the extent that psychotherapeutic modalities can produce benefits, they may also cause harm. Accordingly, patients need to be informed of both the benefits and the risks of specific psychotherapies. For example, a lawsuit alleging that therapists negligently created false memories of sexual abuse invariably has as an element of the claims the therapist's failure to obtain informed consent from the patient about the dangers of the treatment undertaken (Osheroff v. Chestnut Lodge 1984). Any limitations on treatment and confidentiality under managed care contracts should be explained at the beginning of treatment.

An initial period of evaluation allows the patient time to consider his or her "fit" with the therapist, the therapist's technique, and the interactional process between the therapist and the patient. This time also allows the therapist to make an initial diagnostic and treatment assessment of the patient. The nature of the patient's difficulties should be described in plain language using descriptive terms that underlie psychiatric nosology. Table 5–4 lists the main areas for informed consent for psychotherapy.

Table 5–4.　Informed consent for psychotherapy

- Anticipated benefits
- Potential risks
- A prognostic assessment
- Expected outcome with and without treatment
- Available alternative treatments, including risks and benefits

Alternative therapeutic modalities need to be carefully discussed with patients. The therapist can no longer recommend just one form of treatment. Although therapists may not be proficient in using more than a few treatment approaches, they should be knowledgeable about the available treatments used by competent, ethical therapists. At a minimum, therapists should be able to intelligently explain alternative therapies, including risks and benefits, to the patient. If a patient requires another method of treatment for which the therapist lacks proficiency, the patient should be referred to a therapist who can provide such treatment.

In managed care settings, patients requiring long-term psychotherapy will need to be informed of the limitations of treatment. Patients who have recovered or who are currently recovering memories of childhood sexual abuse will likely need extended psychotherapy. Patients with personality disorders, especially borderline personality disorder, may require long-term treatment These patients should be referred to competent therapists outside the managed care plan or treated by the current therapist under a private arrangement. Psychiatrists should refer to their contracts concerning the permissibility of billing patients directly.

In Osheroff v. Chestnut Lodge (1984; see also Gutheil and Simon 1997), long-term psychotherapy was prescribed for an inpatient with major depression. After 7 months of psychotherapy the patient's psychiatric condition had worsened. The plaintiff was transferred to another hospital, where treatment with an antidepressant medication was initiated. Improvement occurred rapidly. After the lawsuit was filed, an arbitration panel found for the plaintiff. Both sides exercised their right to a trial. Before trial, the case was settled for an undisclosed amount.

The treatment of a psychiatric disorder exclusively by psychotherapy when proven, effective biological treatments exist can bring a lawsuit for negligent treatment. An intense debate concerning biological versus psychodynamic treatment of psychiatric disorders grew out of the *Osheroff* case (Klerman 1990; Stone 1990). Even when the psychiatrist is only providing medication management, brief, supportive psychotherapy takes place. The standard of care requires that some form of psychotherapy, often brief, accompany the prescribing of medications.

Recovered Memories of Sexual Abuse

The recovered memory debate has generated intense passions that have driven a number of recovered memory cases into the courts. Patients alleging recovered memories of abuse have sued parents and other alleged perpetrators. In a number of instances, the alleged victimizers have sued therapists who, they claim, negligently induced false memories of sexual abuse. In an about-face, some patients have recanted and joined forces with others (usually their parents) to sue the therapists.

The memory debate has polarized most therapists into believers and disbelievers. Strongly held personal biases about recovered memories represent an occupational hazard for clinicians. Such feelings can undermine the therapists' duty of neutrality to their patients, creating deviant treatment boundaries and the provision of substandard care.

Litigation in recovered memory cases continues, although the rancorous debate has settled down. A jury awarded more than $10 million to the plaintiffs in a case alleging that therapists implanted memories of satanic sexual abuse. A fundamental allegation in these cases is that the therapist abandoned a position of neutrality to suggest, persuade, coerce, and implant false memories of childhood sexual abuse. The guiding principle of clinical risk management in recovered memory cases is maintenance of therapist neutrality and establishment of sound treatment boundaries.

Valid risk management has a solid clinical footing and is secondarily informed by awareness of the legal issues. Table 5–5 lists management principles that should be considered when evaluating or treating a patient in psychotherapy who recovers memories of abuse.

Prescribing Medications and Collaborative Treatment

In managed care or other treatment settings, the prescribing of medication in the absence of a working doctor–patient relationship does not meet generally accepted standards of good clinical care. Such a practice is a prime example of fragmented care. It diminishes the efficacy of the drug treatment itself and may even lead to the patient's failure to take the prescribed medication. Fragmented care, in which the psychiatrist functions only as a prescriber of medication while remaining uninformed about the patient's overall clinical status, constitutes substandard treatment that may lead to a malpractice action if the patient is harmed.

Split-treatment situations require that the psychiatrist stay fully informed of the patient's clinical status as well as of the nature and quality of treatment

Table 5–5. Risk management principles

- Maintain therapist neutrality; do not suggest abuse.

- Stay clinically focused; provide adequate evaluation and treatment for patients presenting specific problems and symptoms.

- Carefully document the memory recovery process.

- Manage personal bias and countertransference.

- Avoid mixing treater and expert witness roles.

- Closely monitor supervisory and collaborative therapy relationships.

- Clarify nontreatment roles with family members.

- Avoid special techniques (e.g., hypnosis or sodium amytal) unless clearly indicated; obtain consultation first.

- Stay within professional competence; do not take cases you cannot handle.

- Distinguish between narrative truth and historical truth.

- Obtain consultation in problematic cases.

- Foster patient autonomy and self-determination; do not suggest lawsuits.

- In managed care settings, inform patients with recovered memories that more than brief therapy may be required.

- When making public statements, distinguish personal opinions from scientifically established facts.

- Stop and refer, if uncomfortable with a patient who is recovering memories of childhood abuse.

- Do not be afraid to ask about abuse as part of a competent psychiatric evaluation.

the patient is receiving from the nonmedical therapist (Meyer and Simon 1999a, 1999b). Split-treatment situations are collaborative arrangements (Sederer et al. 1998). In a collaborative relationship, responsibility for the patient's care is shared according to the qualifications and limitations of each discipline. The responsibilities of each discipline do not diminish those of the other disciplines. Patients should be informed of the separate responsibilities of each discipline. Periodic evaluation of the patient's clinical condition and needs by the psychiatrist and the nonmedical therapist is necessary to determine if the collaboration should continue. On termination of the collaborative relationship, the patient should be informed by both the psychiatrist and the nonmedical therapist, either separately or jointly. If negligence is claimed on the part of the nonmedical therapist, it is likely that the collaborating psychiatrist will also be sued (Woodward et al. 1993).

Psychiatrists who prescribe medications in a split-treatment arrangement should be able to hospitalize patients if that becomes necessary. If the psychiatrist does not have admitting privileges, then prior arrangements should be made with other psychiatrists who can hospitalize patients in an emergency. Some patients with severe mental disorders are being seen in split-treatment arrangements. The psychiatrist should determine whether the patient's condition is appropriate for split treatment. Acutely disturbed patients will likely require that their entire management and follow-up be provided by a psychiatrist. Split treatment is increasingly used by managed care organizations and represents a potential malpractice minefield.

In managed care settings, psychiatrists increasingly may be asked to prescribe medications from a restrictive or closed formulary. Psychiatrists, at their professional discretion, should determine which medications will be prescribed according to the special clinical needs of the patient. Psychiatrists should vigorously resist attempts to limit their choice of drugs by a restrictive or closed formulary or by therapeutic substitution (i.e., interchanging a different chemical agent from the same therapeutic class—for example, substituting a tricyclic antidepressant for a selective serotonin reuptake inhibitor; tricyclic antidepressants have a much greater lethality than selective serotonin reuptake inhibitors for patients who overdose). The prescribing of specific medications should be determined by the psychiatrist alone based on the clinical needs of the patient. An appeal should be filed if a prescription for a nonformulary-approved drug is denied.

References

American Psychiatric Association: The Practice of Electroconvulsive Therapy: Recommendations for Treatment, Training, and Privileging, 2nd Edition (A Task Force Report of the American Psychiatric Association). Edited by Weiner RD. Washington, DC, American Psychiatric Association, 2000

Glazer WM: Expected incidence of tardive dyskinesia associated with atypical antipsychotics. J Clin Psychiatry 61:21–26, 2000

Greenberg SA, Shuman DW: Irreconcilable conflict between therapeutic and forensic roles. Prof Psychol Res Pr 28:50–57, 1997

Gutheil TG, Simon RI: Clinically based risk management principles for recovered memory cases. Psychiatr Serv 48:1403–1407, 1997

Health Care Financing Administration: Medicare and Medicaid requirements for long-term care facilities: final rule with request for comments. Federal Register, February 12, 1989, pp 5316–5336

Hendrickson RM: New federal regulations, psychotropics, and nursing homes. Drug Ther 20:101–105, 1990

Henry VR: Off-label prescribing: legal implications. J Leg Med 20:365–383, 1999

Joint Commission on Accreditation of Healthcare Organizations: Consolidated Standards Manual. Oak Brook Terrace, IL, Joint Commission on Accreditation of Healthcare Organizations, 1999

King SM: Legal and risk management concerns relating to the use of non-FDA approved drugs in the practice of psychiatry. Rx for Risk 6:1–5, 1998

Klerman GL: The psychiatric patient's right to effective treatment: implications of Osheroff v Chestnut Lodge. Am J Psychiatry 147:409–418, 1990

Lewis DA: Unrecognized chronic lithium neurotoxic reactions. JAMA 250:2029–2030, 1983

Meyer DJ, Simon RI: Split treatment: clarity between psychiatrists and psychotherapists, part I. Psychiatr Ann 29:241–245, 1999a

Meyer DJ, Simon RI: Split treatment: clarity between psychiatrists and psychotherapists, part II. Psychiatr Ann 29:327–332, 1999b

Newell ER: Competency, consent, and electroconvulsive therapy: a mentally ill prisoner's right to refuse invasive medical treatment in Oregon's criminal justice system. Lewis & Clark Law Review 9:1019, 2005

Physicians' Desk Reference, 60th Edition. Oradell, NJ, Medical Economics, 2006

Schatzberg AF, Cole JO: Manual of Clinical Psychopharmacology, 2nd Edition. Washington, DC, American Psychiatric Press, 1991

Sederer LI, Ellison J, Keyes C: Guidelines for prescribing psychiatrists in consultative, collaborative and supervisory relationships. Psychiatr Serv 49:1197–1202, 1998

Simon GE, Savarino J, Operskalski B, et al: Suicide risk during antidepressant treatment. Am J Psychiatry 163:41–44, 2006

Simon RI: Somatic therapies and the law, in American Psychiatric Press Review of Clinical Psychiatry and the Law, Vol 1. Edited by Simon RI. Washington, DC, American Psychiatric Press, 1990, pp 3–82

Simon RI: The practice of psychotherapy: legal liabilities of an "impossible" profession, in American Psychiatric Press Review of Clinical Psychiatry and the Law, Vol 2. Edited by Simon RI. Washington, DC, American Psychiatric Press, 1991a, pp 3–91

Simon RI: Psychological injury caused by boundary violation precursors to therapist–patient sex. Psychiatr Ann 21:614–619, 1991b

Simon RI: Clinical Psychiatry and the Law, 2nd Edition. Washington, DC, American Psychiatric Press, 1992a

Simon RI: Treatment boundary violations: clinical, ethical, and legal considerations. Bull Am Acad Psychiatry Law 20:269–288, 1992b

Simon RI: Clinical risk management of the rapid cycling bipolar patient. Harv Rev Psychiatry 4:245–254, 1997

Simon RI: Assessing and Managing Suicide Risk: Guidelines for Clinically Based Risk Management. Washington, DC, American Psychiatric Publishing, 2004

Stone AA: Law, science, and psychiatric malpractice: a response to Klerman's indictment of psychoanalytic psychiatry. Am J Psychiatry 147:419–127, 1990

Winslade WJ, Liston EH, Ross JW, et al: Medical, judicial, and statutory regulation of ECT in the United States. Am J Psychiatry 141:1349–1355, 1984

Woodward B, Duckworth K, Gutheil TG: The pharmacotherapist–psychotherapist collaboration, in American Psychiatric Press Review of Psychiatry, Vol 12. Edited by Oldham J. Washington, DC, American Psychiatric Press, 1993, pp 631–649

Legal References

American Cyanamid v Frankson, 732 S.W.2d 648 (Tex. App., 1987)

Barclay v Campbell, 704 S.W.2d 8 (Tex., 1986)

Clites v State, 322 N.W.2d 917 (Iowa App., 1982)

Femrite v Abbott Northwestern Hosp., 568 N.W.2d 535 (Minn. App., 1997)

Osheroff v Chestnut Lodge, Inc., 490 A.2d 720, 62 Md.App. 519 (Md. App., 1984), cert denied, 304 Md. 163, 497 A.2d 1163 (1985)

Ramon v Farr, 770 P.2d 131 (Utah, 1989)

Rennie v Klein, 462 F.Supp. 1131 (D.N.J., 1978), suppl., 476 F.Supp. 1294 (D.N.J., 1979), modified, 653 F.2d 836 (3d Cir., 1981), vacated and remanded, 458 U.S. 1119 (1982), on remand, 720 F.2d 266 (3d Cir., 1983)

Taylor v Smith, 892 So.2d 887 (Ala., 2004)

United States v Evers, 453 F.Supp. 1141 (M.D. Ala., 1978)

Laws

21 U.S.C. § 355

Cal. Gen. Stat. Ann. § 52-184c (2006)

6

Seclusion and Restraint

Overview of the Law

Seclusion and restraint, which may be necessary as a last resort to avoid irreparable harm to patients or staff when less drastic measures have failed, entails a limitation on the patient's autonomy. Seeking to balance these interests, the law has permitted limited intrusions on patient autonomy but has not given clinical psychiatrists blanket authority to seclude or restrain patients whenever they conclude it would be in the patient's best interest to do so. When the patient is grateful for the intrusion on his or her autonomy once stabilized, there is unlikely to be a legal accounting of the decision-making process resulting in seclusion or restraint. However, when the patient is not grateful for the intrusion on his or her autonomy once stabilized, a tort claim, a civil rights civil claim for monetary damages or injunctive relief (i.e., an order that a psychiatrist do or refrain from doing something), or a civil rights criminal prosecution may be sought. Whether the disgruntled patient's legal response is a minor annoyance or a major difficulty for a psychiatrist turns on the legal rules that have arisen to govern the use of seclusion and restraint. There are myriad sources of regulation of the use of seclusion and restraint.

The federal government's Center for Medicare Services (CMS), the Joint

Commission on Accreditation of Healthcare Organizations (JCAHO), and most states have developed requirements designed to minimize and avoid the use of seclusion and restraint wherever possible. Under the overlapping system of regulations, federal requirements may be superseded by more restrictive state laws. Thus the federal requirements, where they apply, provide a floor to which states or JCAHO may add but may not lessen requirements. For these purposes the CMS regulations define *seclusion* and *restraint* as follows: *Seclusion* is the involuntary confinement of a person alone in a room where the person is physically prevented from leaving or the separation of the patient from others in a safe, contained, controlled environment. *Restraint* is the direct application of physical force to an individual, with or without the individual's permission, to restrict his or her freedom of movement. Physical force may be human touch, mechanical devices, or a combination thereof. The use of drugs is also included in the definition of *restraint*. The CMS regulatory scheme is based on the conclusion that the use of seclusion and restraint presents an inherent risk to the patient's physical safety and well-being and therefore must be used only as a last resort to avoid harm that the patient would inflict on him- or herself or others (Donat 2005). It should never be used for the convenience of staff. The overarching therapeutic goal is to protect the patient's safety and dignity.

Some courts and state statutes outline certain due-process procedures that must be followed before a restraint-seclusion order can be implemented. Typical due-process requirements include some form of notice, a hearing, and the involvement of an impartial decision-maker. The process that is due in any given case is determined by the circumstances. For example, when the necessity to use seclusion and restraint occurs in the early morning hours, a less formal or less timely process may be justified than when its use is called for during the day. Due process does not go away in emergencies; however, the process that is due must account for the circumstances in which it arises.

Some question exists whether seclusion and restraint are ever appropriate other than as a safety measure. Although there is not much authority on point, the acceptability of restraint or seclusion for the purposes of training was recognized in a brief statement without embellishment in the landmark case Youngberg v. Romeo (1982). *Youngberg* challenged the "treatment" practices at the Pennhurst State School and Hospital in Pennsylvania. The U.S. Supreme Court held that patients enjoyed a right to freedom from bodily restraint and could not be restrained except to ensure their safety or—in certain (undefined) circumstances—"to provide needed training." The court reasoned that the liberty interests in safety and freedom from bodily restraint were not absolute and were not in conflict with the need to provide training: "As we have recognized that there is a constitutionally protected liberty interest in safety and freedom from restraint...training may be necessary to avoid unconstitutional infringement of those rights" (p. 318).

Much litigation involving seclusion and restraint of psychiatric patients addresses constitutional issues (Perlin 1989) in civil rights claims (Atkins v. County of Orange 2005). Negligence in the use of seclusion and restraint, however, has been litigated in malpractice cases (Diversicare General Partner, Inc. v. Rubio 2005). For example, in Fleming v. Prince George's County (1976), a physician was found to have violated the standard of care by placing the plaintiff in restraints without attempting to determine the cause of her "obstinate and stubborn" behavior. The plaintiff was severely injured when she attempted to escape. In another seclusion and restraint malpractice case, Pisel v. Stamford Hospital (1980), the plaintiff was found unconscious and without a pulse, with her head wedged between the bed's steel railing and mattress. The evidence showed that the appropriate standard of care required that "no objects or furniture should be left [in the seclusion room] that could cause the patient harm" (e.g., the steel bed frame). The jury awarded $3.6 million in damages, which was upheld on appeal.

It is often not possible when providing psychiatric care to avoid choices that pose equal and opposing risks. Psychiatrists and other mental health professionals must manage the tension between patient safety and freedom of movement (Simon 2006). Failing to initiate seclusion or restraint in a case in which a patient harms him- or herself or others risks a negligence claim. Initiating seclusion or restraint risks a malpractice claim. The stringent legal and administrative control of seclusion and restraint should not deter the psychiatrist from using these emergency, often lifesaving, modalities in appropriate cases.

Clinical Management of Legal Issues

Indications for Seclusion and Restraint

There are three main clinical indications for seclusion and/or restraint (Gutheil and Tardiff 1984):

- To prevent harm either to the patient or to others when control by other means is ineffective or inappropriate
- To prevent significant disruption of the treatment program or damage to the physical surroundings
- To assist in treatment as part of ongoing behavior therapy

Absent a valid informed consent from a competent patient, the legal and clinical appropriateness of using seclusion and restraint for the purpose of behavior modification treatment is unclear and poses an unspecified risk of liability. Behavior therapy methods such as contingent restraint and locked time-out may be used to manage patients who are assessed to become violent. There are two other clinical indications applicable only to seclusion: to decrease sensory overstimulation and to provide seclusion at the patient's voluntary request.

Voluntary requests for seclusion made by competent patients may be honored in order to provide support for weakening impulse control, to diminish seriously threatening contact with others, and to lessen the frightening experience of "flashbacks" and overstimulation in patients recovering from toxic reactions. A viable therapeutic alliance with the staff usually exists when a patient can ask for seclusion. Manipulative patients may try to use seclusion to avoid ward activities and treatment programs, to test the staff's resolve, or to draw the staff into sadomasochistic power struggles. Therefore the motivation behind requests for seclusion must be carefully evaluated.

In addition to federal regulations, many states have freedom-from-restraint-and-seclusion statutes. Mental health professionals who use these management modalities should be familiar with the relevant regulations and laws. Professional opinions on the clinical use of physical restraints and seclusion vary considerably. Unless precluded by federal or state law or by JCAHO and hospital policies, seclusion and restraint can be justified on both clinical and legal grounds for a number of clinical situations. For example, the American Psychiatric Association's (1996) *Guidelines for Inpatient Psychiatric Units* regarding HIV-infected patients states, "If a patient known to be infected with HIV engages, or threatens to engage, in behavior that places other individuals at risk, the responsible physician should assure the appropriate steps are taken to control the behavior and, if necessary, isolate and/or restrain the patient" (p. 542).

The Health Care Financing Administration (now CMS; 42 Code of Federal Regulations 482.13 [f][3][ii][C] [1999]) issued rules governing the use of restraints for hospitals that wish to participate in Medicaid or Medicare. These rules limit the use of seclusion and restraint to emergencies in which their use is necessary to ensure patient safety and in which less restrictive interventions are ineffective. The rules require that seclusion and restraint end at the earliest possible time. Seclusion or restraint requires a physician's written order and a physician examination within 1 hour after the intervention begins. All use of seclusion or restraint requires close monitoring of the patient, and the simultaneous use of seclusion and restraint demands a heightened level of patient observation.

The Omnibus Budget Reconciliation Act of 1987 provides stringent rules for the use of restraint in nursing homes. Most states have enacted statutes regulating the use of restraints, specifying the circumstances in which restraints can be used. Most state rules regarding seclusion and restraint require some type of documentation of their usage. Specifically, the federal rule promulgated by CMS requires that hospital patients be seen face-to-face by a physician or licensed independent practitioner within 1 hour from the time they are restrained (42 Code of Federal Regulations 482.13 [f][3][ii][C] [1999]). A licensed independent practitioner is an individual who is recognized by both state law and hospital policy as having the independent authority to order restraints and seclusion for patients. This requirement is part of expanded policies regulating seclusion and restraint applicable to all hospitals receiving Medicare and Medicaid funds. The 1-hour requirement differs from the corresponding JCAHO mandate because the latter allows nurses to undertake evaluation and management tasks (Joint Commission on Accreditation of Healthcare Organizations 2006).

The JCAHO standard also permits the physician or licensed practitioner to conduct an in-person evaluation of the patient within 4 hours of the initiation of restraint or seclusion for patients age 18 years or older, renewable up to 24 hours. For children and adolescents age 17 years and younger, the in-person evaluation must be conducted within 2 hours of the initiation of restraint and seclusion. The 1-hour visit requirement is also recommended by the American Psychiatric Association Task Force on the Psychiatric Uses of Seclusion and Restraint (American Psychiatric Association 1985). The psychiatrist must document his or her visit and describe the patient's condition, the need for restrictiveness, and any plans for further special monitoring or precautions to be taken by the staff. Regardless of accreditation status, Medicare- or Medicaid-participating hospitals must meet the standards in the Patient's Rights Condition of Participation (U.S. Department of Health and Human Services 1999). New Medicare requirements are incorporated into applicable JCAHO standards.

The JCAHO has made major revisions to its standards for the use of restraint and seclusion, effective January 2001, that seek to reduce use of restraint and seclusion in order to provide greater safety and protection of patients with psychiatric or substance abuse disorders. The revised standards restrict the use of restraint and seclusion to emergency situations in which there is "imminent" risk that the patient may inflict self-harm or harm others. Restraints are to be used only as a last resort. The JCAHO has agreed to enforce the 1-hour rule in hospitals receiving Medicare and Medicaid funds.

Contraindications

Seclusion of patients with medical and psychiatric conditions that are extremely unstable requires the close attention of staff. The staff of psychiatric units that have seclusion rooms some distance from the nursing station must carefully consider which patients they place in seclusion. Patients with dementia who cannot tolerate decreased stimulation (e.g., so-called sundowners among the elderly) or patients who are delirious may represent contraindications to seclusion. Patients with severe drug reactions or overdoses, patients who require close monitoring of their dosages, or extremely self-destructive patients at high risk for suicide should not be placed in seclusion unless close supervision and direct observation can be provided (Simon 2006).

Seclusion and restraint, however, may be necessary for the patient assessed at high risk for suicide in order to prevent self-harm. If the patient can be engaged by the staff shortly after admission, a nascent therapeutic alliance may develop. Appropriate medications given at therapeutic levels often stabilize the high-risk patient. If the suicidal patient is placed in seclusion and restraint, direct observation is required, according to regulatory and hospital policies. Seclusion rooms should have windows or audiovisual surveillance capability (Lieberman et al. 2004). Open-door seclusion is preferable when clinically appropriate.

Using seclusion as a punishment or for the convenience of staff is absolutely contraindicated. A clear indication for secluding a patient is to protect the patient as well as others from harm. For patients who are well known to the hospital staff, the emergence of obnoxious behavior may be an early warning signal of an impending loss of control and physical violence. However, the mere expression of rude behavior is not, by itself, a legitimate reason for seclusion. The potential for misuse of seclusion and restraint is always present. Sometimes it is not clear whether the seclusion is motivated by staff anxiety concerning management of the patient or is based on the legitimate clinical needs of the patient. Seclusion may be requested in desperation to gain the psychiatrist's attention when staff members feel that the psychiatrist has been unresponsive to their concerns about the patient. Close supervision by the psychiatrist of the use of restraint and seclusion is necessary. These procedures must be used only when indicated and are never routine. Seclusion and restraint must never be used in place of proper care.

Implementing Seclusion and Restraint

The rules and regulations set by CMS and JCAHO, described above, should be followed when implementing seclusion and restraint. National guidelines for the proper use of seclusion and restraint also have been established by the American Psychiatric Association Task Force on the Psychiatric Uses of Seclusion and Restraint (American Psychiatric Association 1985). The following pertain to the emergency use of seclusion and restraint:

- The physician should visit the patient within 1 hour of seclusion or restraint.
- Secluded patients should be visited at least once a day and the need for continued restraint or seclusion reviewed.
- When a patient is restrained or secluded for more than 72 consecutive hours, the case should be reviewed by the hospital director.
- Restraint techniques should be rehearsed and approved by the facility's staff, and the facility's legal counsel should advise staff whether such techniques are in accord with state and federal statutes governing the use of seclusion and restraint.

The task force examined the indications for seclusion and restraint in three critically sensitive areas: treatment of children and adolescents, of the elderly, and of individuals with developmental disabilities. Although the task force report was published in 1985, the guidelines continue to represent good clinical practice that helps protect patients from abuse and practitioners from legal liability. Since the task force report was published, a number of the report's recommendations have been adopted or independently formulated as federal, state, JCAHO, CMS, or hospital policies and regulations.

Initiation of emergency restraint and seclusion procedures by nursing and other professional staff, in accordance with established hospital policy, requires the psychiatrist's review and order for continuation (Lion and Soloff 1984). In such a case the psychiatrist should be notified immediately. Emergency implementation of restraint and seclusion generally should not exceed 1 hour without a physician staff member's oral order. Subsequent visits by the psychiatrist are a matter of clinical judgment. Although a patient may need to be seen more frequently, a minimum of one visit a day is usually appropriate. The seclusion and restraint orders should be reviewed on each visit and the need for continued restriction documented (Lion and Soloff 1984). A risk-benefit analysis should be conducted describing the benefits (e.g., improvement in physical state, mental status, and control of violence) balanced against the adverse physical and emotional consequences of seclusion and restraint. The ability of the staff to handle the patient, with and without restriction, should also be evaluated.

The patient in seclusion or restraint must be observed every 15 minutes by members of the nursing staff. With some violent patients, observation may be possible only through a window. The patient may need to be observed continuously or to have a staff member in the seclusion room. If a relationship can be established with the acutely disturbed patient the time in seclusion may be significantly reduced, particularly when the relationship permits smooth transition to the open ward. If the door can be left open when the patient is quiet ("open seclusion"), nursing staff may not need to check more than every 30 minutes. The clinical observations made during these checks should be recorded and used in assessing the patient's progress and readiness to leave restraint or seclusion.

Toileting should be done at least every 4 hours. If the patient cannot use an adjoining toilet, then a bedpan will be necessary. Toileting can be one of the most difficult management problems in seclusion. Lion and Soloff (1984) reported that assaults by patients are most apt to occur during toileting. This is not surprising, considering that issues of control, humiliation, and invasion of privacy are all intimately involved with toileting.

If possible, patients should not be allowed to eat alone, because meals are important occasions for social interaction. Assaultive patients, however, may use food or utensils as weapons against themselves or others and thus require supervision. Adequate administration of fluids is essential because of profuse sweating and the potential for dehydration. This is particularly true of seclusion rooms that tend to have inadequate air conditioning or poor ventilation.

The process of removing a patient from seclusion and restraint is initiated when the initial goals of restriction have been met: the patient no longer poses a threat to others or him- or herself and is no longer disruptive to the therapeutic setting of the ward. Incremental steps are usually required in removing the patient from seclusion and restraint. As each step of a ward transition plan is successfully negotiated, the next step is taken. Introduction to ward routine can be done while the patient is still spending some time in seclusion. It is possible that the patient might suddenly regress or become assaultive. Accordingly, a risk-benefit assessment should be made prior to final separation from seclusion. If the patient can form reasonably stable relationships with staff members, chances of successfully negotiating transfer to the open ward are maximized.

Mechanical restraints should be used only as clinical interventions. Tinetti et al. (1991) found that the use of mechanical restraints in nursing homes for safety and behavioral management rather than to treat medical conditions is a prevalent practice. These findings confirm earlier data from the Health Care Financing Administration (1989a). Stringent guidelines for the use of restraints in nursing homes were included in the federal Omnibus Budget Reconciliation Act of 1987. According to guidelines issued by the U.S. Department of Health and Human Services, restraints should be limited to treating a resident's medical symptoms. A treatment plan must carefully consider less restrictive alternatives, and specific informed consent must be obtained from the patient, a family member, or a legal representative (Health Care Financing Administration 1989b).

Chemical Restraints

Psychotropic medications, such as neuroleptics or atypical antipsychotics, should not be used for the purpose of physically immobilizing a patient (Pinals and Appelbaum 2003). Psychotropic medications are indicated for the treatment of a patient's psychiatric disorder that is the cause of behavior requiring emergency control and containment. "Chemical straitjackets" have no place in the treatment of the mentally ill. Patients in long-term care facilities may present chronic personality and behavioral problems that are difficult for the staff to manage. On occasion, cantankerous and difficult, but not mentally ill, residents have been placed on long-term psychotropic medications by exasperated clinical staffs. In response to these and other abuses, the Omnibus Budget Reconciliation Act of 1987 regulates the use of psychotropic drugs in long-term care facilities receiving funds from Medicare and Medicaid (Hendrickson 1990). The CMS rules addressing the use of neuroleptic drugs should be assumed to also be applicable to atypical antipsychotics (Health Care Financing Administration 1989b) and include the following:

- Documentation of the psychiatric diagnosis or specific condition requiring neuroleptic
- Prohibition of neuroleptics if certain behaviors alone are the only justification
- Prohibition of as-needed neuroleptic use
- Gradual dosage reductions of neuroleptics combined with attempts at behavioral programming and environmental modification

In Rogers v. Commissioner of Department of Mental Health (1983), a landmark right-to-refuse-treatment case, the Massachusetts Supreme Judicial Court held that the administration of drugs for the purpose of restraint rather than treatment violated state law.

Seclusion and Restraint in Managed Care Settings

The treatment of psychiatric inpatients has changed dramatically in the managed care era. Most psychiatric units, particularly those in general hospitals, have become short-stay, acute-care psychiatric facilities. Generally, only suicidal, homicidal, and gravely disabled patients with major psychiatric disorders pass strict precertification review for hospitalization. Approximately half of these patients have comorbid substance-related disorders. The purpose of hospitalization is crisis intervention and management to stabilize patients and to ensure their safety.

Under these circumstances, insufficient time, a severely ill patient population, and rapid turnover do not ordinarily allow for development of the therapeutic alliances with psychiatrists and staff that are essential to patient stabilization and management. Thus there is often a reliance on medications to curb violent, destructive behaviors. The temptation is great to use chemical straitjackets solely for the purpose of physically immobilizing the out-of-control patient. Furthermore, managed care organizations (MCOs) do not ordinarily pay additional benefits for intensive care such as seclusion and restraint. One-to-one monitoring of patients may be required but is not usually covered by MCOs. The patient's family or the hospital will have to absorb the additional costs of such intensive care. Nevertheless, the use of seclusion and restraint may be required by the emergency clinical needs of the patient, even though insurance coverage is denied by an MCO.

The clinical staff can become temporarily overwhelmed by the rapid admission of very sick patients. The psychiatric unit may need to briefly restrict or curtail new admissions. Patients should not be placed in seclusion or restraint for the convenience of the staff or because of insufficient staffing. The indications and safety precautions for seclusion and restraint should be thoroughly documented. Seclusion and restraint should be utilized only when all other treatment and safety measures have failed.

References

American Psychiatric Association: The Psychiatric Uses of Seclusion and Restraint (Task Force Report No. 22). Washington, DC, American Psychiatric Association, 1985

American Psychiatric Association: AIDS policy: guidelines for inpatient psychiatric units. Am J Psychiatry 145:542, 1996

Donat DC: Encouraging alternatives to seclusion, restraint and reliance on prn drugs in a public psychiatric hospital. Psychiatr Serv 56:1105–1108, 2005

Gutheil TG, Tardiff K: Indications and contraindications for seclusion and restraint, in The Psychiatric Uses of Seclusion and Restraint. Edited by Tardiff K. Washington, DC, American Psychiatric Press, 1984, pp 11–17

Health Care Financing Administration: Medicare/Medicaid Nursing Home Information, 1987–1988. Washington, DC, U.S. Department of Health and Human Services, 1989a

Health Care Financing Administration: Medicare and Medicaid requirements for long-term care facilities: final rule with request for comments. Federal Register, February 12, 1989b, pp 5316–5336

Hendrickson RM: New federal regulations, psychotropics, and nursing homes. Drug Ther 20:101–105, 1990

Joint Commission on Accreditation of Healthcare Organizations: Comprehensive Accreditation Manual for Behavioral Health Care: Restraint and Seclusion Standards for Behavioral Health. Oak Brook Terrace, IL, Joint Commission Accreditation of Healthcare Organizations, 2006

Lieberman DZ, Resnik HLP, Holder-Perkins V: Environmental risk factors in hospital suicide. Suicide Life Threat Behav 34:448-453, 2004

Lion JR, Soloff PH: Implementation of seclusion and restraint, in The Psychiatric Uses of Seclusion and Restraint. Edited by Tardiff K. Washington, DC, American Psychiatric Press, 1984, pp 19–34

Perlin ML: Mental Disability Law: Civil and Criminal, Vol 3. Charlottesville, VA, Michie, 1989, pp 50–51

Pinals DA, Appelbaum PS: Impact of new legal framework for chemical restraints. Dir Psychiatry 23:317–323, 2003

Simon RI: Patient safety versus freedom of movement: coping with uncertainty, in American Psychiatric Publishing Textbook of Suicide Assessment and Management. Edited by Simon RI, Hales RE. Washington, DC, American Psychiatric Publishing, 2006, pp 423–439

Tinetti ME, Liv WL, Marottoli R, et al: Mechanical restraint use among residents of skilled nursing facilities. JAMA 265:468–471, 1991

U.S. Department of Health and Human Services: Medicare and Medicaid programs. Hospital conditions of participation: patient's rights; interim final rule. Federal Register, July 2, 1999, pp 36069–36089

Legal References

Atkins v County of Orange, 372 F.Supp.2d 377 (S.D.N.Y., 2005)

Diversicare General Partner, Inc. v Rubio, 185 S.W.3d 842 (Tex., 2005)

Fleming v Prince George's County, 277 Md. 655, 358 A.2d 892, 895–897 (1976)

Pisel v Stamford Hospital, 180 Conn. 314, 430 A.2d 1, 12–14 (Conn., 1980)

Rogers v Commissioner of Department of Mental Health, 390 Mass. 489, 458 N.E.2d 308 (Mass., 1983), cert denied, 484 U.S. 1010 (1988)

Youngberg v Romeo, 457 U.S. 307, 102 S.Ct. 2452, 73 L.Ed.2d 28 (1982), on remand 687 F.2d 33 (3rd Cir., 1982)

Laws

42 Code of Federal Regulations 482.13 (f)(3)(ii)(C) (1999)

Omnibus Budget Reconciliation Act of 1987 (Pub. L. No. 100-203, § 9133[b][2])

7

Involuntary Hospitalization

Overview of the Law

Involuntary Hospitalization: Rationale

There is a long history of state detention of individuals for noncriminal acts that threaten public health and safety. The mentally ill have consistently been subject to detention under these laws. The civil deprivation of a mentally ill person's freedom is premised on two sources of state authority: police power and *parens patriae*. The police power permits the state to take certain actions necessary to safeguard the welfare of its citizens (e.g., detaining a person who is mentally ill in a psychiatric hospital when that person presents a risk of danger to society). The *parens patriae* power permits the state to act on behalf of those citizens unable to care for themselves because of an infirmity (e.g., mental disability).

Civil Commitment: Usage of the Term

The term *civil commitment* is not used in this book in its strict legal sense, which encompasses both voluntary and involuntary commitment. Psychiatrists do not usually think of a voluntary hospitalization as a commitment, even though patients who undergo conditional voluntary admission may be detained against their will for varying periods of time. When psychiatrists speak of involuntary hospitalization, they usually just say "commitment." In order not to confuse the reader, the terms *voluntary* and *involuntary hospitalization* are used whenever possible. Civil commitment is used synonymously with involuntary hospitalization, except when referring to outpatient commitment.

Criteria

A person may be involuntarily hospitalized only if certain statutorily mandated criteria are met. Although state statutes vary, three main substantive criteria—whether found alone or grouped together or with other miscellaneous criteria—serve as the foundation for all commitment requirements (see Table 7–1). Generally, each state spells out which criteria are required and what each means. Terms such as *mentally ill* are often loosely defined without reference to standardized psychiatric criteria (see D.C. Code § 21-501 [2006], which defines *mental illness* as "a psychosis or other disease which substantially impairs the mental health of a person"). As a result, the responsibility for implementation of these legal standards relies heavily on clinical judgment.

In addition to permitting commitment of individuals with mental illness, certain states have enacted legislation adding three other distinct groups: 1) those who are developmentally disabled (mentally retarded); 2) those with substance abuse problems (alcohol, drugs); and 3) minors who are mentally disabled. Special commitment provisions may govern requirements for admission and discharge of minors who are mentally disabled, in addition to the numerous due-process rights afforded these individuals. There is a fourth group of persons subject to commitment under specialized procedures: sexually violent predators (Kansas v. Hendricks 1997). We choose not to address that statutory scheme here because it is a specialized practice not addressed by most clinical psychiatrists.

Procedures and Standards

Procedures for involuntary civil commitment vary from state to state according to three principal factors: 1) the nature of the commitment, 2) the purpose of the commitment, and 3) the primary authority seeking the commitment.

Table 7–1. Typical substantive and miscellaneous criteria or civil commitment

Substantive criteria

- Mentally ill
- Dangerous to self or others
- Unable to provide for basic needs

Miscellaneous criteria (in conjunction with one or more of above criteria)

- Gravely disabled (unable to care for self to the point of likely self-harm)
- Refusing hospitalization
- In need of hospitalization
- Danger to property
- Lacks capacity to make rational treatment decisions
- Hospitalization represents least restrictive alternative

Note. Criteria are statutorily determined and vary from state to state.

Hospitalization of patients is either voluntary or involuntary. *Voluntary hospitalization* consists of two types: informal and conditional. They are distinguished by the degree of freedom a patient is given in leaving the hospital. An *informal* voluntary admission permits a patient to leave at any time during the hospitalization, although minimal conditions may be attached (e.g., the discharge can only occur during a day shift, Monday through Friday). Unless the patient meets the criteria for involuntary hospitalization, only moral suasion can be used to induce the patient to stay in the hospital. A *conditional* voluntary admission statutorily authorizes the hospital to detain a patient for a specified number of days after the initial written notice of discharge is given so that the patient may be evaluated for involuntary hospitalization.

Involuntary hospitalization, or civil commitment, is the hospitalization of a person against his or her will based on an assessment that the person is mentally ill and a danger to self or others.

The last factor, *primary authority,* refers to the decision-maker under the statutory scheme. Essentially, there are two commitment authorities: judicial decision-makers and administrative decision-makers.

Statutes Addressing the Purpose of Commitment

Generally, statutory schemes addressing commitment are of three types: emergency detention, hospitalization for observation, and extended custody. Each state has a variety of statutory procedures for voluntary and involuntary hospitalization of a person who is mentally ill. Clinicians should be familiar with the procedures and standards in their state.

Most states provide for *emergency hospitalization,* which is a brief, temporary measure implemented when an individual presents an "imminent" risk of harm to self, others, or—in some states—property. For example, in Virginia, to authorize emergency involuntary detention, the magistrate must have probable cause to believe the person 1) has a mental illness, 2) presents an imminent danger to him- or herself or others as a result of a mental illness or is so seriously mentally ill as to be substantially unable to care for him- or herself, 3) is in need of hospitalization or treatment, and 4) is unwilling to volunteer or incapable of volunteering for hospitalization or treatment (Va. Code Ann. § 37.2-808 [2006]; see also N.Y. C.L.S. Men Hyg § 9.39 [2006]). The "emergency hold period" until a hearing is conducted usually lasts 24–72 hours (see N.Y. C.L.S. Men Hyg § 9.39 [2006]; Va. Code Ann§ 37.2-814 [2006]).

Observational hospitalization, or short-term commitment, is for a designated period of time in order to adequately observe and diagnose an individual's condition and to provide limited treatment. Although only approximately one-half of the states have formal observational commitment statutes, nearly every state has some functional equivalent. Short-term commitment involves a longer period of time than emergency commitment. Greater procedural protection is required. Substantive standards for short-term commitment may not be as stringent as standards for long-term commitment. At the end of an observational period, either the patient must be discharged or extended commitment procedures must be instituted (see 405 ILCS 5/3-813 [2005]; Tex. Health & Safety Code § 574.034 [2005]).

The last category, *extended custody,* is procedurally the most formal. Because the duration of the detention is generally longer, a number of due-process protections are afforded an individual to ensure that the commitment is not unduly burdensome or unnecessarily long term (see Tex. Health & Safety Code § 574.035 [2005]).

Liability

The most common patient lawsuit involving involuntary admission is the claim that gross errors in professional judgment led to a wrongful commitment, which is addressed by the tort of false imprisonment. Other areas of liability that may arise from an alleged wrongful commitment include assault and battery, malicious prosecution, abuse of process, and intentional infliction of emotional distress. States grant psychiatrists who participate in the commitment process immunity from tort liability as long as they use reasonable professional judgment and act in good faith when petitioning for involuntary hospitalization (see Tex. Health & Safety Code § 571.019 [2005]). Evidence of willful, blatant, or gross failure to adhere to statutorily defined commitment procedures does not meet the good-faith provision. However, erring in favor of liberty is no guarantee of nonliability. Psychiatrists have also been successfully sued for failure to commit an individual who subsequently committed suicide or violent acts toward others (Simon 2004).

In extreme cases, psychiatrists and other mental health professionals have been found liable for infringement of civil rights under Section 1983 of the Civil Rights Act (42 U.S.C. § 1983 [1982]). The patient must establish that the conduct in question was committed by an individual acting "under color of state law, and the conduct deprived the patient of rights, privileges or immunities secured by the constitution or United States laws."

Clinical Management of Legal Issues

Current Trends in Civil Commitment

The movement of the law in the 1970s and 1980s in most states was away from *parens patriae*–based commitments in favor of police power commitments that relied on dangerousness as the standard for civil commitment and limited extrajudicial decision making regarding patient liberty. Patients were granted procedural protections similar to those granted to criminal defendants. Based primarily on the due-process and equal-protection clauses of the Fourteenth Amendment, all states now require some form of judicial hearings with notice to the patient, representation by counsel, and proof of mental disorder and dangerousness by at least clear and convincing evidence (see 405 ILCS 5/3-601 [2005]; Addington v. Texas 1979; Tex. Health & Safety Code § 572-574 [2005]).

More recently there has been a shift to revise commitment statutes to respond to the treatment needs of individuals who are seriously mentally ill before they become a danger to themselves or to society. Some patient advocates, psychiatrists, and state legislators have sought to move away from the dangerousness standard as the primary basis for civil commitment, seeking to meet the treatment needs of individuals with severe mental illness in a timely manner (Appelbaum 1994).

Procedures and Types of Commitment

Mental health professionals do not make commitment decisions about patients. Commitment is a judicial decision that is made by the court or by a mental health commission. The clinician may only file a petition or medical certification that initiates the process of involuntary hospitalization or evaluate a patient's suitability for hospitalization.

Emergency Commitment

State laws vary substantially regarding procedures and types of commitment. Most states provide for brief emergency hospitalization until a hearing is held. A majority of states have a short hold period of 24–72 hours, particularly those states that require probable-cause hearings. Probable-cause hearings determine whether substantial evidence exists that the patient meets the standards for involuntary hospitalization (see Tex. Health & Safety Code § 574.025 [2005]). If sufficient evidence is found, the patient may be hospitalized until the formal hearing. The basis for emergency commitment is that the patient has a mental illness and presents a danger to self or others. A number of states require that dangerousness be manifested by a recent overt act or threat and that it present an "imminent" risk of substantial harm to the patient or others.

Commitment statutes do not require involuntary hospitalization of persons under defined circumstances. Rather, commitment statutes are permissive—that is, they enable mental health professionals and others to seek involuntary hospitalization for persons who meet certain substantive criteria (Appelbaum et al. 1989). The duty to seek involuntary hospitalization of a patient under the clinician's care is a standard-of-care issue. In Schuster v. Altenberg (1988) the Wisconsin Supreme Court found an affirmative duty to commit in appropriate cases. In most other jurisdictions, however, clinicians *may* seek commitment of patients who meet the statutory standards for commitment.

Procedures for initiating commitment vary considerably from state to state. A report or form is usually required in which the reasons for emergency hospitalization are stated, along with a description of the recent statements and behaviors of the patient (see 405 ILCS 5/3-601 [2005]; Tex. Health & Safety Code § 573.011 [2005]). Police officers, next of kin, psychiatrists, other physicians, psychologists, social workers, or even interested parties may file a petition for emergency hospitalization. If the psychiatrist is concerned about endangering the treatment alliance with the patient, the patient's next of kin or others may be asked to petition for involuntary hospitalization.

Short-Term and Long-Term Commitment

A number of states provide for short-term commitment in addition to emergency commitment (see D.C. Code § 21-523 [2006]). The periods of detention specified for emergency, short-term, and long-term commitment vary considerably from state to state. For long-term commitment, all states require judicial or administrative determinations. Long-term commitment procedures vary considerably among jurisdictions, although the requirement that the substantive criteria of mental illness and dangerousness be met is usually followed. Hospitalization for indeterminate durations has given way to periodic review for serial involuntary hospitalization. Such reviews are usually done by the court that conducted the original hearing. Reviews may be made every 3, 6, or 12 months.

Release of Patients

Typically psychiatrists have discretion to release civilly committed patients who no longer meet the commitment standards but not patients who have been criminally committed. Release of the latter commonly requires an order for release from the committing court. Psychiatrists have been successfully sued when a criminally committed patient was released without court approval and subsequently harmed another person (Semler v. Psychiatric Institute of Washington, D.C. 1976).

Minors

Minors may be hospitalized under "voluntary" provisions, which vary considerably from state to state (see 405 ILCS 5/3-502 [2006] applying this provision to minors age 16 years or older, but see Fla. Stat. § 394.4785 [2005] explaining that children may not be admitted to a state-owned or state-operated mental health treatment facility). In some states, a minor is given limited discretion over the voluntary admission. If a minor refuses to consent when his or her consent is statutorily required, the parent may initiate involuntary hospitalization. In Parham v. J.R. (1979), the U.S. Supreme Court held that in addition to prescribed state law procedures, the federal due-process clause required review by an independent and neutral physician of a parental decision to commit a minor child. The court rejected the argument that the due-process clause necessitated more rigorous procedural safeguards.

Outpatient Commitment

Depending upon statutory authority and fiscal resources, outpatient civil commitment may be one alternative for the pressing problem of the individual who is mentally ill, homeless, but nondangerous and in dire need of treatment and care. The "revolving-door" patient is the person for whom outpatient commitment may be most beneficial. Approximately one-quarter of violent patients who are involuntarily hospitalized subsequently experience another violent episode that requires rehospitalization (Miller 1991).

Standard of Proof

The minimum standard of proof constitutionally required for long-term commitment was determined by the U.S. Supreme Court in Addington v. Texas (1979). The court held that the standard of proof required before depriving an individual of his or her liberty was "clear and convincing evidence" that the individual meets civil commitment requirements. This standard of proof is a midway position between the standards of "a preponderance of the evidence" in civil cases and "beyond a reasonable doubt" in criminal cases.

Substantive Standards for Long-Term Commitment

Involuntary hospitalization represents, to varying degrees, the exercise of the state's *parens patriae* and police powers. Mental illness is a basic requirement for civil commitment, although state statutes define mental illness differently. For example, some states list specific psychiatric disorders, whereas others apply an impairment requirement that leaves the diagnosis to the professional judgment of the certifying clinician.

In addition to requiring mental illness, all state statutes permit commitment upon a finding of dangerousness. The dangerousness standard refers to "dangerous to self or others" as the most common basis for long-term commitment, but definitions of dangerousness also vary considerably. In many states recognizing an alternative *parens patriae* ground for commitment, "inability to provide for basic needs" has replaced the old criterion of "in need of treatment."

"Gravely disabled" is another criterion in some states that may justify involuntary hospitalization of an individual. The definition of *gravely disabled* varies from state to state but generally encompasses life-threatening self-neglect or the inability to provide for such basic needs as food, clothing, or shelter. Some states have additional criteria allowing involuntary hospitalization for patients who refuse voluntary admission, patients who are expected to benefit from treatment, and patients who are unable to make rational decisions about treatment, as well as requirements that involuntary hospitalization practices follow the principle of the least restrictive alternative.

Maintaining Clinical Roles

Proper clinical procedures for civil commitment that maintain the traditional treatment role of psychiatrists include conducting a careful examination of the patient, abiding by the requirements of the law, and ensuring that sound reasoning motivates the certification of those who are mentally ill. *The Principles of Medical Ethics With Annotations Especially Applicable to Psychiatry* (American Psychiatric Association 2001) provides, in part, that "the psychiatrist may permit his/her certification to be used for the involuntary treatment of any person only following his/her personal examination of that person" (p. 11, Section 7, Annotation 4).

Dangerousness, by itself, is not a sufficient basis for involuntary hospitalization, nor is mental illness by itself a sufficient basis for involuntary hospitalization. The person must have a mental illness that causes his or her potential for violence. Persons who are deemed dangerous but who are not mentally ill according to current diagnostic criteria are the responsibility of the police and the courts, not the psychiatrist. Table 7–2 lists the main clinical tasks confronting the psychiatrist participating in the commitment process.

Assessing a person's suitability for involuntary hospitalization requires careful diagnostic and risk assessment for violence to self or others. Minimizing the potential adverse consequences of involuntary hospitalization depends on the patient's ability to understand an empathic explanation of the

Table 7–2.   Clinical management of the commitment process

- Assessing the patient's suitability for involuntary hospitalization
- Minimizing the threat to the therapist–patient relationship
- Managing tensions between legal requirements and professional duties owed to the patient

---

commitment process as an emergency intervention. Maintaining even the semblance of a therapeutic alliance during involuntary hospitalization can be a daunting task with those who are severely ill. A clinician may be "pressured" to involuntarily hospitalize an individual who is dangerous but who does not have a treatable mental disorder (e.g., sociopathic personality disorder). Psychiatrists should resist being placed in the position of being society's police. Involuntary hospitalization should be a clinical intervention.

Stone's (1976) "thank you" theory of civil commitment, which has not been accepted by the courts, captures the essence of the clinical approach. It asks the psychiatrist to focus inquiry on illness and treatment while asking the law to guarantee treatment before intervening in the name of *parens patriae.* Stone opined that moral and legal justification for the doctrine of *parens patriae* can be achieved if the three essential ingredients of reliable criteria are present: diagnosis of illness, incompetent refusal, and a decent institution. Stone's "thank you" theory divests civil commitment of a police function and returns dangerousness to the province of criminal law. Only the mentally ill, treatable, and incidentally dangerous patient would be confined in mental health systems, ideally prompting a "thank you" from an ultimately grateful patient.

Dangerousness

The statutory definitions of the dangerousness requirement are often vague and reflective of the value judgments of the statute's authors. As influenced by societal and political agendas, the term *dangerousness* ordinarily refers to legal rather than psychiatric criteria. Instead of *dangerousness,* the term *risk of violence* is preferable (Simon 2006). The validity of violence risk assessments performed by the clinician, however, is only modestly greater than chance (Monahan et al. 2001). Furthermore, violence is multifactorial (social, clinical, personality, situation). Violence is also the product of the unique interaction between the individual and the environment and, as such, defies predictability. Therefore, psychiatrists and other mental health practitioners should refrain from making predictions of violence and instead limit themselves to "here-and-now" assessments of the risk of violence that informs patient treatment and management (see Chapter 9 in this volume, "Psychiatric Responsibility and the Violent Patient").

Comprehensive violence risk assessment is not a crystal ball. The clinician's task is to identify and assess acute, high-risk factors for violence that need immediate treatment and management. Clinicians are not able to predict dangerousness. The court will decide whether the patient meets substantive standards for civil commitment. The court's decision making is better informed by systematic risk assessment than by conclusary statements of "imminent" violence for which no risk factors exist (Simon 2006). *Imminent* is a subjective term that can be used to deny mentally ill individuals needed treatment.

For clinicians who are asked by attorneys or judges to opine about an individual's dangerousness, Dvoskin and Heilbrun (2001) advised as follows: "If the court is interested, entirely or in part, on the best available prediction of violence risk, then one should rely on an applicable actuarial tool. If a court wants to know an individual's violence risk might be reduced through hospital or community interventions, then one should provide a strategy that encompasses interventions that have empirically demonstrated risk reduction value" (pp. 9–10). Clinician assessment, however, can be assisted by actuarial tools if the court requires the clinician's opinion about future dangerousness. Most psychiatrists, however, are not proficient in the adjunctive use of actuarial instruments. Courts and attorneys are aware of psychiatrists' limitations in predicting violence (American Bar Association 1998).

Grave Disability

Assessment difficulties arise from the almost universal requirement that a prediction of dangerousness to self or others be made prior to commitment. The assessment of grave disability has received much less attention in the literature than has that of overt dangerousness. The psychiatrist is on firmer ground when assessing a patient's ability to properly care for him- or herself during an acute psychotic episode or whether he or she has an advanced form of dementia. In reality, there may be a disjunction between the presence of certain severe mental disorders and the ability to take day-to-day care of oneself. Some patients with chronic schizophrenia manage their lives reasonably well in the presence of hallucinations, delusions, and thought disorders. Assessment of functional ability for this group should focus on survival tasks. Can the patient manage food, finances, clothing, and shelter requirements? Is a support system in place? Are any changes occurring in the environment that may be destabilizing?

Therapeutic Alliance

Involuntarily hospitalization may severely strain the psychiatrist–patient relationship. Once a treatment relationship is damaged or destroyed, the patient's subsequent relationships with other mental health caregivers may be adversely affected. Therefore, a psychiatrist should strive to keep the patient informed of, or even involved with, the decision-making process concerning involuntary hospitalization. Family involvement, if available and supportive of the patient's welfare, can often help mitigate the trauma of involuntary hospitalization. As a result, the therapeutic alliance may be preserved. Controlled studies have found that involuntary hospitalization is a valid intervention for appropriate patients. In retrospect, patients involuntarily hospitalized have mostly been appreciative for the care they were given (Gove and Fain 1977; Spensley et al. 1980).

Questionable Commitments

Even when patients who do not meet commitment criteria might benefit from hospitalization, they may not be involuntarily hospitalized. Doubtful situations arise in which the psychiatrist has reason to believe that a patient is at significant risk for violence but remains uncertain about this conclusion. In these situations, psychiatrists should rely on their training and clinical experience to determine which course is in the patient's best interest and to communicate this to the courts, integrating clinical information with legal standards.

The threat of involuntary hospitalization should not be used to coerce patients into accepting treatments or procedures. If a psychiatrist expects to seek involuntary hospitalization for a patient, the patient should be informed of this action. Failing to inform the patient may deal a severe blow to the patient's trust and may adversely affect future treatment efforts. Malcolm (1992) noted the subtle differences in the concepts of coercion and persuasion; *persuasion* is defined as the physician's aim "to use the patient's reasoning ability to arrive at a desired result" (p. 241), whereas *coercion* occurs "when the doctor aims to manipulate the patient by introducing extraneous elements that undermine the patient's ability to reason" (p. 241).

Lidz et al. (1995) demonstrated that patients' feelings of being coerced into mental hospital admissions appear to be closely related to their sense of procedural justice. *Procedural justice* refers to the patient's perception of being treated with concern, respect, and fairness and being taken seriously. Even among patients legally committed, the authors advised that patients' experiences of coercion can be minimized by the clinician's paying closer attention to procedural-justice issues.

Using the *Diagnostic and Statistical Manual of Mental Disorders*

One of the two essential prongs of all commitment statutes is the presence of mental illness as defined by the relevant statute. Persons who are dangerous but not mentally ill do not qualify. When there is a link between the statutory criteria and DSM, psychiatrists should use the diagnostic criteria contained in DSM-IV-TR (American Psychiatric Association 2000). Such a practice is also an effective antidote to the temptation to finesse the mental-illness requirement in order to circumvent a perceived legal impediment to involuntary hospitalization (Simon 1992).

Managed Care and Involuntary Hospitalization

In managed care settings, only suicidal, homicidal, or gravely disabled patients with major psychiatric disorders pass strict precertification review for hospitalization. Usually, in order to gain precertification for admission in managed care settings, patients must meet "medically necessary" criteria, the stringency of which often equals or exceeds that of the substantive criteria for involuntary civil commitment. If a patient cannot be managed on a psychiatric unit and continues to pose a danger to self or others, involuntary hospitalization should be considered only when the patient meets civil commitment criteria for mental illness and dangerousness. In a large majority of states, involuntary hospitalization is permissible only when a less-restrictive, clinically appropriate setting is not available. Patients should not be involuntarily hospitalized solely because a managed care organization denies insurance coverage for continued hospitalization. The usual candidate for involuntary hospitalization is a patient with psychosis who poses a significant risk of violence to self or others, who refuses treatment, or who signs a formal request for discharge against medical advice.

References

American Bar Association: National Benchbook on Psychiatric and Psychological Evidence and Testimony. Washington, DC, American Bar Association, 1998

American Psychiatric Association: Diagnostic and Statistical Manual of Mental Disorders, 4th Edition, Text Revision. Washington, DC, American Psychiatric Association, 2000

American Psychiatric Association: The Principles of Medical Ethics With Annotations Especially Applicable to Psychiatry. Washington, DC, American Psychiatric Association, 2001, p 11, Section 7, Annotation 4

Appelbaum PS: Almost a Revolution: Mental Health Law and the Limits of Change. New York, Oxford University Press, 1994

Appelbaum PS, Zonana H, Bonnie R, et al: Statutory approaches to limiting psychiatrists' liability for their patients' violent acts. Am J Psychiatry 146:821–828, 1989

Dvoskin JA, Heilbrun K: Risk assessment and release decision-making: toward the great debate. J Am Acad Psychiatry Law 29:6–10, 2001

Gove WR, Fain T: A comparison of voluntary and committed psychiatric patients. Arch Gen Psychiatry 34:669–676, 1977

Lidz CW, Hoge SKI, Gardner W, et al: Perceived coercion in mental hospital admission: pressures and process. Arch Gen Psychiatry 52:1034–1039, 1995

Malcolm JG: Informed consent in the practice of psychiatry, in American Psychiatric Press Review of Clinical Psychiatry and the Law, Vol 3. Edited by Simon RI. Washington, DC, American Psychiatric Press, 1992, pp 223–281

Miller RD: Involuntary civil commitment, in American Psychiatric Press Review of Clinical Psychiatry and the Law, Vol 2. Edited by Simon RI. Washington, DC, American Psychiatric Press, 1991, pp 95–172

Monahan J, Steadman HJ, Silver E, et al: Rethinking Risk Assessment: The MacArthur Study of Mental Disorder and Violence. New York, Oxford, 2001

Simon RI: Clinical Psychiatry and the Law, 2nd Edition. Washington, DC, American Psychiatric Press, 1992

Simon RI: Assessing and Managing Suicide Risk: Guidelines for Clinically Based Risk Management. Washington, DC, American Psychiatric Publishing, 2004

Simon RI: The myth of "imminent" violence in psychiatry and the law. Univ Cincinnati Law Rev 75:2, 2006

Spensley J, Edwards DW, White E: Patient satisfaction and involuntary treatment. Am J Orthopsychiatry 50:725–727, 1980

Stone AA: Mental Health and Law: A System in Transition (Publication No. ADM-76–176). Rockville, MD, National Institute of Mental Health, 1976

Legal References

Addington v Texas, 441 U.S. 418, 99 S.Ct. 1804, 60 L.Ed.2d 323 (1979)

Kansas v Hendricks, 521 U.S. 346 (1997)

Parham v J.R., 442 U.S. 584 (1979)

Schuster v Altenberg, 424 N.W.2d 159, 144 Wis.2d 223 (Wis., 1988)

Semler v Psychiatric Institute of Washington, D.C., 538 F.2d 121 (4th Cir., 1976), cert denied, 429 U.S. 827 (1976)

Laws

42 U.S.C. § 1983 (1982)

405 ILCS 5/3-502 (2006)

405 ILCS 5/3-601 (2005)

405 ILCS 5/3-813 (2005)

D.C. Code § 21-501 (2006)

D.C. Code § 21-523 (2006)

Fla. Stat. § 394.4785 (2005)

N.Y. Consolidated Laws of State Men Hyg § 9.39 (2006)

Tex. Health & Safety Code § 571.019 (2005)

Tex. Health & Safety Code § 572-574 (2005)

Tex. Health & Safety Code § 573.011 (2005)

Tex. Health & Safety Code § 574.025 (2005)

Tex. Health & Safety Code § 574.034 (2005)

Tex. Health & Safety Code § 574.035 (2005)

Va. Code Ann. § 37.2-808 (2006)

Va. Code Ann. § 37.2-814 (2006)

8

The Suicidal Patient

Overview of the Law

Psychiatrists owe a duty to their patients to provide competent professional care. When patients in psychiatric care take their own lives, the question whether competent care might have prevented the harm is understandably an issue for the patient's family as well as the psychiatric community. Thus it should not be surprising, given the number of psychiatric patients who seek to harm themselves, that the claim that the patient would not have successfully committed suicide but for a breach of the duty to provide competent care is the most frequent claim faced by psychiatrists.

The types of substandard professional care resulting in tort claims after patient suicide can be grouped into two categories: 1) failure to properly diagnose (assess suicide risk); and 2) failure to implement an appropriate treatment plan (use reasonable treatment interventions and precautions).

These categories of professional wrongdoing apply to the duties psychiatrists owe both outpatients and hospitalized patients, although what may be reasonable in one setting may not be in another. As with all actions grounded in negligence, the claimant is required to demonstrate that the defendant breached a duty, which proximately caused harm. Wrongful death claims arising out of

131

patient suicide require proof of a duty (which ordinarily turns on the existence of a physician–patient relationship); a breach of that duty (was there an unreasonable failure to foresee or assess suicide risk or to implement reasonable interventions?); and that the breach proximately caused the harm (would the harm have occurred anyway even if the psychiatrist acted reasonably?). If there was no physician–patient relationship or it had been properly terminated (absent unique *Tarasoff* kinds of cases), the claim fails for lack of duty. If the psychiatrist's failure to correctly assess the risk of harm or to prevent harm through intervention was a "reasonable" error, the claim fails for lack of breach. Finally, if other factors would have resulted in the same outcome, regardless of the psychiatrist's actions, the claim fails for lack of causation.

Foreseeable Suicide

An evaluation of suicide risk should be done with all patients. The case law incorporates the accepted standard of practice, which recognizes the obligations owed a patient who may be at risk for suicide. A failure to either reasonably assess a patient's suicide risk or implement an appropriate precautionary plan once the risk is recognized falls short of that standard of care.

Each state defines the standard of care required of physicians as a matter of state law, and variations exist from state to state. For example, in Stepakoff v. Kantar (1985), a suicide case, the standard applied by the court was the "duty to exercise that degree of skill and care ordinarily employed in similar circumstances by other psychiatrists." The standard of care articulated to measure the defendant's conduct was imposed by professional custom. Although there is variation across the states, this approach is generally applied across medical specialties, deferring to the profession in determining the standard of care. Thus, in general, the standard of care is defined by professional custom in the relevant field of practice.

Because customary practice does not yield error-free risk determinations, the law does not demand that all assessments prove to be right, only that they be reasonably conducted and implemented. The law's approach to what is reasonable under any set of circumstances is dependent in large part on what risk was foreseeable. As noted by Justice Cardozo in the famous case of Palsgraf v. Long Island Railroad (1928), "The risk reasonably to be perceived defines the duty to be obeyed" (p. 100). This use of risk and foreseeability is a commonsense, probabilistic concept, not a scientific construct.

Foreseeability, in this context, is used to mean harm that is reasonably anticipated to result from certain acts or omissions (Garner 1996). Because courts tend to focus on the process used in judging what might reasonably have been anticipated, recording the results of any suicide risk assessments that direct clinical interventions is sound clinical practice as well as sound legal strategy (Simon 2002).

Inpatients

Intervention in an inpatient setting usually requires 1) screening evaluations, 2) case review by clinical staff, 3) development of an appropriate treatment plan, and 4) implementation of that plan.

Clinically and legally, careful documentation of suicide risk assessments and management interventions with responsive changes to the patient's clinical situation are necessary components of competent psychiatric care. The importance of this documentation is illustrated when a psychiatric inpatient commits suicide, which is an event for which psychiatrists are likely to be sued. The case law assumes that the opportunities to foresee (anticipate) and control (treat and manage) suicidal patients are greater in the hospital and is therefore more likely to recognize a duty to protect the patient from him- or herself there than in the outpatient setting.

Outpatients

Outpatient therapists face a somewhat different situation. Although psychiatrists are expected to assess all patients' level of suicide risk, psychiatrists' accountability for failing to do so or failing to implement precautionary measures has often turned on patient status. Furthermore, although psychiatrists' duty to protect an inpatient from self-harm is typically clear, the existence of a similar duty to an outpatient has been more acknowledged more grudgingly and does not lend itself as well to succinct summary. Factors such as the time between the patient's act and the psychiatrist's last visit with the patient and whether the patient's behavior would have supported commitment are some of the considerations taken into account by the courts when deciding whether to recognize a duty to protect an outpatient from self-harm (Speer v. United States 1982).

Legal Defenses

Some defense strategies focus on the potential therapeutic benefits of the psychiatrist's acts that put the patient at risk. For example, one approach to justify as reasonable an absence of close supervision that might have protected the patient from self-harm is the use of an "open-door" policy in which hospitalized patients are allowed freedom of movement for therapeutic purposes. The response of courts to this argument that the duty was not breached has been mixed (see Ellis v. United States 1978). The results seem to be fact specific, particularly with regard to the staff's application of the open-door policy.

Immunity is a defense that insulates a person or an entity from a claim without regard to the claim's merits. Unless repealed, common law sovereign and charitable immunity limit the liability of government and charitable hospitals and their employees. Although much abrogation of these immunities has occurred, in some instances of waiver of governmental immunity only the state and not its employees can be sued (Federal Tort Claims Act [28 U.S.C.A. §§ 2671 et seq. (2006)]).

Because the plaintiff's proof on causation must show that but for the defendant's conduct the harm most likely would not have occurred, one successful defensive strategy is to prove that the same outcome would have occurred even if the defending psychiatrist had acted "reasonably." Thus, if a psychiatrist negligently fails to warn an outpatient's family about the risk of suicide and the necessity to secure the patient's gun collection, but the patient committed suicide with a gun he kept hidden at another location of which the family was unaware, the psychiatrist's negligence is not the cause of the harm. Just as a psychiatrist is not liable for negligence when his unreasonable behavior was not the cause of the harm, so a psychiatrist who acts reasonably is not liable for negligence when a patient commits suicide anyway (Robertson 1991).

Clinical Management of Legal Issues

Assessment

The evaluation of suicide risk by the practitioner is one of the most complex, difficult, and challenging tasks in psychiatry. The psychiatrist's ability to perform an adequate suicide risk assessment is basic to clinical practice (Simon 1998a); it is a core clinical competency. Clinical standards do not exist for the prediction of suicide (Simon 1992a). The law does not subject psychiatrists' inaccurate assessments of suicide risk to liability as such; rather, the law's focus in judging liability is the reasonableness of the psychiatrist's conduct of the process—the proper collection and logical evaluation of necessary data in making an assessment of suicide risk.

All suicide risk assessments should be recorded in the patient's chart at the time of evaluation. For the outpatient who is at risk of suicide, an assessment should be made at each session. The hospitalized patient should also have frequent assessments, particularly when a change in status is considered, such as room or ward change, pass, or discharge. When a suicide risk assessment is noticeably absent, the court is less able to evaluate the appropriateness of the decision-making process in assessing the risk of suicide. Suicide risk assessment is a continuing process, not an event (see Table 8–1).

Risk-Benefit Analysis

In the treatment and management of the suicidal patient, assessing suicide risk alone is usually insufficient. The benefits of treatment and management interventions must also be considered. Risk-benefit analysis provides a systematic assessment of the balance of clinical factors favoring or opposing the treatment intervention under consideration. A risk-benefit evaluation allows the psychiatrist more therapeutic latitude with the suicidal patient in situations in which fears of malpractice may inhibit appropriate therapeutic interventions. If, after reasonable clinical examination and evaluation, the clinician concludes that the potential benefits to the patient of a given psychiatric intervention outweigh the specific risks of that intervention, then these judgments should be recorded in a risk-benefit note in the patient's chart. The record should reflect what sources of information were consulted, what factors went into the clinical decision, and how the factors were balanced by the use of risk-benefit analysis.

Risk-benefit notes are decisional road marks. When in doubt about a particular intervention, a risk-benefit analysis should be conducted and recorded. For example, when considering a hospital discharge, both the risks and the benefits of discharging the patient as well as the risks and benefits of keeping him or her in the hospital should be considered.

Patient Safety Versus Freedom of Movement

The tension between promoting individual freedom and protecting a patient from self-injury is often encountered in the clinical management of suicidal patients (Amchin et al. 1990). For example, discharging patients from the hospital is usually a more difficult decision than admitting them. Although keeping the patient hospitalized may reduce the immediate chance of suicide

---

Table 8–1.   Assessing the risk of suicide

- Identify patients with individual, clinical, interpersonal, situational, and epidemiologic risk factors associated with suicide.

- Assess the overall risk of suicide based on the weighing of specific risk factors and protective factors.

- Implement treatment and preventive interventions that bear a logical nexus to the overall suicide risk assessment.

- Evaluate effectiveness of treatment and other interventions.

- Continue the process of suicide risk assessment.

---

and also diminish the psychiatrist's anxiety, resumption of the patient's usual lifestyle as soon as clinically feasible can be therapeutic. For suicidal patients requiring greater restrictions, the situation is complicated by court directives that require such patients to be treated by the least restrictive means. The psychiatrist can feel caught on the horns of this dilemma. Nevertheless, clinical judgment based on the treatment needs of the patient takes precedence. An open-door policy cannot be applied in stock fashion to all psychiatric patients. Autonomy in the hospital setting must bear a rational nexus to the patient's diagnosis, clinical condition, and level of functional mental capacity (Simon and Hales 2006). Before the patient who has seriously contemplated or attempted suicide can be given off-ward privileges or discharged, the psychiatrist needs to consider a number of factors (Table 8–2). A similar analysis applies when the clinician decides to continue outpatient treatment or to hospitalize the patient at risk for suicide.

The therapeutic alliance is usually a solid indicator of a patient's subsequent adjustment outside of the hospital. The patient who does not have a working relationship with the psychiatrist or the treatment team or a supportive relationship with others is often at increased risk for self-destructive behavior on discharge. In managed care settings, sufficient time may not be available for the psychiatrist or treatment team to develop an alliance with the patient. Moreover, only the sickest patients are admitted, and they may not have the capacity to establish a working alliance. Discharge of these patients should be carefully planned, structured, and followed up on for compliance.

In reviewing the records of patients who have successfully committed sui-

Table 8–2.   Suicidal patients: discharge considerations

Benefits of release versus risk analysis

- Readiness for discharge: Clinician and patient collaborative assessment
- Consultation with all appropriate staff
- Review of patient's course of hospitalization

Evidence of posthospitalization self-care ability

- Can patient function without significant affective and cognitive impairment?

Capability and accessibility for obtaining assistance

- Is patient physically and mentally able to employ others for support?.

Remission of illness

- What remains unchanged and can be managed as an outpatient?

Medication side effects and patient adherence

- Can side effects be tolerated and managed outside the hospital and will patient comply with treatment?

Support

- Are family members or significant others available and, if so, are they stabilizing or destabilizing?

Timing of proposed release

- Does staff adequately know the patient?
- Has the patient been acclimated adequately to the therapeutic milieu, with sufficient time allowed to develop meaningful relationships?
- Has sufficient time elapsed to evaluate the effectiveness of treatment (e.g., medication)?
- Have the stressful factors in the patient's environment that precipitated hospitalization improved?

Therapeutic alliance

- Will the patient continue to work with the psychiatrist or other mental health professionals?

cide, one invariably finds frequent notations of seclusive behavior, lack of involvement in ward activities, and the avoidance of meaningful personal relationships with other patients and staff (Simon and Gutheil 2002). In patients with serious depression, the therapeutic alliance with the clinician, present during the therapy hour, may dissipate between treatment sessions and increase the risk of suicide.

The 3 months after hospitalization is a time of significantly increased suicide risk. In one diagnostically heterogeneous sample of 94 patients, 65% of suicides occurred within 3 months of discharge from the hospital (Roy 1986). A Veterans Administration study of outpatient referrals found that of 47 inpatients referred to a Veterans Administration mental health clinic, 21 did not keep their first appointments (Zeldow and Taub 1981).

The patient's willingness to cooperate is crucial to appropriate follow-up. The clinician's obligation is to structure the follow-up to encourage compliance (e.g., scheduling an initial appointment prior to releasing the patient, using reminder letters or phone calls, recruiting family members to ensure that the patient comes to appointments and takes medications). Once a patient is discharged from the hospital, the psychiatrist's intervention options may be limited or nonexistent (Simon 1997).

Patients who are no longer at acute risk of suicide may nevertheless remain at chronic risk. All the psychiatrist can do is carefully note that the patient is not at acute risk at the time of discharge. Once the patient is discharged, the potential for violence will depend on the patient's mental disorder, compliance with treatment, course of illness, and unpredictable situational factors. Violent behavior toward self or others is the result of dynamic, complex interactions among a variety of clinical, personality, social, and environmental factors whose relative importance varies across time and situations (Widiger and Trull 1994).

Suicide Risk Factors

There are no pathognomonic predictors of suicide. Some of the major clinical indicators of suicide risk reported in the psychiatric literature are shown in Table 8–3. This list of suicide risk factors, by no means exhaustive, separates risk indicators into individual, clinical, interpersonal, situational, and statistical categories. The table also distinguishes short-term and long-term risk factors for suicide. In their study of suicide among 954 persons with major affective disorders, Fawcett et al. (1990) found the following short-term suicide indicators to be statistically significant within 1 year of assessment: panic attacks, psychic anxiety, loss of pleasure or interest, alcohol abuse, depressive turmoil, diminished concentration, and global insomnia. They demonstrated in their prospective study that the suicide risk factors for individuals with major affective disorders who committed suicide within 1 year of assessment were different from the suicide risk factors found among individuals who committed suicide within 2–10 years of assessment. In the former group, the anxiety-related symptoms of panic attacks, psychic anxiety, global insomnia, diminished concentration, alcohol abuse, and loss of interest and pleasure were significantly more severe. Clinical interventions directed at treating anxiety-related symptoms (treatable risk factors) in patients with major affective disorders may significantly diminish a number of short-term suicide risk factors.

The more traditional suicide risk factors—including hopelessness, suicidal ideation, suicidal intent, and a history of previous suicide attempts—were not associated with short-term suicide but were significantly associated with long-term suicide. Long-term suicide risk factors are derived from community-based psychological autopsies and the retrospective study of completed suicide by psychiatric patients (Fawcett et al. 1993). Long-term suicide risk factors are severe, depression-driven symptoms (traditionally assessed by clinicians) that are significantly associated with completed suicides 2–10 years after assessment. The National Comorbidity Survey (Kessler et al. 1999) demonstrated that the transition probabilities from suicide ideation to suicide plan were 34% and from plan to attempt were 72%. Approximately 90% of unplanned and 60% of planned first attempts happened within 1 year of suicide ideation onset.

The short-term and long-term distinctions among suicide risk factors have important treatment implications. There are, however, no short-term suicide risk factors that predict when, or even if, a patient will attempt suicide. The concept of "imminent" suicide is illusory. Additional prospective studies are needed to confirm the findings that distinguish short-term from long-term suicide risk factors.

Some patients exhibit suicide risk factors that are uniquely individual. For example, one patient who had a severe stutter began to speak clearly as he became suicidal. A clinician's awareness of such an individually unique suicide risk factor can come only from knowing the patient well. In the managed care era, this degree of knowledge about patients is usually difficult or impossible to obtain. A managed care setting can become a suicide risk factor if the clinician allows the managed care organization (MCO) to dictate treatment.

Suicide is a multidetermined act that results from a complex interplay of several factors. Clinicians rely on a number of clinical risk variables in assessing

Table 8–3. Systematic suicide risk assessment: a conceptual model.

Assessment factors	Risk	Protective
Individual		
Distinctive clinical features (prodrome)		
Clinical		
Current attempt (lethality)		
Panic attacks[a]		
Psychic anxiety[a]		
Loss of pleasure and interest[a]		
Alcohol abuse[a]		
Depressive turmoil[a]		
Diminished concentration[a]		
Global insomnia[a]		
Suicide plan		
Suicidal ideation[b]		
Suicide intent[b]		
Hopelessness[b]		
Prior attempts (lethality)[b]		
Psychiatric diagnoses (Axes I and II)— symptom severity		
Recent discharge from psychiatric hospital (within 3 months)		
Drug abuse		
Impulsivity		
Physical illness		
Family history of suicide		
Mental competency		
Recent humiliation		

Table 8–3.   Systematic suicide risk assessment: a conceptual model. *(continued)*

Assessment factors	Risk	Protective
Interpersonal		
Therapeutic alliance		
Work relations		
Family relations		
Spousal or partner relations		
Children		
Situational		
Living circumstances		
Employment status		
Financial status		
Availability of lethal means (e.g., guns)		
Managed care setting		
Demographic		
Age		
Gender		
Marital status		
Socio-cultural group (base rates)		

Overall Risk Rating:

Instructions:
1. Rate risk and protective factors present as low (L), moderate (M), high (H), nonfactor (0).
2. Judge overall suicide risk as low, moderate, or high.

Note.   Tables 8–3 and 8–4 represent a conceptual model of suicide risk assessment and intervention. The purpose of these tables is to encourage a systematic approach to risk assessment. The practitioner's clinical judgment concerning the patient remains paramount. Because suicide risk variables will be assigned different weights according to the clinical presentation of the patient, the method presented in these tables cannot be followed rigidly.
[a]Risk factors statistically significant within 1 year of assessment.
[b]Associated with suicide 2–10 years following assessment.

the suicide potential of a patient. Suicide is a rare event. Some of the suicide risk variables are vague and difficult to interpret. Furthermore, it is extremely difficult for the practitioner to assign accurate clinical weight to the various factors that might signal suicide risk. Risk variables identify too many false-positive situations to be useful in long-range suicide prediction.

Suicide Risk Assessment

Systematic suicide risk assessment identifies acute, treatable, and modifiable risk and protective factors that inform the treatment and management of the suicidal patient. A conceptual model for assessing suicide risk as a low, moderate, or high potential for suicide is given in Table 8–3. In this table, suicide risk factors are not listed in order of clinical importance; that determination depends on the patient's clinical presentation. These tables may be used for comprehensive assessment of suicide risk when time does not allow for consultation. Some psychiatrists use a method similar to the one presented in Table 8–3 for patient self-assessment of suicide risk. This should be done only in conjunction with the psychiatrist's own assessment. The clinician cannot rely solely on the patient's assessment of suicide risk. The systematic assessment of suicide risk is good clinical practice and also a sound risk-management technique.

A number of suicide risk assessment methods are available to clinicians (Simon 2004). No suicide risk assessment model has been empirically tested for reliability and validity. Additionally, no method of suicide risk assessment can reliably identify who will commit suicide (sensitivity) and who will not (specificity). Attempts to predict suicide result in high false-positive and negative predictions. To assist clinicians, the American Psychiatric Association has published suicide assessment and treatment guidelines (American Psychiatric Association 2003).

Weather forecasting is analogous to the process of suicide risk assessment: Astronomical events such as eclipses can be predicted with 100% accuracy, wherease short-term and long-term weather predictions (24–48 hours, 7–10 days) are made within certain probabilities. The assessment of a patient's suicide risk is a here-and-now determination, the accuracy of which, like the weather, can change quickly and without warning. It requires frequent updates. Accordingly, a patient undergoing a suicidal crisis should be seen frequently and the suicide risk assessed from session to session.

Overall suicide risk assessments of low, moderate, or high risk are based on reasonable clinical judgment (see Table 8–4). There is no clinical standard for predicting the *occurrence* of a suicidal act, only for the assessment of suicide risk. Once an assessment is made, however, appropriate clinical interventions must be initiated (e.g., hospitalization, more frequent patient visits, or medication adjustments).

Risk factors may be also evaluated along a variety of parameters that enhance suicide risk assessment (see Table 8–5). For example, a suicide risk factor can be rated as acute or chronic. Demographic or statistical suicide risk factors such as age, gender, and race are generally considered to be relatively fixed. Acute risk factors are the focus of current clinical evaluation. Chronic risk factors have been present for 1 year or longer before assessment. Patients with Axis I disorders, especially schizophrenia, anxiety, and major affective disorders, may present with acute (state) suicide risk factors. Patients with Axis II disorders may display chronic (trait) suicide risk factors. Patients with comorbid Axis I and II disorders can have both acute and chronic risk factors present. Comorbidity is an important "predictor" of suicide attempts (Kessler et al. 1999). A suicide risk factor may also be both acute and chronic, as with recurrent depression. Other assessment parameters include risk and protective (unique, characteristic) and situational (usually loss), and necessary and sufficient.

Most depressed patients do not kill themselves. For example, the suicide rate in the general population has ranged between 10 and 11 per 100,000 per year. The suicide rate for individuals with affective disorders is 180 per 100,000 per year. Turning this statistic on its head, 99,820 out of 100,000 patients with depression will not commit suicide in a single year (Simon 2004). Thus, on a statistical basis alone, the vast majority of patients with depression will not commit suicide. The clinical challenge is to identify those patients with depression who are at significant risk for suicide (Jacobs et a l. 1999).

Suicides usually occur when both necessary (depression) and sufficient (perturbation) factors are present (Goodwin and Runck 1992; Schneidman 1985). For instance, the patient with major depression who is also experiencing an interpersonal or occupational crisis may have both necessary and sufficient suicide risk factors operating. Many suicide risk factors listed in Table 8–3 can be evaluated on necessary-sufficient parameters. The individual (state or trait)–situational (loss) parameter can be also applied to the example just given and to some of the suicide risk factors in Table 8–3. Usually a num-

Table 8–4. Assessment of suicide risk and examples of outpatient psychiatric intervention options

Suicide risk	Psychiatric interventions
High	Immediate hospitalization
Moderate	Consider: Hospitalization Frequent outpatient visits Reevaluate treatment plan frequently Remain available to patient
Low	Continue with current treatment plan

Table 8–5. Assessment parameters for suicide risk factors

- Risk–protective
- Acute–chronic
- Necessary–sufficient
- Individual–situational

ber of risk factor parameters are considered simultaneously.

The assessment factors listed in Table 8–3 are evaluated as risk and protective factors. Supportive relationships, responsibility for children, religious beliefs, and gratifying work may act as protective factors. However, suicide risk increases with the total number of risk factors, also providing a quasi-quantitative dimension to suicide risk assessment (Murphy et al. 1992).

The method of suicide risk assessment presented here is for educational purposes only. It is not necessary to reproduce Tables 8–3 and 8–4 in the patient's chart. A note containing an adequate suicide risk assessment based on the parameters in Table 8–5 is all that is necessary. This conceptual model of suicide/violence risk assessment is derived from the author's clinical experience and the evidence-based psychiatric literature but has not been empirically tested for reliability and validity. Each practitioner's clinical experience is singular and unique. Competent suicide risk assessments will vary accordingly. As noted earlier, other approaches to suicide risk assessment are also available to the clinician (Chiles et al. 2005; Clark and Fawcett 1992; Maris et al. 1992). Regardless of which method is used, suicide risk assessments must be made and contemporaneously recorded in the patient's chart.

The standard of care requires that the clinician be able to perform an adequate suicide risk assessment. Simply asking a patient whether he or she is suicidal and obtaining a "no-harm" contract is insufficient. Especially with new patients, there is no credible basis for relying on such reassurances. Moreover, approximately 25% of suicidal patients do not admit to being suicidal (Fawcett et al. 1990). The clinician should be able to identify suicide risk factors and perform suicide risk assessments that inform appropriate clinical interventions. Suicide prevention contracts, either oral or written, should not be used as a substitute for adequate suicide risk assessments.

A patient's denial of suicidal ideation, even if the patient is telling the truth, should not be equated with the absence of suicide risk. A patient may be at increased risk for suicide because of the heightened presence of other significant suicide risk factors, particularly impulsivity. A patient's suicide risk can change quickly. Fawcett (1999) noted impulsivity as a high-risk "pathway" for suicide. Impulsivity, usually a chronic trait factor, may be acutely exacerbated by stressful events (e.g., loss of a relationship, substance abuse). In patients with suicidal ideation, the probability of transition from suicidal thoughts to unplanned attempt is 26% (Kessler et al. 1999). Observational data obtained from the general psychiatric examination and the mental status examination can provide objective information about the patient's clinical status that does not depend on the patient's subjective reporting (e.g., depressive turmoil, diminished concentration, acute symptoms of drug or alcohol withdrawal, agitation isolation, impulsivity, self-destructive behaviors, responding to auditory or visual hallucinations, and other observable risk data).

Single scores of suicide risk assessment scales and inventories should not be relied upon (Beck et al. 1999; Busch et al. 1993; Simon 1998a). Structured or semistructured suicide scale questionnaires may complement but should not take the place of a thorough clinical assessment of suicide risk. Self-administered suicide scales have the disadvantage of being oversensitive and underspecific. The reliance on clinical checklists alone creates the danger that the practitioner will reflexively suspend clinical skills and judgment in assessing suicide risk. No checklist can encompass all pertinent suicide risk factors. Plaintiffs' attorneys are quick to point out omissions on checklists that were used to assess the patient who committed suicide. Furthermore, a checklist can neither replace a psychodynamic understanding of the patient nor assess suicide risk factors unique to the individual patient.

The Therapeutic Alliance

No one suicide risk variable can be counted on exclusively in the assessment of suicide risk. Nonetheless, one of the most significant suicide risk factors is the lack of a therapeutic alliance with the patient. The *therapeutic alliance* is defined as the conscious and unconscious working relationship between therapist and patient in which each implicitly agrees to collaborate in the process of treatment. The presence of a therapeutic alliance is a solid indicator of the patient's willingness to seek help and support during serious emotional crises. The presence or absence of the therapeutic alliance can be used by clinicians as a here-and-now indicator of the patient's suicidal vulnerability. For new patients or for patients seen in emergencies, sufficient time may not have elapsed for a therapeutic alliance to be evaluated or established. In addition, for a variety of clinical reasons, the therapist may not be able to develop a working alliance with the patient.

The therapeutic alliance, however, can be ephemeral. During the treatment session, a depressed patient may be able to maintain a working therapeutic alliance. After leaving the therapist, however, the patient's depression may worsen. An impulsive act can momentarily overwhelm the alliance, leading the patient to attempt or commit suicide. The therapist should assess the status of the therapeutic alliance outside of the sessions. A viable, sustainable therapeutic alliance with the patient is a powerful factor that minimizes suicide risk. This clinical phenomenon often accounts for the shock and bewilderment therapists experience after a patient, with whom a working therapeutic alliance existed, commits suicide.

Prior Suicide Attempts

Studies show that between 9% and 33% of individuals with previous suicide attempts eventually go on to completed suicide (Perr 1984). Placing significant clinical weight on the distinction between a suicide gesture and a suicide attempt can be perilous, particularly if the act occurred some time ago. Without question, some suicide attempts can be identified as gestures because the patient does not have the slightest intention of self-destruction. Unconscious distortion or retrospective falsification by the patient, however, may disguise a genuine attempt as a gesture.

Upon proper authorization, medical and psychiatric records should be obtained regarding previous diagnoses, treatments, or suicidal acts. Vital information pertinent to the current treatment and management of the patient is usually contained in previous medical records. If there is a history of psychiatric treatment, some psychiatrists call the patient's previous therapist. Summaries of prior treatments and hospitalizations may be obtained quickly via fax. With the patient's permission, family members should be contacted or interviewed to obtain additional history. Questions concerning past suicidal attempts should include the following: Did the patient intend to die? What was the lethality of the method used? Did the patient expect to be found in time? Was there some obvious manipulation or secondary gain? Was the patient overtly depressed?

Weisman and Worden (1972) devised a risk-rescue rating utilizing a descriptive and quantitative method for assessing the lethality of suicide attempts. For example, a patient who takes a few minor tranquilizers and immediately calls the physician is at low risk and high rescue. The patient who makes superficial slashes with a razor while in the psychiatric unit but remains alone is at low risk and low rescue. A high-risk, high-rescue patient attempts hanging in the presence of a friend. The high-risk, low-rescue situation occurs, for example, when the patient buys a hose to fit a car exhaust and waits for everyone to leave the house. The hypothesis underlying the suicide risk rating is that the *lethality* of the method of suicide, defined as the probability of inflicting irreversible damage, may be expressed as a ratio of factors influencing risk and rescue. The risk-rescue rating correlates with the level of treatment recommended, the subject's sex, and whether the subject lived or died. The risk-rescue rating is not a predictive instrument, but when considered along with other factors, such as explicit intention to die, prior history of mental illness, and availability of family and community support, the risk-rescue rating can assist the clinician in making an individualized suicide risk assessment.

Demonstration of Suicide Risk Assessment

After doing a complete psychiatric examination, a competent suicide risk assessment can be performed and recorded within a few minutes. One way of conducting a competent suicide risk assessment is to follow a conceptual model as demonstrated in Table 8–6. The patient's risk factors can be rated as low (L), moderate (M), high (H), or nonfactor (0). This dimensional model assesses risk factor severity and protective resource factors. Severity is a measure of intensity and duration (acute or chronic). For example, does the patient experience fleeting suicidal ideation or persistent, overwhelming thoughts of suicide? The rating of protective factors against suicide includes internal and external resources—for example, adequate coping skills and family support. After weighing all of the risk factors, the overall assessment of suicide risk is rated as low, moderate, or high.

The following clinical vignette illustrates the importance of assessing a patient's suicide risk at the time of a contemplated discharge. After reviewing the vignette, the reader is encouraged to do an independent suicide risk assessment before considering the psychiatrist's assessment.

A 36-year-old woman is transferred from the obstetrical service to the psychiatric unit of a general hospital with a diagnosis of major depressive episode following the delivery of her first son. She was discovered trying to climb onto the fifth floor windowsill in order to jump.

After 3 weeks in the psychiatric unit, the patient's depression improves with supportive psychotherapy and the administration of an antidepressant. In particular, she sleeps and eats better and has more energy. She continues, however, to display a lack of pleasure and interest in her newborn child. Occasionally, she experiences brief episodes of intense anger followed by anxiety, depression, and moderate agitation. She denies suicidal impulses but occasionally has unbidden ruminations about "what it would be like to be dead." She also denies having a suicide plan. Her initial suicide attempt arose from a momentary impulse that now seems frightening and unacceptable to her. Cognitive mental capacity is intact.

The patient develops a working alliance with her psychiatrist. She is cooperative and agrees to a contract to inform him if suicidal impulses reoccur. She also has a good marital relationship. Her husband, an engineer, is very supportive but is not psychologically minded. He feels very threatened by his wife's depression. Her husband is extremely happy about "finally having a son."

After her first child was born, the patient willingly gave up a position as an accountant. She enjoys staying home to raise her two daughters, ages 2 and 3 years, whom she loves.

The patient's past history reveals no psychiatric disorders. There is no history of alcohol or drug abuse. Her mother had a successful course of electroconvulsive therapy for recurrent depression. Her father is a recovered alcoholic who was abusive toward the patient throughout her childhood. Ten years ago, the father stopped drinking. A paternal uncle was treated for a bipolar disorder. During a depressive episode, this uncle committed suicide with a handgun. The patient has been devoutly religious from her early teen years. Her religion is an important source of solace during periods of crisis. A downturn in her husband's business during this last pregnancy caused considerable emotional distress. Money matters have been a source of worry and anxiety. Financial prospects are not favorable for the coming year. The couple's comfortable home, however, is not in jeopardy.

While a patient in the psychiatric unit, she is accompanied by a staff member when visiting her baby in the maternity ward. These visits are productive but are preceded by a moderate amount of anxiety. Occasionally, the visits end with an increase in her feelings of depression. She tends to be seclusive on the psychiatric unit. She avoids other patients and staff, preferring to stay in her room. A loss of interest and pleasure in reading and in her needlepoint are evident. She complains of some difficulty concentrating. There is no evidence of an Axis II personality disorder or history of impulsive behavior.

After 10 days the psychiatrist requests an additional week of inpatient treatment. The MCO authorizes two additional hospital days after a doctor-to-doctor appeal. The MCO will not provide further coverage for continued hospital treatment. The patient also requests discharge. The patient wants to resume full care of her baby. She misses her daughters and feels guilt about "not being able to take care of my children." The patient's parents will be staying with the patient after she is discharged. The husband is a sportsman who has a collection of guns at home that he keeps locked away. The key to the gun cabinet is kept at his office outside the home. The psychiatrist requests and receives a callback from the patient's husband that the guns have been removed from the home and secured elsewhere. The psychiatrist conducts a systematic suicide risk assessment, judging the patient's overall risk to be in the moderate to high range (see Table 8–6). The suicide risk assessment is included in the risk-benefit evaluation for both continued hospitalization and discharge. The psychiatrist concludes that the patient can be discharged but must attend a partial hospitalization program. An appointment is arranged with the psychiatrist for the day after discharge.

This vignette has been presented at clinical conferences where clinicians were asked to assess the patient's suicidal risk and appropriateness for discharge. Most of the practitioners rated the patient's suicide risk as moderate to high. Suicide risk assessments varied substantially among clinicians because of differences in training, experience, and whether the clinician had lost a patient to suicide. A number of practitioners would not discharge the patient until her suicide risk diminished in response to antidepressant medication.

Table 8–6.   Demonstration of a rapid, competent suicide risk assessment

Assessment factors	Risk	Protective
Anxiety	M	
Loss of pleasure and interest in child	H	
Depressive turmoil	M	
Diminished concentration	L	
Therapeutic alliance		H
Family relations		M
Hopelessness	L	
Psychiatric diagnosis	M	
Prior attempts	0	
Current attempt (lethality)	H	
Specific plan	0	
Living situation		H
Employment		L
Availability of gun	M	
Suicidal ideation/intent	L (passive)	
Family history	H	
Impulsivity	M–H	
Drug/alcohol	0	
Depression/postpartum	M	
Religion		L–M
Insomnia	L	
Other children		H
Physical condition		M
Cognition/competence		M–H
Marital relationship		M–H
Overall Risk Rating:	Moderate-high (at discharge)	

Others felt that it would be impractical to continue hospital treatment without insurance coverage. Moreover, the patient was worried about money matters. Incurring a substantial debt for an uninsured hospitalization could exacerbate the patient's depression and risk for suicide. They thought that patients at moderate to even high suicide risk are currently managed as outpatients and that close, continuing follow-up would be necessary for this patient immediately after discharge.

This situation arises frequently and poses a difficult problem for clinicians who do not receive authorization from the MCO for additional hospital days for patients who require continuing treatment. A managed care setting should not be allowed to become a suicide risk factor. In a crisis, the practitioner may decide to continue treatment until the patient is clinically stabilized or make other suitable arrangements for care.

Suicide Prevention Contracts

Some therapists attempt to formalize the alliance with the patient by a verbal or even a written contract stating that the patient will call on the psychiatrist if he or she becomes suicidal. Suicide prevention contracts have no legal force (Simon 1999). They neither bind patients nor immunize psychiatrists. No evidence exists that suicide prevention contracts reduce or eliminate suicide risk (Stanford et al. 1994). The patient who refuses a no-harm contract gets the attention of the clinician and staff as an important indicator of significant suicide risk. Thus a patient's contract refusal is of greater clinical value than a patient's acquiescence to the agreement. A suicide prevention contract can falsely reassure the therapist and lower vigilance without having any appreciable effect on the patient's suicidal intent. Frequently, such contracts reflect the therapist's attempt to control the inevitable anxiety associated with treating suicidal patients. Contracts against suicide may be of therapeutic value when used to affirm the therapeutic alliance, but their limitations should be understood by the therapist. Moreover, contracts must not be used as a substitute for the adequate assessment of suicide risk (Simon 1991). Finally, suicide prevention contracts should not be a criterion for discharge of patients from an inpatient unit or emergency department.

Treatment

The clinician must fully commit time and effort to the overall care and treatment of the patient at risk for suicide. Clinicians have a professional, ethical, and legal duty to provide adequate care to their patients, regardless of managed care protocols and restriction of benefits. The clinician's duty of care is not a function of payment. Moreover, clinicians should make a realistic self-appraisal regarding the number of suicidal patients he or she can competently treat at any given time. Some clinicians have neither the time, the inclination, nor the temperament to treat suicidal patients. The treatment and management of the suicidal patient can be enormously emotionally taxing and disturbing of the clinician's equanimity. Clinicians must acknowledge these limitations (Simon 2004). Patients at risk for suicide require aggressive treatment and safety management. Time works against reduction of suicide risk if treatment is delayed or ineffectual. Loss of employment, disruption of relationships, and demoralization increase the likelihood that the illness will become entrenched. Because antidepressants take time to work, other more immediate interventions must be implemented. Temporizing can increase the depressed patient's risk of suicide.

Inpatient and Outpatient Settings

The opportunities to monitor the patient and to anticipate suicide are greater in the hospital setting, although hospitalization does not guarantee that suicide will not be attempted. Often, the hospitalized patient will put the psychiatrist on notice by a prior attempt or by exhibiting suicidal behaviors on the ward. A patient at suicide risk may not exhibit any signs or symptoms of self-destructive behavior after hospital admission. Because a patient can be placed on suicide precautions (e.g., constant one-on-one supervision, observations every 15-minutes or more frequently) in the hospital, a higher level of awareness and diligence is expected in reducing the likelihood that the patient will commit suicide. Patients can and sometimes do commit suicide in the interval between 15-minute checks. Suicide precautions should be tailored to the safety needs of the patient. Definitions of suicide precautions and observation usually vary from hospital to hospital. The clinician should clearly understand how these terms are being used. A consistently heightened awareness that patients can, and do, commit suicide as inpatients enhances patient safety. Nevertheless, there is no such thing as a suicide-proof psychiatric unit (Benesohn and Resnik 1973).

It is more difficult for the psychiatrist to supervise a patient outside than inside the hospital. Thus, asking a patient specifically about suicide should be part of every psychiatric evaluation. For outpatients at moderate to high risk for suicide, one treatment option is to see the patient more frequently. Time attenuates assessments of suicide risk. Daily or even more frequent visits may be required with patients at high risk for suicide who refuse hospitalization and do not meet criteria for involuntary hospitalization. The therapist must be readily available to the patient and monitor closely any medications that are administered.

Involuntary hospitalization may be a final option for the high-risk suicidal patient who refuses treatment and meets involuntary hospitalization criteria and for whom no less-restrictive treatment option exists. Liability may be incurred for the suicide of an outpatient if a gross error is made in deciding not to seek civil commitment of the patient (Simon 2004).

Informing Third Parties of a Patient's Suicidal Intent

The competent patient's request to maintain confidentiality must be honored absent countervailing interests resulting in an exception to the duty of confidentiality, as in the case of the patient who is a danger to self or to others. Reflecting this need to balance confidentiality against other interests, *The Principles of Medical Ethics With Annotations Especially Applicable to Psychiatry* (American Psychiatric Association 2001) states: "Psychiatrists at times may find it necessary, in order to protect the patient or the community from imminent danger, to reveal confidential information disclosed by the patient" (p. 8, Section 4, Annotation 8). This same balance is reflected in state confidentiality laws that permit a breach of confidentiality for disclosures to law enforcement when the patient poses what the court terms an imminent risk of harm to self or others (Thapar v. Zezulka 1999).

The question of whether a psychiatrist must breach confidentiality by disclosure to a third party (friend or family member) in order to protect the patient from harm to self is complex. Unlike Tarasoff v. Regents of the University of California (1976), where the injured third party was not someone for whom the psychiatrist had agreed to care, when the patient under the care of a psychiatrist causes harm to self, the victim has a psychiatrist–patient relationship that gives rise to certain professional duties. For example, the patient or his or her estate may sue the psychiatrist for malpractice if the psychiatrist's unreasonable failure to order suicide precautions was a proximate cause of the patient's death. Nonetheless, on policy grounds, several courts have limited the obligation to warn third parties when the risk is only harm to self, without regard to the foreseeability of harm (Bellah v. Greenson 1978). In most other jurisdictions, the issue turns on the foreseeability of harm to the patient and the reasonableness of the psychiatrist's response (Smith v. New York City Health and Hospitals Corp. 1995).

It is standard practice to take reasonable preventive measures to keep patients from harming themselves. Such measures may include communicating with family members about the patient's case, attempting to modify pathological interactions between the patient and family members, and mobilizing family support (e.g., removing lethal weapons, poisons, and drugs; administering and monitoring prescribed medications) (Simon 2004).

Suicide as a Function of Psychiatric Illness

Suicide is the result of dynamically interactive, complex factors, including diagnostic (psychiatric and medical), constitutional, occupational, environmental, social, cultural, existential, situational, and chance factors. Although there is a loose fit between diagnosis and suicide, suicide rarely occurs in the absence of psychiatric illness. Every psychiatric diagnosis is associated with an increased risk of suicide (see Table 8–7).

Individuals who make serious suicide attempts have high rates of mental disorders and comorbid conditions (Beautrais et al. 1996). Impulsivity and opportunity can be unanticipated factors in suicide. For example, a patient may be determined to attempt suicide for just a few seconds, minutes, or hours during the course of a psychiatric hospitalization. If the patient then discovers an unlocked window, an area under construction, or a lethal instrument carelessly left about, she or he may take advantage of the opportunity to impulsively commit suicide.

Acutely suicidal patients usually have Axis I disorders such as major affective or schizophrenic illnesses that often require immediate hospitalization and aggressive treatment. The acute risk of suicide usually passes with the amelioration of the acute episode of illness. Patients with chronic waxing and waning suicidal ideation are usually treated as outpatients. The most frequent

Table 8–7. Mortality associated with selected mental and physical disorders

Disorder(s)	SMR[a]
Eating disorders	23.14
Major depression	20.35
Sedative abuse	20.34
Mixed drug abuse	19.23
Bipolar disorder	15.05
Opioid abuse	14.00
Dysthymia	12.12
Obsessive-compulsive disorder	11.54
Panic disorder	10.00
Schizophrenia	8.45
Personality disorders	7.08
AIDS	6.58
Alcohol abuse	5.86
Epilepsy	5.11
Child and adolescent	4.73
Cannabis abuse	3.85
Spinal cord injury	3.82
Neuroses	3.72
Brain injury	3.50
Huntington's chorea	2.90
Multiple sclerosis	2.36
Malignant neoplasms	1.80
Mental retardation	0.88

[a]SMR (standardized mortality ratio) is calculated by dividing observed mortality by expected mortality.
Source.   Adapted from Harris and Barraclough 1997.

diagnoses are Axis II personality disorders, especially borderline personality disorder. These patients may require psychiatric hospitalization if their suicidal impulses are exacerbated because of some life crisis or if they develop a comorbid Axis I psychiatric disorder (usually a major depression).

Exacerbations in the chronic suicidal state of patients with personality disorders are often the result of intense rage and unstable self-esteem regulation, triggered by an interpersonal crisis. The possibility of suicide is seized upon as a comforting means of escape and control. At times of crisis, real suicide risk may exist. If not hospitalized, these patients should be seen frequently and reevaluated for suicide risk from session to session. Their medication should be monitored closely. The patient's support system should be mobilized, if available. The psychiatrist needs to be accessible. The psychiatrist must be able to tolerate a patient's chronic, recurrent exacerbations of suicidal risk to continue the work of therapy (Simon 1992b).

Psychiatric Residents and Training Program Orientation

Psychiatric residents who treat patients at acute risk of suicide should increase the frequency of supervision with their attending psychiatrists. Not only is this policy clinically prudent, but it will help to ensure that the resident treats the patient as required by the standard of care.

Psychiatric residents should consider the theoretical orientation and possible treatment biases of their training program and supervisors. Psychodynamic approaches to treatment may tend to deemphasize strategies such as a discussion of the suicidal patient's condition with family members or the use of organic therapies such as pharmacotherapy or electroconvulsive therapy. Organic therapies that may be the treatment of choice for certain psychiatric disorders may be given insufficient consideration. Conversely, biologically oriented training programs and supervisors may not place enough emphasis on the need for an ongoing treatment relationship with the patient as the essential context for psychopharmacological interventions. Also, too many medications may be prescribed in place of seeing the patient more frequently. Psychodynamic understanding of the patient may be deemphasized or even disparaged. Psychiatrists are most effective when they can provide balanced treatment approaches tailored to the clinical needs of patients.

Managed Care and the Suicidal Patient

The treatment of psychiatric inpatients has changed dramatically in the managed care era. The number of reimbursed outpatient visits has been severely curtailed. Most psychiatric units, particularly those in general hospitals, are now short-stay, acute-care psychiatric facilities. Mainly only suicidal, homicidal, or gravely disabled patients with major psychiatric disorders pass strict precertification review for hospitalization. Approximately half of these patients have comorbid substance-related disorders.

The goal of hospitalization is crisis intervention and management to stabilize severely ill patients and to ensure their safety. The close scrutiny by utilization reviewers generally allows only brief hospitalization. In addition, the hospital administration may exert pressure for early discharge in order to maintain length-of-stay statistics within predetermined limits. Treatment of acutely and chronically ill patients is provided by a variety of mental health professionals. With reduced provider reimbursement for inpatient treatment, the psychiatrist may be tempted to turn over more of the patient's care to the multidisciplinary team. Irrespective of payment, the psychiatrist is responsible for the care of the patient (Simon 1998b).

The psychiatrist is liable for psychiatric treatments gone awry. Unfortunately, limited opportunity exists during the hospital stay to develop a therapeutic alliance with seriously ill suicidal patients. The ability to communicate with patients, the psychiatrist's stock-in-trade, is usually severely curtailed by the patient's condition and the conditions for hospitalizations. Usually, in order to gain precertification for admission in managed care settings, patients must meet "medically necessary" criteria, the stringency of which often equals or exceeds that of the substantive criteria for involuntary civil commitment. All of these psychiatric risk factors contribute to the increased risk of malpractice suits against psychiatrists, especially suits alleging premature or negligent discharge of suicidal patients due to cost-containment policies (Cruzan v. Director, Missouri Department of Health 1990).

In both the outpatient and inpatient managed care settings, psychiatrists continue to be responsible for the care of acutely suicidal patients, even if further insurance benefits are denied by the MCO. The psychiatrist's professional, ethical, and legal duty to provide care to the patient is not dependent on payment. MCOs can limit or deny *payment* for services but not the actual services themselves. After the emergency is over, the psychiatrist may refer the patient to other appropriate health care providers, see the patient at a reduced fee, or discharge the patient if no further treatment is deemed necessary.

The psychiatrist should record in the discharge note that the suicide risk assessment is a "here-and-now" evaluation. The discharge note should detail the acute suicide risk factors that have abated along with chronic suicide risk factors that persist. The note should also document that patients at chronic suicide risk can become acutely suicidal, depending on the nature and course of their mental illness, the adequacy of future treatment, adherence to treatment recommendations, and exposure to life's unpredictable vicissitudes. Suicidal behaviors are the result of a dynamic, complex interaction among a variety of clinical, personality, social, and environmental factors that vary across time and situations.

Supervision by Family or Friends

Whether one practices in a jurisdiction that recognizes a duty to breach confidentiality to protect patients at risk of suicide or one that does not (Bellah v. Greenson 1978), good clinical practice frequently requires that significant others be apprised of the patient's risk of suicide or be included in the treatment. Because of MCO limitations on inpatient length of stay, supervision by significant others after discharge is important. The stability of the patient and the family and their interaction should be assessed before discharge. It is usually not possible to wait for patients to become totally free of suicide ideation before discharge. Most patients at moderate or even moderate to high suicide risk are treated as outpatients.

There are potentially two basic problems with suicidal patients and their families. First, the interaction between the patient and the family may be impaired. Seriously mentally ill patients rarely come from families whose members are without substantial psychological impairment. Some members of the patient's family may be more disturbed than the patient. Releasing a patient at suicide risk to a troubled family could cause the patient to abandon treatment and regress, increasing the risk of suicide.

A patient may withhold permission for the clinician or hospital staff to contact his or her family for no good reason or for good reason, such as appraisal that the family's involvement is potentially destructive. This situation often arises when the patient has been physically or sexually abused by family members. Absent what the courts term as an "imminent" risk of harm to the patient or others, a competent patient's refusal to waive confidentiality must be respected.

Secondly, family members are not trained to diagnose and manage suicidal patients. Asking family members to supervise the patient places on them a burden that they often may not be able to manage. Specifically, asking family members to keep constant watch on the patient will likely fail. Family members usually will not follow the patient into the bathroom or stay up all night to observe the patient. Family members often fall asleep, especially if they worked all day and must go to work again the next day. Moreover, family members usually make exceptions, due to denial, fatigue, or the pressing need to attend to other matters. Thus, when clinicians advise a responsible, designated family member or other person to remove guns from the patient's home or office, a callback is necessary to confirm that the guns were removed and safely secured (R.I. Simon, "Suicidal Patients With Guns at Home," unpublished data, August 2006).

There is an important role for the family, but it is not as a substitute for the care provided by trained mental health professionals. Family support and feedback about the patient's thoughts and behaviors is an appropriate, helpful role. Family members that have a reasonably sound relationship with the patient are usually sensitive to reportable changes in the patient's mental condition.

Physician-Assisted Suicide

With increasing legal recognition of physician-assisted suicide, psychiatrists are likely to be called on to act as gatekeepers. Such a role represents a radical departure from the physician's code of ethics, which prohibits an ethical doctor's participation in any intervention that hastens death. In the case of Cruzan v. Director, Missouri Department of Health (1990), the U.S. Supreme Court ruled that terminally ill persons could refuse life-supporting medical treatment. Every proposal for physician-assisted suicide requires a psychiatric screening or consultation to determine the terminally ill person's competency to choose suicide. The presence of psychiatric disorders associated with suicide, particularly depression, will have to be ruled out as the driving factor behind the request (Simon 1989). Much controversy rages over the ethics of this gatekeeping function (American Medical Association 1994).

Recently, in Gonzales v. Oregon (2006), the U.S. Supreme Court interpreted the Controlled Substances Act as not permitting the U.S. attorney general to prosecute Oregon physicians prescribing drugs under the Oregon Death With Dignity Act for use in physician-assisted suicide. Although the major portion of the opinion is devoted to the authority granted the attorney general under federal drug law, a portion of the opinion addresses the authority of the states to regulate the practice of medicine, including authorizing physicians to administer lethal doses of drugs.

References

Amchin J, Wettstein RM, Roth LH: Suicide, ethics, and the law, in Suicide Over the Life Cycle. Edited by Blumenthal SJ, Kupfer DJ. Washington, DC, American Psychiatric Press, 1990, pp 637–663

American Medical Association: Physician-Assisted Suicide: Code of Medical Ethics Reports, Vol 5, No 2. Chicago, IL, American Medical Association, 1994, pp 269–275

American Psychiatric Association: The Principles of Medical Ethics With Annotations Especially Applicable to Psychiatry. Washington, DC, American Psychiatric Association, 2001

American Psychiatric Association: Practice guidelines for the assessment and treatment of patients with suicidal behaviors. Am J Psychiatry 160:1–60, 2003

Beautrais AL, Joyce PR, Mulder RT, et al: Prevalence and comorbidity of mental disorders in persons making serious suicide attempts: a case-control study. Am J Psychiatry 153:1009–1014, 1996

Beck AT, Brown GK, Steer RA, et al: Suicide ideation at its worst point: a predictor of eventual suicide in psychiatric outpatients. Suicide Life Threat Behav 29:1–9, 1999

Benesohn H, Resnik HLP: Guidelines for "suicide-proofing" a psychiatric unit. Am J Psychother 26:204–211, 1973

Busch KA, Clark DC, Fawcett J, et al: Clinical features of inpatient suicide. Psychiatr Ann 23:256–262, 1993

Chiles JA, Strosahl KD: Clinical Manual for Assessment and Treatment of Suicidal Patients. Washington, DC, American Psychiatric Publishing, 2005

Clark DC, Fawcett J: An empirically based model of suicide risk assessment for patients with affective disorders, in Suicide and Clinical Practice. Edited by Jacobs D. Washington, DC, American Psychiatric Press, 1992, pp 55–73

Fawcett J: Profiles in completed suicides, in Guide to Suicide Assessment and Intervention. Edited by Jacobs JG. San Francisco, CA, Jossey-Bass, 1999, pp 115–124

Fawcett J, Scheptner WA, Fogg L, et al: Time-related predictors of suicide in major affective disorder. Am J Psychiatry 147:1189–1194, 1990

Fawcett J, Clark DC, Busch KA: Assessing and treating the patient at risk for suicide. Psychiatr Ann 23:244–255, 1993

Garner BA: Black's Law Dictionary, Pocket Edition. St. Paul, MN, West Publishing, 1996

Goodwin FK, Runck BL: Suicide intervention: integration of psychosocial, clinical, and biomedical traditions, in Suicide and Clinical Practice. Edited by Jacobs DG. Washington DC, American Psychiatric Press, 1992, pp 1–22

Harris EC, Barraclough B: Suicide as an outcome for mental disorders. A meta-analysis. Br J Psychiatry 170:205–228, 1997

Jacobs DG, Brewer M, Klein-Benheim M: Suicide assessment: an overview and recommended protocol, in Guide to Suicide Assessment and Intervention. Edited by Jacobs JG. San Francisco, CA, Jossey-Bass, 1999, pp 3–39

Kessler RC, Borges G, Walters EE: Prevalence of and risk factors for lifetime suicide attempts in the National Comorbidity Survey. Arch Gen Psychiatry 55:617–626, 1999

Maris RW, Berman AL, Maltsberger JT, et al: Assessment and Prediction of Suicide. New York, Guilford, 1992

Murphy GE, Wetzel RD, Robins E, et al: Multiple risk factors predict suicide in alcoholism. Arch Gen Psychiatry 49:459–463, 1992

Perr IN: Suicide liability: a clinical perspective. Legal Aspects of Psychiatric Practice 1:5–8, 1984

Robertson JD: The trial of a suicide case, in American Psychiatric Press Review of Clinical Psychiatry and the Law, Vol 2. Edited by Simon RI. Washington, DC, American Psychiatric Press, 1991, pp 423–441

Roy A (ed): Suicide. Baltimore, MD, Williams & Wilkins, 1986

Schneidman ES: Definition of Suicide. New York, Wiley, 1985

Simon RI: Silent suicide in the elderly. Bull Am Acad Psychiatry Law 17:83–95, 1989

Simon RI: The suicide prevention pact: clinical and legal considerations, in American Psychiatric Press Review of Clinical Psychiatry and the Law, Vol 2. Edited by Simon RI. Washington, DC, American Psychiatric Press, 1991, pp 441–451

Simon RI: Clinical Psychiatry and the Law, 2nd Edition. Washington, DC, American Psychiatric Press, 1992a, pp 283–284

Simon RI: Clinical risk management of suicidal patients: assessing the unpredictable, in American Psychiatric Press Review of Clinical Psychiatry and the Law, Vol 3. Edited by Simon RI. Washington, DC, American Psychiatric Press, 1992b, pp 3–66

Simon RI: Discharging sicker, potentially violent psychiatric inpatients in the managed care era: standard of care and risk management. Psychiatr Ann 27:726–733, 1997

Simon RI: Psychiatrists awake! Suicide risk assessments are all about a good night's sleep. Psychiatr Ann 28:479–485, 1998a

Simon RI: Psychiatrists' duties in discharging sicker and potentially violent inpatients in the managed care era. Psychiatr Serv 49:62–67, 1998b

Simon RI: The suicide prevention contract: clinical, legal, and risk management issues. J Am Acad Psychiatry Law 27:445–450, 1999

Simon RI: Suicide risk assessment: what is the standard of care? J Am Acad Psychiatry Law 30:340–344, 2002

Simon RI: Assessing and Managing Suicide Risk: Guidelines for Clinically Based Risk Management. Washington, DC, American Psychiatric Publishing, 2004

Simon RI: Imminent suicide: the illusion of short-term prediction. Suicide Life Threat Behav 36:296–301, 2006

Simon RI, Gutheil TG: A recurrent pattern of suicide risk factors observed in litigated cases: lessons in risk management. Psychiatr Ann 32:384–387, 2002

Simon RI, Hales RE: American Psychiatric Publishing Textbook of Suicide Assessment and Management. Washington, DC, American Psychiatric Publishing, 2006

Stanford EJ, Goetz RR, Bloom JD: The no harm contract in the emergency assessment of suicide risk. J Clin Psychiatry 5:344–348, 1994

Weisman AD, Worden JW: Risk-rescue rating in suicide assessment. Arch Gen Psychiatry 26:553–560, 1972

Widiger TA, Trull TJ: Personality disorders and violence, in Violence and Mental Disorder: Developments in Risk Assessment. Edited by Monahan J, Steadman HJ. Chicago, IL, University of Chicago Press, 1994, pp 203–226

Zeldow PB, Taub HA: Evaluating psychiatric discharge and aftercare in a VA medical center. Hosp Community Psychiatry 32:57–58, 1981

Legal References

Bellah v. Greenson, 81 Cal.App.3d 614, 146 Cal.Rptr. 535 (Cal. App. 1 Dist., 1978)

Cruzan v Director, Missouri Department of Health, 497 U.S. 261 (1990)

Ellis v United States, 484 F.Supp. 4 (S.C., 1978)

Gonzales v Oregon, 126 S. Ct. 94 (2006)

Palsgraf v Long Island Railroad, 248 N.Y. 339, 162 N.E. 99 (N.Y., 1928)

Smith v New York City Health and Hospitals Corp., 211 A.D.3d 483, 621 N.Y.S.2d 319 (1st Dep't., 1995)

Speer v United States, 512 F.Supp. 670 (N.D. Tex., 1981), aff'd, Speer v. United States, 675 F.2d 100 (5th Cir., 1982)

Stepakoff v Kantar, 393 Mass. 836, 473 N.E.2d 1131 (Mass., 1985)

Tarasoff v Regents of the University of California, 17 Cal.3d 425; 551 P.2d 334 (Cal. Rptr., 14 1976)

Thapar v Zezulka, 994 S.W.2d 635 (Tex., 1999)

Laws

Federal Tort Claims Act (28 U.S.C.A. §§ 2671 et seq. [2006])

9

Psychiatric Responsibility and the Violent Patient

Overview of the Law

As a general rule, in the absence of a special relationship (e.g., jailer–prisoner), one person has no legal duty to control the conduct of a second person in order to prevent that person from harming a third person (Restatement [Second] of Torts § 315[a] [1965]). Under this rule, psychiatrists traditionally have only owed a duty to third persons for their patients' actions in limited circumstances, such as the negligent discharge of a hospitalized dangerous patient who causes harm to a third person. However, in the main, psychiatrists were not held accountable for the actions of their outpatients, who were alone liable for their own actions. In the wake of the Tarasoff v. Regents of the University of California (1976) decision, the therapist's legal duty and potential liability significantly expanded. In *Tarasoff,* the California Supreme Court reasoned that the special relationship required to recognize a duty to a third party was satisfied in this circumstance based on assumptions the court made regarding the ability of mental health professionals to predict dangerousness. The court held that "the single relationship of a doctor to his [or her] patient is sufficient to support the duty to exercise reasonable care to protect others" from the violent acts of patients.

Other jurisdictions have also concluded that the need to safeguard the public may override confidentiality and call for a psychotherapist to contact the police or the potential victim, hospitalize the patient, or take other measures that would protect a third party. In most states, a psychotherapist owes a legal duty to protect identifiable persons from reasonably foreseeable patient violence. In jurisdictions that recognize such a duty, there are typically requirements that the threat of serious violence be reasonably foreseeable if no protective action is taken and that the victim be identifiable. Several states have rejected recognition of a legal obligation by a doctor to persons injured by the acts of his patient (Evans v. United States 1995; Green v. Ross 1997). For example, in Thapar v. Zezulka (1999), the Texas Supreme Court ruled that the state statute *permits* but does not *require* disclosures by therapists of threats of harm by patients against others (see Quattrocchi and Schopp 2005). Others have enacted legislation to make clear what circumstances trigger the duty and how it may be met. For example, California statutory law now limits a psychotherapist's liability for failure "to warn of and protect from a patient's threatened violent behavior or failing to predict and warn of and protect from a patient's violent behavior except where the patient has communicated to the psychotherapist a serious threat of physical violence against a reasonably identifiable victim or victims" (Cal. Civ. Code § 43.92 [2006]). When a duty arises, it may be met by "the psychotherapist making reasonable efforts to communicate the threat to the victim or victims and to a law enforcement agency."

When Does the Duty to Protect Arise?

The duty to protect arises, where it is recognized, to avoid serious violence that would otherwise likely occur without a timely opportunity for other intervention. Thus one dimension of the requirements often imposed for a duty to arise is temporal—the patient must pose an imminent threat of serious harm to an identifiable third party. Whatever legal balance this term strikes between patient privacy and public safety, it is clinically problematic. Imminence of violence is an illusion of short-term prediction for which no risk factors exist (Simon 2006). Determining what the "standards of the profession" are in evaluating an imminent threat (i.e., predicting dangerousness) and how the duty should be carried out is unsettled. As a result, this area of law is controversial and vexing. In jurisdictions that have statutorily specified the circumstances triggering a duty to protect, clinicians have found that a duty to protect that contains more concrete thresholds provides more latitude for treatment interventions. For example, Colorado statutory law provides that liability for a mental health professional who fails to warn or protect is limited to circumstances in which "the patient has communicated to the mental health care provider a serious threat of imminent physical violence against a specific person or persons" (Colo. Rev. Stat. Ann. § 13-21-117 [2006]). Absent such statutory thresholds, courts typically focus on whether the violence was foreseeable and whether a sufficient element of control was present.

Three threshold factors need to be addressed by the clinician in a potential duty-to-protect situation:

1. Assess the threat of violence to another.
2. Identify the potential object of that threat.
3. Implement some affirmative, preventive act.

The law assumes that the foreseeability of violence provides an intended victim an opportunity to avoid harm that the law should value. Thus, if the fact finder determines that but for the psychiatrist's failure to identify or take action to protect against foreseeable violence it would not have occurred, the psychiatrist is liable for the harm caused. Foreseeability, however, is a legal term of art that asks what should have reasonably been anticipated. It asks but does not answer questions about the ability of clinicians to predict violent behavior. Foreseeability also should not be confused with preventability. In hindsight, some violent acts seem *preventable* that were not *foreseeable*.

Assessing the Threat

Recognizing the inability to predict the occurrence of violence reliably, the law does not demand that all predictions be correct but instead requires only that psychiatrists exercise reasonable care in making such assessments. This requires compliance with ordinary violence assessment procedures used in the profession. Steps such as taking a thorough pretreatment history, asking about and exploring past or present violence, and attending to factors reasonably thought to contribute to violent behavior are likely to satisfy a reasonable standard of care (see Tables 9–1 and 9–2 later in this chapter).

Identifying the Intended Victim

If the clinician determines that a threat of violence exists, it is clinically and legally necessary to follow up that assessment with a determination of the person(s) who might be the object of the threat. Early cases and an increasing number of recent decisions have held that the duty to protect applies only when there is a "specific or identifiable threat to a specific or identifiable victim" (Brady v. Hopper 1984; Thompson v. County of Alameda 1980; White v. United States 1986). A few courts have broadened this finding by requiring the duty to protect whenever there is a "foreseeable risk of harm" to the public at large (Lipari v. Sears, Roebuck and Co. 1980; Schuster v. Altenberg 1988).

Discharging the Duty

A number of courts and state statutes have addressed what is required to discharge the duty to protect. The statutes usually provide that the duty is met when an identifiable victim is warned and/or the police notified (Appelbaum et al. 1989). Judicial decisions are, by nature, more pragmatic and less comprehensive about how the duty to protect may be met. For example, although the issue was never decided, the therapist in *Tarasoff* had notified the campus police of his concerns. The broad language used in the cases affords a therapist a certain latitude in determining "whatever steps are reasonably necessary" to discharge that duty.

A conceptual model for assessing violence and implementing suggested psychiatric interventions is outlined in Tables 9–1 and 9–2. The legal reasoning applied in cases involving the duty to warn and protect suggests a number of factors to consider in order to reduce the risk of potential liability, if a patient threatens harm to others.

Special Considerations

Time Limitations

The courts have not clarified important temporal aspects of the duty to protect. Specifically, for how long after the last patient contact will a therapist be held accountable for the patient's act? Rather than drawing lines, the time between the last patient contact and the injury of a third party is simply one factor for the jury's consideration. For example, in Naidu v. Laird (1987), the Delaware Supreme Court upheld a finding that an inpatient psychiatrist was negligent in failing to foresee a former patient's potential to commit a violent act 5½ months after discharge. The court stated that the lapse of time, by itself, was not a bar to recovery but one factor to be weighed by the jury.

Confidentiality and Liability

The recognition of a duty to warn does not eliminate the necessity to resolve an opposing risk of lawsuit for breach of confidentiality in unreasonably discharging the duty to protect (i.e., unnecessary disclosures where a duty to protect exists or any disclosures where a duty to protect does not exist). Because fulfilling the duty to protect through disclosure to the police or hospitalization of the patient helps to prevent patient violence, the question of whether the risk of violence was correctly assessed and the breach of confidentiality justified remains unresolved. At the least, a disclosure must be made with discretion and in a manner that will preserve the patient's privacy while preventing potential harm. Moreover, the disclosure must be based on a well-documented, reasonable risk assessment of violence.

Unforeseeable Violence

Liability for failing to act to prevent third-party injury is not appropriate if the evaluation leading to the conclusion that a patient is at low risk for violence is based on acceptable and reasonable clinical judgment. Although a finding that an evaluation was based on accepted standards for clinical judgment should not result in a finding of liability, some analysis suggests that deviations from clinical practice that may be professionally acceptable are nonetheless troubling to jurors.

Unreachable Identified Victims

In situations in which the patient is judged to be a threat to a third party, but the third party cannot be reached in order to be warned, the therapist must consider notifying the police or contacting someone in close relationship with the potential victim. If clinically indicated, the patient may require hospitalization. Documenting that the therapist was unable to reach the identified victim and that alternative approaches were used may be important in determining liability.

Evolving Trends

An important, evolving trend is the application of the *Tarasoff* duty to protect third persons from sexual abuse by a pedophile treated by the therapist. In one reported decision, Garamella v. New York Medical College (1998), the appellate court upheld the denial of a psychiatrist's motion to dismiss a tort claim

Table 9–1.　Systematic violence risk assessment: a conceptual model

Assessment factors	Risk	Protective
Individual		
Specific person threatened[a]		
Past violent acts[a]		
Accessible victim		
Motive		
Clinical		
Psychiatric diagnosis (Axis I and II)		
Thought insertion or control		
Command hallucinations		
Control of anger		
Syntonic or dystonic violence		
Nonspecific threats		
Childhood abuse (or witnessing parental spouse abuse)		
Alcohol abuse		
Drug abuse		
Mental competency		
History of impulsive behavior		
Neuropsychiatric disorder		
Interpersonal		
Therapeutic alliance (ongoing patient)		
Family, partner, work, other relationships		
Fear of control by others		
Situational		
Stressor(s) specify		
Living environment		
Employment status		
Availability of lethal means (e.g., guns)		

Table 9–1.   Systematic violence risk assessment: a conceptual model *(continued)*

Assessment factors	Risk	Protective
Epidemiological		
Age		
Gender		
Sociocultural group (base rates)		
Marital status		
Violence base rates		

Overall risk rating:

Instructions:
1. Rate risk factors present as low (L), moderate (M), high (H), nonfactor (0).
2. Judge overall violence risk as low, moderate, or high.

Note.   Tables 9–1 and 9–2 represent a conceptual model of violence risk assessment and intervention. The purpose of these tables is to encourage a systematic approach to risk assessment. The therapist's clinical judgment concerning the patient remains paramount. Because violence risk factors will be assigned different weights according to the clinical presentation of the patient, the method represented in these tables should not be followed rigidly.
[a]When a specific person is threatened and past violence has occurred, the patient is at high risk to commit violence.

for not reporting to the medical school that his student/patient was a pedophile. The student/patient, a psychiatric resident, engaged in child molestation at a hospital crisis center. Reasoning that the outpatient setting did not present an insurmountable problem for the plaintiff because of the supervising psychiatrist's control over his student, the court left for trial the matter of the plaintiff's foreseeability. A *Tarasoff* duty was also found in a case in which a spouse had knowledge of her husband's sexually abusive behavior against children in the neighborhood (J.S. v. R.T.H. 1998; Touchette v. Ganal 1996). In another case, the court found that a *Tarasoff* duty could exist but declined to find the parents of a babysitter liable for his dangerous sexual behavior (Popple v. Rose 1998). The court determined that no evidence existed that the parents knew of their son's proclivity to commit a sexual assault.

Table 9–2. Assessment of violence risk and examples of outpatient psychiatric intervention options

Violence risk	Psychiatric interventions
High	Immediate hospitalization if mentally ill and likely to benefit from hospitalization
Moderate	Hospitalization Frequent outpatient visits Consider warning endangered person(s) and calling the police Reevaluate patient and treatment plan frequently Remain available to the patient
Low	Continue with current treatment plan

Summary

Although the potential for psychiatrists to be held liable for their patients' violent acts toward third parties has expanded, only a relatively small number of psychiatrists and other mental health professionals have been found liable. In 1990, Beck estimated that approximately 50 psychiatrists were sued each year for breach of the duty to protect. Of these cases, roughly two-thirds settled before trial. Of the 17 trials, approximately two-thirds resulted in defendant verdicts. Thus six psychiatrists a year were found liable for violating a duty to protect third parties from their patients. For a psychiatrist who is a member of the American Psychiatric Association (APA; total membership in 1990 of approximately 35,000), Beck estimated that the odds of being found liable for a breach of the duty to protect are 5,800 to 1 in any given year. Nonetheless, prudent practice demands that *Tarasoff* be considered a national standard for psychiatrists and other mental health professionals (Beck 1987).

Clinical Management of Legal Issues

Predicting Violent Behavior

The term *dangerousness* is a legal, not a psychiatric, construct. Accordingly, instead of *dangerousness,* the term *risk of violence* is used in this book. A robust pattern of findings across studies supports a causal connection only between some mental disorders and violence (Monahan 1992). The National Institute of Mental Health Epidemiologic Catchment Area Study estimated that 90% of persons with current mental illnesses are not violent (Swanson et al. 1990). If a person was not having an acute psychotic episode or if psychotic symptoms were not part of the psychiatric problems, the individual was no more likely to be involved in violent behavior than the average person. Even when psychotic symptoms were present, there was only a modest increase in risk of violence above the norm. The persons with the highest risk of violence were young, substance-using males from lower socioeconomic classes. Seriously mentally ill patients with schizophrenia, major depression, mania, or bipolar disorder had an incidence of violence five times higher than that of persons with no diagnosed mental illness. The incidence of violence was 12–16 times higher among persons who were alcohol and substance abusers.

Violent behavior is a function of the dynamic interaction between social, clinical, personality, and environmental factors over situations and time (Widiger and Trull 1994). "Second-generation" research on violence prediction shows that certain elements of the clinical situation contribute to imminent violence by the patient, thereby allowing appropriate interventions to be made. Violence is a function of the dynamic interaction between a specific individual and a specific situation for a given period of time. Nevertheless, because of the lack of clinical standards for the prediction of violence in any context or time frame, the prediction of violence becomes an unreliable exercise.

Stone (1984), however, contended that psychiatrists do have some expertise in determining whether a patient manifests violent tendencies based on the mental status evaluation. Therapists' predictions of the actual occurrence of violent acts by patients, however, cannot be made with any degree of professional skill. As noted earlier, no short-term risk factors identify the imminence of violent behavior. Nevertheless, Tardiff (1991) maintained that well-trained clinicians should be able to predict a patient's short-term *potential* for violence by using evaluation techniques similar to those used in the short-term assessment of suicide risk. Binder (1999) posed the question, "Which mentally ill, under what circumstances, are dangerous?" Her research data show that although short-term predictions of violence can be relatively accurate, clinicians are better at predicting violence for certain patients and specific acute symptom patterns are related to violent acts.

The notion that therapists have no more skill than laypersons in predicting imminent violence was derived from "first-generation" research studies on the long-term clinical prediction of violent behavior in populations of people convicted of criminal offenses (Binder 1999). It should be noted that a number of these studies, however, were methodologically flawed. Nevertheless, according to these studies, the accuracy level has been roughly one correct prediction out of every three predictions made. These predictions have been limited by emphasis on certain traits of those guilty of criminal offenses, without the benefit of any situational analysis.

Because of psychiatrists' high false-positive prediction rate, combined with a low base-rate occurrence of violence in outpatient psychiatric populations, accurate prediction of long-term violence to endangered third parties remains elusive. The MacArthur Violence Risk Assessment Study was established to help rectify this situation. Its purpose was to improve clinical risk assessment validity, to enhance effective clinical risk management, and to provide data on mental disorders and violence for informing mental health law and policy (Dix 1980). In this study, violence risk assessments were found to have a validity that was modestly better than chance. Until more studies are available, sound clinical practice requires that thorough violence risk assessments be routinely performed on potentially violent patients, relying on evidence-based violence risk factors.

An accurate assessment of a high risk of violence may be more likely for some patients when the unique interplay of patient and situational factors is psychodynamically understood. Assessment accuracy also can be improved when dealing with defined homogeneous populations with high base rates of violence. For example, a closed psychiatric unit containing very disturbed patients may have a violence base rate of 25%–35%. Epidemiologic data containing known base rates for specific groups are an important assessment variable. Studies that focus on inpatient populations have demonstrated significantly improved predictability (Steadman et al. 1998).

The best protection against allegations of negligence when assessing the risk of violence is to evaluate the patient according to methods and procedures that take into account known violence risk factors (Tables 9–1 and 9–2). Because the clinician is likely to be wrong more often than not, humility and sound clinical judgment dictate careful documentation of how the assessment of violence is conducted.

In Barefoot v. Estelle (1983), a review of the constitutionality of a state court's imposition of capital punishment, the U.S. Supreme Court reasoned that if jurors are authorized to bear responsibility for a death penalty based on predictions of future behavior, then psychiatrists should not be prohibited from testifying about dangerousness by the Eighth Amendment's ban on cruel and unusual punishment, despite the low predictive ratio of one out of three. Although this may appear to set a judicial benchmark for prediction accuracy, the logic of using this constitutional decision to determine the professional standard of care for risk assessment in duty-to-protect cases addressing a different issue is problematic. Moreover, duty-to-protect issues are creatures of state tort law, in which the U.S. Supreme Court's constitutional authority is rarely pertinent.

Violence Risk Factors

Certain personal, socioeconomic, situational, and clinical risk factors are associated with violence. Monahan (1981, 1991) demonstrated a statistical association between violence and epidemiologic data (see Table 9–3). Tardiff (1988) disputed race as a factor in violence. Studies of patients with and without criminal convictions do not uniformly find a correlation in the incidence of violence with race (Monahan 1981, 1991).

Situational factors associated with violence include an unstable family, a violent environment, a violent peer group, and availability of weapons (e.g., handguns). Some of the risk factors reported to be associated with violence in the psychiatric literature are listed in Table 9–4.

Every study on the assessment of violence risk factors has found that the single factor most highly correlated with the potential for future violence is a history of violence (Tardiff 2002). Violent patients should be asked how they feel about having committed or threatened to commit violent acts. Determining whether violent behavior is syntonic or dystonic for the patient is an essential element of violence risk assessment. The therapeutic alliance can be an effective deterrent to violence. With new patients or patients seen in an emergency, sufficient time may not have elapsed for an alliance to form.

Link and Stueve (1994) found a relationship between a subset of psychotic symptoms and violence, specifically thought insertion, thought control, and the fear of being harmed by others. The index of suspicion for potential violence should be high in patients with acute psychosis who are substance abusing, angry, fearful of being harmed, and experiencing delusions of being controlled or

Table 9–3.   Epidemiologic risk factors associated with violence

- Previous violence
- Sex (males 10 to 1 over females in the United States)
- Race (controversial)
- Younger age
- Employment and residential instability
- History of alcohol abuse
- History of drug abuse

influenced. Substance abuse significantly raises the rate of violence in both patient and comparison groups (Dix 1980). A number of factors have been identified in young persons that should alert mental health professionals to an increased potential for future violence (Monahan 1981, 1991; Table 9–5).

Motive is a very important clinical variable in the assessment of violence (Beck 1987). When the patient responds affirmatively to the question about wanting to hurt someone, the therapist must further ask, "Who?" "When?" "Where?" "Why?" and "For how long?". Information gleaned from these inquiries is critical to the evaluation of the following: 1) how acutes the threat of violence is, 2) who the object of potential violence is, and 3) what can be done to treat the patient and protect potential victims.

Careful assessment and documentation of pertinent risk and protective factors used in assessing the potentially violent patient is an important way to avoid allegations of negligence. Even if the therapist is wrong in the assessment of the risk of violence, a reasonable mistake is not malpractice. Nevertheless, systematic assessment of the risk of violence is good clinical practice and only secondarily a risk management technique.

Violence risk assessments, both actuarial and clinical, have been compared to weather forecasting (Monahan and Steadman 1996; Simon 1992). The clinical assessment of the risk of violence is a here-and-now (current weather) determination. Clinical assessments of the risk of violence, like weather forecasts, require frequent updating. Actuarial assessments are similar to short- and long-term weather predictions (24–48 hours, 7–10 days). Clinical assessment directs treatment. Actuarial assessment makes a prediction of

Table 9–4.   Clinical risk factors associated with violence

- History of violence
- A stated desire to hurt or kill another
- Alcohol and substance abuse
- Inability to control anger (e.g., intermittent explosive disorder)
- Impulsivity (e.g., previous violence toward others or self, reckless driving, unrestrained spending, sexual promiscuity)
- Paranoid ideation, thought insertion or control, fear of harm
- Command hallucinations
- Psychosis
- Personality disorders: antisocial, borderline
- "Soft" neurological signs (e.g., neuropsychiatric disorders)
- Substance abuse
- Mental retardation

violence. The assessment model presented in Tables 9–1 and 9–2 is suggested only as a coneptual model and an educational clinical guide. Professional judgment concerning the unique clinical presentation of the patient and the associated specific situational factors should dictate appropriate decision making. Accordingly, with the exception of *specific person threatened* and *past violent acts,* violence risk factors in Table 9–2 are not listed in order of clinical importance. That determination depends on the patient's clinical presentation. It is not necessary to reproduce the tables in the patient's chart. A standard note containing an adequate violence risk assessment is all that is necessary. The weather forecast model provides one way of thinking about violence risk assessment. This conceptual model of suicide-violence risk assessment is derived from the author's clinical experience and the evidence-based psychiatric literature. Each practitioner's clinical experience is singular and unique. Competent violence risk assessments will vary accordingly.

Other approaches to violence risk assessment exist (Monahan 1991). Actuarial analysis is useful in identifying diagnostic groups at higher risk for violence rather than for trying to predict the violent acts of a specific patient

Table 9–5. Risk factors in young persons associated with increased potential for violence

- Violence as a juvenile
- Conduct disorder
- Psychosis
- Substance abuse or dependence
- Neurological impairment or head injury
- Childhood abuse
- Witnessing parental spouse abuse
- Psychiatric hospitalization
- Mental retardation

(Monahan et al. 2001). Actuarial analysis does not identify patient-specific treatable risk and modifiable protective factors. Actuarial instruments are not sensitive to patients' clinical changes that guide treatment interventions or gauge the impact of treatment (Norko and Baranoski 2005). No method of violence risk assessment can predict who will commit violent acts and when. Regardless of which method is used, the important point is that in the management of violent patients, violence risk assessments need to be made and recorded in the medical chart as required.

Demonstration of Violence Risk Assessment

After doing a complete psychiatric examination, the clinician should perform, record, and document a competent violence risk assessment. The patient's risk factors should be rated as low (L), moderate (M), high (H), or nonfactor (0). This dimensional model method assesses risk factor severity. Risk factor severity is a measure of intensity and duration (acute or chronic). For example, does the patient experience fleeting thoughts of violence or escalating impulses for violence? The rating of protective factors against violence include internal and external resources, for example, adequate coping skills and family support. After weighing risk factors, the overall assessment of violence risk should be rated as low, moderate, or high. The following case example illustrates the importance of assessing a patient's violence risk at the time of a contemplated discharge from a psychiatric unit. After reviewing the case example, the reader is encouraged to do an independent violence risk assessment before reading the psychiatrist's assessment.

A 35-year-old patient with chronic schizophrenia is admitted to the psychiatric unit of a general hospital because of auditory hallucinations commanding him to kill his mother. He also expresses the delusion that his mother is poisoning him. The patient has not lived apart from his mother. He works sporadically as a laborer. His only income is from Social Security Disability Insurance. The patient is treated with antipsychotic medication and individual and group therapies. Because the patient speaks only broken English, verbal interaction between the psychiatrist and the patient is minimal. The psychiatrist relies on observation of the patient's behavior on the ward and the input from the treatment team.

The psychiatrist learns from the patient's mother that the patient has been involuntarily hospitalized three times in the past 10 years. An assault preceded each of the previous hospitalizations. Before the second hospitalization, the patient stabbed a cousin. He was criminally charged with felonious assault but found not guilty by reason of insanity. The psychiatrist feels that she needs more information. She asks the unit secretary to call and request fax copies of the patient's previous hospital summaries.

After 10 days of hospitalization, the psychiatrist reviews the clinical course of the patient with the staff. The patient stays to himself most of the time. There is no evidence of any violent behavior. He is described in the nursing notes as "very cooperative." He complies with ward routine and regulations. Medication is taken. After the fourth day of hospitalization, the patient denies hallucinations or delusions. The staff informs the psychiatrist that the patient becomes sullen and withdrawn when his mother visits. No off-ward privileges are requested by the patient.

A discharge conference is held with the treatment team. The conference participants conclude that the patient is ready for discharge. The patient denies any intent to harm his mother or anyone else. At the discharge conference, the just-received fax summaries of the previous hospitalizations are reviewed. The summaries reveal that the patient was diagnosed with paranoid schizophrenia on each admission. The history is also consistent for each hospitalization. The patient fails to keep his outpatient visits, stops taking his medication, and begins drinking. He then becomes delusional, begins to hear voices, and becomes assaultive. The psychiatrist and the treatment team are concerned about the patient's revolving-door history of paranoid schizophrenia, alcohol dependence, noncompliance with treatment, decompensation, violence, and rehospitalization. The patient's history is similar to that of a number of other patients with schizophrenia admitted to the unit. The treatment team concludes that the patient has received maximal therapeutic benefit from inpatient treatment. The patient has one more hospital day authorized by the managed care organization. The psychiatrist performs a violence risk assessment, judging that the patient's overall lifetime risk of violence is high but is low *at the time of discharge* (see Table 9–6). The violence risk assessment is included in a risk-benefit assessment that weighs the risks and benefits for both continued hospitalization and discharge. The risk-benefit assessment favors discharge.

The psychiatrist is careful to note that the violence assessment is a here-and-now evaluation. At the time of discharge, the patient's risk of violence is assessed as low. The patient, however, is at a high risk for future violence if there is an exacerbation of his severe psychiatric disorder, noncompliance with treatment, alcohol abuse, an altercation with his mother, and other unforeseen, situational stress factors.

Psychiatric facilities for long-term hospitalization are not available. Because the patient has progressed so well, the psychiatrist decides to discharge the patient. The psychiatrist discusses the discharge with the patient's mother. The psychiatrist advises the mother to remove any potentially lethal weapons from the home and requests a callback to confirm their secure storage elsewhere. She agrees but expresses trepidation to have her son live at home. She hopes her son will be able to go back to his job as a laborer. The patient rejects referrals to Alcoholics Anonymous and the hospital's day treatment program. The social worker arranges an appointment for the patient at the community outpatient center for the first available session. His appointment is scheduled for 1 week after discharge. The patient is seen on the day of discharge and is stable and eager to leave.

This case example has been presented at clinical conferences where clinicians were asked to assess the patient's risk of violence and the appropriateness for discharge. The clinicians were clustered into two groups on the violence risk rating. All agreed the patient was at high risk of future violence. Disagreement arose, however, about the psychiatrist's low violence risk rating at the time of discharge. Some clinicians (Group A) felt that the distinction between the low risk of violence at the time of discharge versus the patient's high risk of future violence was a distinction without a difference. This group explained that the patient was at just as high a risk of violence at discharge. They observed that, as expected, the patient functioned quite well in a structured hospital environment where he was monitored for medication compliance. It was entirely foreseeable, however, that the patient would repeat the prior cycles that led to violence and rehospitalization. These clinicians recommended

Table 9–6.   Demonstration of a rapid, competent violence risk assessment.

Assessment factor	Risk	Protective
Specific person threatened	0 (in hospital)	0
Past violence	H (stabbed cousin)	
Accessible victim	H (mother)	
Therapeutic alliance		L–M (with staff)
Psychiatric diagnosis	H	
Command hallucinations	0 (in hospital)	0
Employment		L
Specific plan	0	0
Treatment response		H
Medication compliance		H (in hospital)
Structured environment		H
Alcohol dependence	H	
Substance abuse	0	0
History of impulsivity	H	
Guns		L (none at home)
Compliance with aftercare	H	
Relationships	M–H (loner)	
Overall risk rating:	Low (at discharge)	

that the patient be involuntarily hospitalized and then transitioned to outpatient commitment status to ensure follow-up and compliance.

The other group of clinicians (Group B) felt that Group A's recommendations were impractical. The purpose of hospitalizing a patient in the managed care era was rapid stabilization and referral to outpatient treatment. Inpatient psychiatrists provide acute care for very sick patients, similar to the intensive care unit for medical-surgical patients. Involuntary hospitalization would be inappropriate because the patient would not meet the standards for involuntary commitment, especially the usual requirement of "imminent" danger to self and others. Moreover, hospitals receiving involuntary patients discharge them rapidly if the patients are stable.

Long-term private psychiatric hospitalization was not an option for this patient who, except for receiving Social Security disability benefits, was impecunious. Group B felt that the best course of action was to carefully structure outpatient follow-up for compliance with treatment. Because the potential for violence toward the mother existed, referral of the patient should be made to a supervised residential setting where his condition and medication could be monitored. The conferees were in agreement that managed care pressures should not lead to a premature discharge. A lively debate invariably occurred about clinicians' responsibility for continuing care of an unstable inpatient after a managed care organization refuses to authorize payment for additional stay. Younger clinicians with families to support had greater difficulty in assuming the financial loss of caring for acutely ill patients until they were stabilized and discharged.

The *Tarasoff* Duty and Psychiatric Practice

The *Tarasoff* duty of the therapist to protect foreseeable victims of patient violence applies to outpatient as well as inpatient cases. In treating an outpatient, the *Tarasoff* duty generally is triggered by a patient's expressed or implied threats or acts directed to a specific, foreseeable victim. The violence threatened must be substantial, involving serious bodily harm or death. If no threats or violent acts are uncovered after careful clinical evaluation, liability is unlikely even if violence occurs.

In inpatient release cases, the duty to protect does not require a specific foreseeable victim as long as there is reasonable evidence that the patient may be dangerous. An appropriate evaluation of the patient for potential violence satisfies the *Tarasoff* duty. If hospitalization is based on a court order and the court releases a patient deemed to pose a high risk of violence, the psychiatrist should attempt to make known his or her concerns about the patient's potential for violence. However, the judicial decision to release insulates the psychiatrist from liability.

In some states with statutory provisions limiting the *Tarasoff* duty to warning an endangered, identifiable victim, the clinician may be distracted from providing the full spectrum of clinical interventions (Klassen and O'Connor 1994). Warning, by itself, is often insufficient as a clinical intervention. Usually, more needs to be done clinically. Whenever possible, the *Tarasoff* duty should be integrated into the clinical work with the patient.

Beck (1985) noted that once the clinical assessment is made that a patient is potentially violent, three basic options are open to the clinician: 1) deal with the violence in the therapy, 2) warn the victim and/or the police, or 3) hospitalize the patient voluntarily or involuntarily.

Systematic assessment of risk and protective factors informs the therapist's clinical options. Accordingly, potentially violent patients should be seen face-to-face frequently and their risks for violence reassessed at each visit. Documentation that a violence risk assessment was conducted evidences adherence to the standard of care. Violence risk assessment is, however, a process, not an event. Clinicians cannot provide a guarantee of accuracy, only an assurance of the process of assessment.

Clinical Considerations

Long before *Tarasoff*, therapists warned endangered third persons as part of their professional and ethical duty when they possessed "insider information" from treatment about the risk of violence posed by a patient to others. The duty to warn should not blind the clinician from implementing other clinical interventions that may be more effective in meeting their professional and ethical duties. The great majority of potentially violent patients can be managed through good clinical practice.

Warning Endangered Third Parties

Simply issuing a warning as a legal formalism is not an acceptable approach to managing the violent patient. Although a number of states have defined the *Tarasoff* duty in statutes and have narrowed the potential liability, the therapist who does not exercise reasonable professional judgment in managing the violent patient may still be vulnerable to a lawsuit by the patient for negligence. Clinical efforts to manage and control the patient should be attempted before a warning is issued to the intended victim. Frequently, the patient's treatment ends when a warning is made to an endangered third party. At this point, the therapist's intervention options are severely limited or nonexistent. Involuntary hospitalization may be an appropriate, last-resort intervention for selected patients who meet the substantive criteria (mentally ill and dangerous) for civil commitment.

Therapists have a moral, ethical, and professional duty to protect patients and their potential victims. The imposition of a legal duty is incidental to the therapist's professional duty. When the duty to protect is implemented, every effort should be made to include the patient in the process.

Giving a warning to meet the duty is not without peril. Many warnings will be based on erroneous predictions, unnecessarily alarming the person warned as well threatening the therapeutic alliance between patient and therapist. Warnings based on accurate assessments provide neither assurance of police protection nor comprehensive guidance to avoid the risks posed by the patient.

In general, if the therapist decides to warn, a phone call is appropriate. A phone call allows the potential victim to ask questions. Nuances and difficulties in communication can also be appreciated by both parties. Telephoning in the patient's presence may help to temper exaggerated remarks by a therapist's overreaction to the threat of violence. In addition, the patient's presence tends to head off suspicions or outright paranoid ideas that the psychiatrist is acting duplicitously. Sometimes, a trusted third party may act as a go-between. The warning should be made clearly. The clarity of the warning has been open to second-guessing by some courts. Successful malpractice suits are unlikely when good-faith warning and reporting are based on reasonable clinical judgment.

The psychology of victimization is pertinent to the decision to warn (Monahan and Steadman 1994). For example, the psychodynamics of victim–victimizer, husband–wife, or partner relationships in which one party is being abused may dictate attempting to move the victim toward a sheltered environment rather than warning the abuser that the abused partner is considering retaliatory violence. To do otherwise might seriously endanger the patient or precipitate mutual violence.

How the warning is given, not *whether* one is given, is sometimes the more critical factor. When the clinician discusses the warning with the patient before giving it, generally the clinical result is positive. Failing to discuss the warning with the patient often harms the therapeutic alliance and the therapy. Potential victims should be warned in a clinically supportive manner. If they feel that evasive action can be taken and that the therapist is acting in a responsible, genuinely concerned manner, the warnings are likely to be received positively.

Generally, courts have been reluctant to impose a duty on psychiatrists to warn the foreseeable victim when the latter knew of the potential for violence from a patient (Lewis et al. 1988). For example, in Estate of Heltsley v. Votteler (1982), the plaintiff had knowledge of the patient's previous aggressive behavior but contended that a warning from the psychiatrist would have made her appreciate the significance of the threat. The Iowa Supreme Court upheld the trial court's summary dismissal, reasoning that the duty should not be imposed when the foreseeable victim knows of the danger. Not all cases place the same emphasis on the victim's knowledge. For example, in Jablonski v. United States (1984), a child brought a wrongful death claim against the government under the Federal Tort Claims Act when her mother was killed by her boyfriend, a patient who was being evaluated at a Veterans Administration hospital, after making earlier threats to the mother. In a judge trial the court found, and the appellate court agreed, that the plaintiff had met the requirements to impose liability under *Tarasoff:* 1) the existence of a psychotherapist–patient relationship; 2) that the psychotherapist knew, or should have known, that the patient was dangerous; 3) that the mother was a foreseeable victim of the patient's violence; and 4) that the psychotherapist did not take the necessary steps to discharge his duty (i.e., failed to secure the patient's prior medical history and to warn the mother that the patient's violence may be directed toward her). Although the victim had been the recipient of the threats for which the patient was being evaluated, the matter of what duty is owed to a knowledgeable victim was not raised by the parties or the court.

The therapist should not assume that an endangered person who has been previously threatened or harmed by the patient fully appreciates the current danger of his or her situation. Denial may cause the person to minimize or ignore the threat. It may be necessary to warn the endangered person of the specific threats made by the patient, despite his or her prior knowledge.

Confidentiality Concerns

Trust is the cornerstone of psychiatric treatment. Without trust, no therapeutic alliance can develop, damaging the patient's chances of receiving psychotherapeutic help. In the real world, however, confidentiality, like trust, cannot be absolute. Exceptions to the maintenance of confidentiality exist for the protection of both the patient and society.

In *Tarasoff,* the court was mindful of the importance of maintaining as much confidentiality as possible in the therapist–patient relationship. The court stated that warning of a victim should be done in such a way as to preserve confidentiality consonant with the prevention of threatened danger.

Confidentiality should not be breached by warning a third party unless the threat is serious and substantial, an identifiable victim is endangered, and there is no alternative way to fulfill the duty to protect (e.g., hospitalization). Nevertheless, a plaintiff may allege breach of confidentiality.

The Principles of Medical Ethics With Annotations Especially Applicable to Psychiatry (American Psychiatric Association 2001) states, "Psychiatrists at times may find it necessary, in order to protect the patient or the community from imminent danger, to reveal confidential information disclosed by the patient" (p. 8, Section 4, Annotation 8). The *Tarasoff* exception to confidentiality is part of the same public policy exception requiring the reporting of contagious diseases, suspected child abuse, and gunshot wounds.

Potential conflicts between the duty to maintain confidentiality and the duty to protect may also arise concerning the capacity of a patient to operate an automobile (Pettis 1992). A duty to protect third parties might demand notification of the bureau of motor vehicles regarding psychiatric patients who should not drive. Indeed, by statute, a number of states require physicians to report cognitive or functional impairments likely to affect the patient's ability to operate an automobile safely (Or. Rev. Stat. § 807.710 [2006]). Another related issue is the psychiatrist's accountability for injuries to third parties when a patient was not informed of medication risks while driving (Levin and Hill 1992).

There is a split of authority regarding the liability of a physician to nonpatient third parties injured as a result of physician negligence in the prescription of medication to a patient (Simon 1992). Although some states have concluded that the driving behavior of outpatients is too remote for a physician to control (Estate of Heltsley v. Votteler 1982), other states have found the injuries to a third person a foreseeable risk of failing to inform a patient of the risks of medications that can cause drowsiness (Kaiser v. Suburban Transp. Sys. 1965).

Although the *Tarasoff* duty arises only occasionally, the maintenance of confidentiality is a constant duty in clinical practice. In 1996, the U.S. Supreme Court ruled in Jaffee v. Redmond (1996) that confidential communications between psychotherapist and patient are privileged from compelled disclosure in federal cases under the Federal Rules of Evidence. Perlin (1999) pointed out that a footnote in *Jaffee* states an exception to the privilege where a serious threat of harm exists to the patient or others that "can be averted only by means of a disclosure by the therapist" (518 U.S. at 18 n.19). Perlin commented that "the relationship of this footnote to the *Tarasoff* doctrine has not yet been fully explored" (pp. 20–21).

To further informed consent, some therapists give *Miranda*-type warnings to new patients about the therapist's duty to protect third parties against harm from violent patients. Others conclude that starting treatment in this way may cast a pall over the fledgling therapeutic process. Patients already frightened of their own aggression may find such a warning confirmatory of their worst fears. Secretive patients may seize upon the warning and withhold verbal expression of violent feelings. When the protection of others from patient violence is necessary, clinical interventions may allow for the preservation of confidentiality.

If a patient gives the therapist good reason to believe that a warning should be issued to an endangered third party, the confidentiality of the communication that gave rise to the warning may be lost. In some states, the warning of endangered third parties has resulted in psychiatrists being compelled to testify in criminal cases, although the matter is unresolved in most states (Leong et al. 1992).

Protecting Endangered Third Parties

Whereas *Tarasoff I* would have recognized a duty to warn, *Tarasoff II,* which vacated the earlier opinion, demanded that the therapist exercise his or her own best judgment consistent with that reasonable degree of skill, knowledge, and care ordinarily exercised by therapists under similar circumstances to *protect* the victim from the foreseeable violence of dangerous patients. The court did not require unerring accuracy but only the skill exercised by therapists in similar circumstances. The duty to protect permits a broader clinical approach to the management of violent patients. Although warning may be part of a therapist's intervention strategy, it rarely should be relied on initially or exclusively. Some clinical options include increasing patient appointments, adjusting medications, consultation, and voluntary or involuntary hospitalization.

The Patient With HIV

With the universal concern about the spread of AIDS, psychiatrists who treat patients testing positive for HIV face special ethical and legal dilemmas. For example, how should the psychiatrist manage the patient who is HIV positive and continues to have multiple sexual relationships but refuses to inform his or her partners? Consent between adults is a sham under this circumstance. Unlike other potentially dangerous patients, the patient who is promiscuous and has concealed HIV infection constantly carries a potentially lethal weapon. The occasion for harm commonly occurs within the unguarded embrace of a sexual relationship. Eth (1988) noted four clinical situations in which violating confidentiality to protect life is ethically indicated: 1) communicable disease, 2) child abuse, 3) threat of violence, and 4) HIV seropositivity.

Psychiatrists treating patients with diagnosed HIV infections who pose a continuing danger of infection to others should evaluate these patients in the same manner as other potentially dangerous patients. It is the patient's behavior, and not the HIV status per se, that represents the immediate danger. The psychiatrist should focus the evaluation particularly on the following questions:

- What is the patient's psychiatric diagnosis (Axis I and Axis II)?
- Is the patient treatable by available psychiatric therapies?
- What is the motivation of the patient for not informing sexual partners of HIV-positive status?
- Can the endangering behavior be contained by and within the treatment?
- Can support groups and organizations be mobilized to help the unemployed, isolated HIV patient?

Often, patients who are HIV positive are unemployable, shunned by society, alone, and terrified. Sexual contact with others may be motivated not so much by sexual interest as by the need for human contact, affection, and support. To expect these patients to be sexually abstinent without providing other sources of emotional sustenance is naive and insensitive. Support groups and organizations are critically important.

In some cases, the patient may be motivated to infect others out of malice or a callous indifference to the welfare of others. If this behavior cannot be managed clinically, serious consideration must be given to telling the patient that a warning will be issued, if the identity of the endangered parties is known. A report to the health department should also be considered if the authorities will conduct tracing and notification. A full notation of all measures taken should be recorded in the patient's chart. Consultation with a colleague should also be considered. As in other *Tarasoff*-type situations, warnings must be discreet, balancing the right of society to be protected from disease against the psychiatrist's duty to maintain patient confidentiality.

Successful malpractice suits for breach of confidentiality are possible, even when good-faith warning and reporting are based on reasonable clinical judgment. Clinicians should become familiar with health regulations and laws governing the reporting of HIV status. Immunity from liability for health care providers may be available, similar to that found in mandatory reporting requirements currently applicable for other contagious diseases.

The APA's Commission on AIDS has revised its confidentiality and disclosure guidelines to permit psychiatrists to notify an endangered identifiable third party at risk from a patient who is unable or unwilling to take precautions, including abstinence (Lester v. Hall 1998). Other important issues covered in the APA guidelines include 1) the use of involuntary hospitalization when an HIV-positive patient's endangering behaviors are the result of mental illness that can be treated by hospitalization, and 2) the permissibility of notifying public health authorities of previously exposed individuals who are no longer in contact with and at risk of exposure to the HIV-positive patient, if the patient is unable or unwilling to cooperate. As with all warnings given to endangered third parties, the psychiatrist must consider the serious emotional impact and adverse consequences that notification may have on the person warned. Appelbaum and Appelbaum (1990) provide an in-depth analysis of confidentiality versus the duty to protect in the management of the patient with HIV.

Assessing and Managing the Risk of Violence

Assessing and managing the risk of violence involves five basic steps (see Tables 9–1 and 9–2):

1. Identify patients with risk factors associated with violence.
2. Assess the overall risk of violence based on the rating of risk and protective factors.
3. Implement treatment and preventive interventions that are informed by the overall violence risk assessment.
4. Evaluate the effectiveness of treatment and other interventions.
5. Continue the process of violence risk assessment.

Based on the assessment of risk and protective factors, a probability determination of low, moderate, or high potential for violence can be made according to a tabulation of clinical factors that increase or decrease the risk of violence. The assessment of the patient's overall risk of violence is based on clinical judgment. No clinical standards exist for predicting the occurrence of a violent act. Psychiatrists are not held liable for mistakes in assessing the risk of violence per se. Rather, liability is imposed for failing to properly collect necessary data and to adequately assess the risk of violence. The method illustrated in Tables 9–1 and 9–2 may be used when time and circumstances do not permit obtaining a consultation (Perlin 1999).

The nexus between mental disorders and potential violence allows for clinical interventions. Psychiatrists possess the ability to treat and manage most patients who are currently or potentially violent. Potential violence rather than dangerousness is a preferable clinical focus for therapists. Legal definitions of *dangerousness* tend to be arbitrary and abstract concepts not readily translatable into the diagnostic and treatment models used by psychiatrists.

The assessment of potential violence involves two major steps: gathering information and assessing the risk of violence. Appelbaum (1985) suggested that clinicians routinely ask patients two questions: "Have you ever seriously injured another person?" and "Do you ever think about harming someone else?" These two questions often yield surprising information that is not usually obtained from a general psychiatric history unless asked. Areas of assessment include the individual, social, situational, and clinical variables related to violence discussed earlier. The most common mistake made by clinicians is to base a violence risk assessment on insufficient information. Although a standard of care does not exist for predicting violent acts, clear standards do exist for gathering sufficient information to satisfy a reasonable standard of care in the assessment of the *risk* of violence. Because the prediction of violence is not possible, careful documentation from visit to visit of the clinical reasoning behind the overall violence risk assessment is essential. Violence assessment is a process, not an event.

The Risk-Benefit Assessment

With any treatment intervention undertaken for health care of a potentially violent patient, a risk-benefit assessment should be conducted and recorded in the patient's chart immediately. In the event of a violent outcome, a documented risk-benefit analysis that considers clinically relevant interventions with potentially violent patients will be useful in demonstrating that reasonable care was taken with the patient. Absolute statements that a patient is no longer at risk of violence are not clinically defensible. Considering risks alone leads to unduly defensive practices. Risk-benefit assessments bring a balanced perspective to clinical decision making.

Risk-benefit assessments should evaluate the risks and benefits both for and against the intervention under consideration. For example, in considering a hospital discharge for a patient who has displayed a potential for violence, the risks and the benefits of the discharge must be considered against the risks and the benefits of continued hospitalization. A note should include a statement about the likelihood of violence, a proposed course of action, and the clinical decision-making rationale.

Consultation with a colleague may be reassuring to both the patient and the therapist. The consultant should document his or her findings. If time does not allow for the patient to be seen, an informal consultation with a colleague can take place over the phone. Although not ideal, such a consultation is better than none at all. The psychiatrist should summarize the consultant's opinion in the patient's record. If legal questions arise later, consultation may help establish that a reasonable standard of care was provided to the patient.

Psychiatric residents should consider increasing the frequency of their clinical supervision when a dangerous patient is undergoing a crisis. Decisions regarding management of the potentially violent patient should be endorsed by the supervisor's signature.

Treatment Refusal

If a potentially violent patient stops taking medication or drops out of treatment, the patient's continued need for treatment should be addressed aggressively. Voluntary or involuntary hospitalization may need to be pursued, depending on the clinical condition of the patient and the assessed risk of violence. The involvement of family members may also be necessary. If the potential for violence is high, endangered third parties and law enforcement agencies may need to be informed. A telephone call or letter (if time permits and if the patient can be located) may be necessary to determine the patient's treatment intentions. If the patient terminates treatment but is not an acute threat to others, a letter should be sent confirming that the patient has terminated treatment unilaterally. The letter may also recommend continued treatment and state the psychiatrist's willingness to provide referral sources and the patient's records to other treaters, on proper authorization (see Chapter 2, "The Doctor–Patient Relationship"). If the patient is transferred to another facility, the assessment of potential violence needs to be communicated to the new treaters. Reassessment of the risk of violence should be made before discharge (see Table 9–6).

When involuntary hospitalization is sought, the final dispositional responsibility rests with the judicial system. If the psychiatrist recommends commitment and the court finds the patient not committable, and the patient subsequently causes harm, the court is not liable for the consequences of the decision not to commit. Similarly, if an appellate court overturns a commitment, neither the committing court nor the psychiatrist is liable for the commitment. Involuntary hospitalization should be pursued when it is in the best interest of the patient (e.g., if the patient is likely to receive benefit from hospitalization) or for the immediate safety of the patient or others. When a less-restrictive alternative is unavailable, clinicians should not shrink from seeking involuntary hospitalization as an important clinical intervention for patients who meet commitment criteria (see Chapter 7, "Involuntary Hospitalization"). However, involuntary hospitalization should not be implemented defensively by the therapist in an attempt to avoid liability. Seeking involuntary hospitalization solely as a risk management technique will likely destroy the treatment relationship. It will also adversely affect future treatment endeavors with the patient, paradoxically increasing the risk of the therapist being sued.

Release of Hospitalized Patients

Voluntary patients who are at risk for violence may not meet the criteria for involuntary hospitalization. If the patient will be discharged, a careful note explaining the decision-making process is essential. Individuals who were threatened or harmed by the patient before hospitalization should be given advance notice of the patient's impending discharge, if the patient is still considered to be at risk of violence. The clinician should inquire about the presence of guns or other lethal weapons at home or easily accessible elsewhere. A responsible, designated person should be advised to remove all lethal weapons and to safely secure them ouside of the home. A callback is necessary to confirm that the instructions were followed.

Appointments need to be scheduled for as soon after discharge as possible.

Violent patients are often noncompliant with treatment recommendations. A Veterans Administration study of outpatient referrals found that of 47 inpatients referred to a Veterans Administration mental health clinic, 21 did not keep their first appointments (Zeldow and Taub 1981).

Every discharge is a complex process that must be tailored to the patient's individual treatment needs and circumstances (Felthous 2004). A risk-benefit assessment should be recorded that evaluates the risks and benefits of continued hospitalization versus discharge. Factors to be considered and weighed in the risk-benefit assessment include the risk of violence (against self or others), the severity of illness, the likely compliance with follow-up care, the availability of family or other support, the presence of substance abuse and/or other comorbid conditions, the need for safety, the importance of resuming life outside the hospital, and other significant individual factors. The absence of violent thoughts, feelings, or impulses is not as important at the time of discharge as an assessment of the patient's ability to control such impulses and the sufficiency of the environment to support the patient's self-control. The majority of patients manifesting violent ideation are treated as outpatients. Clinicians can avoid discharges that are doomed to fail by asking themselves and the clinical staff what is different about the patient's condition and life situation at discharge as compared with those aspects at admission.

Discharge decisions must be carefully documented. Notes should be recorded contemporaneously with decision making. After-the-fact notes are of little value and are legally precarious. A well-reasoned, clearly documented risk-benefit note that reveals the psychiatrist's clinical thinking at the time of discharge will help preempt second-guessing by a court if a lawsuit is later filed. Assessing the risk of violence toward self or others is a here-and-now determination performed at the time of discharge. Once the patient is discharged, the potential for violence will depend on the patient's mental state as well as on concurrent situational factors at any given time. As previously noted, violent behaviors are the result of dynamic, complex interactions among a variety of clinical, personality, social, and environmental factors whose relative importance varies across time and situations.

The clinician's obligation is to structure the follow-up so as to encourage adherence to the outpatient treatment plan. There are limits to psychiatrists' powers to ensure adequate patient follow-up. These limitations must be acknowledged by the psychiatric and the legal communities. Most discharged patients retain the right to refuse further treatment. The American Medical Association Council on Scientific Affairs has developed evidence-based discharge criteria for safe discharge from the hospital (American Medical Association 1996).

Managed Care and Premature Release

The treatment of psychiatric inpatients has changed dramatically in the managed care era. Most psychiatric units, particularly in general hospitals, have become short-stay, acute-care psychiatric facilities. Generally, only suicidal, homicidal, or gravely disabled patients with major psychiatric disorders pass strict precertification review for hospitalization. Approximately half of these patients have comorbid substance-related disorders. Usually, in order to gain precertification for admission in managed care settings, patients must meet "medically necessary" criteria whose stringency often equals or exceeds that of the substantive criteria for involuntary civil commitment.

The purpose of hospitalization is to provide crisis intervention and management to stabilize severely ill patients and to support their safety. Close scrutiny by utilization reviewers, however, permits only brief hospitalization for these patients. In addition, hospital administration may exert pressure on the psychiatrist for early discharge to maintain length-of-stay statistics within predetermined limits. Increasingly, the treatment of these patients is being provided by a variety of mental health professionals. Yet the psychiatrist must often bear the ultimate burden of liability for treatments gone awry. Limited opportunity exists during the hospital stay for psychiatrists to develop a therapeutic alliance with their patients. The ability to communicate with patients, the psychiatrist's stock-in-trade, is often severely curtailed. All of these factors contribute to a greatly increased risk of malpractice lawsuits against psychiatrists that allege premature or negligent discharge of patients due to cost-containment policies (Simon 1997).

Psychiatrists have certain responsibilities and legal duties to patients treated in managed care settings. These include disclosure of all treatment options, exercise of appeal rights, continuance of emergency treatment, and reasonable cooperation with utilization reviewers. Fulfillment of these duties is important in the management of the potentially violent inpatient. The duty to protect endangered third parties will likely arise with increased frequency as cost-containment measures tighten to curtail the length of patient hospitalization.

Psychiatrists are being held to a new standard of efficiency by third-party payers. They are expected to rapidly gather patient information, to determine a diagnosis, and to develop a multidisciplinary treatment plan. Psychiatrists must acquire new treatment skills for the rapid management and discharge of potentially violent patients. In addition, they need to have the personal and professional skills necessary to collaborate effectively with the multidisciplinary team in managing violent patients. Psychiatrists practicing in the managed care era are expected to be knowledgeable in the uses and limitations of a number of treatment modalities and behavioral techniques and in the use of medications to achieve rapid improvement and stabilization. In addition, psychiatrists are expected to provide competent, efficient clinical care despite stringent managed care restrictions on insurance coverage for psychiatric treatment. Psychiatrists have the responsibility for, but not necessarily the control of, treatments provided to patients.

Managed care organizations generally limit or deny payment for services but not the actual services themselves. How a patient is treated is strictly the physician's decision. Although the *quality of care* may be adversely affected by managed care restrictions, the *standard of care* for treating self-destructive or potentially violent psychiatric inpatients has not changed. As a result, psychiatrists often feel that they are practicing under conflicting standards (Simon 1998). As in the past, psychiatrists will be judged by whether they fulfill their professional, ethical, and clinical duties to the patient.

References

American Medical Association: Report of The Council on Scientific Affairs: Evidence-Based Principles of Discharge and Discharge Criteria (CSA Report 4-A-96). Chicago, IL, American Medical Association, 1996

American Psychiatric Association: AIDS policy: position statement on confidentiality, disclosure, and protection of others. Am J Psychiatry 150:852, 1993

American Psychiatric Association: The Principles of Medical Ethics With Annotations Especially Applicable to Psychiatry. Washington, DC, American Psychiatric Association, 2001

Appelbaum K, Appelbaum PS: The HIV antibody-positive patient, in Confidentiality Versus the Duty to Protect: Foreseeable Harm in the Practice of Psychiatry. Edited by Beck JC. Washington, DC, American Psychiatric Press, 1990, pp 121–140

Appelbaum PS: Implications of Tarasoff for clinical practice, in The Potentially Violent Patient and the Tarasoff Decision in Psychiatric Practice. Edited by Beck JC. Washington, DC, American Psychiatric Press, 1985, pp 98–108

Appelbaum PS, Zonana H, Bonnie R, et al: Statutory approaches to limiting psychiatrists' liability for their patients' violent acts. Am J Psychiatry 146:821–828, 1989

Beck JC: The psychotherapist and the violent patient: recent case law, in The Potentially Violent Patient and the Tarasoff Decision in Psychiatric Practice. Edited by Beck JC. Washington, DC, American Psychiatric Press, 1985, pp 10–34

Beck JC: The psychotherapist's duty to protect third parties from harm. Ment Phys Disabil Law Rep 11:141–148, 1987

Beck JC: Current status of the duty to protect, in Confidentiality Versus the Duty to Protect: Foreseeable Harm in the Practice of Psychiatry. Edited by Beck JC. Washington, DC, American Psychiatric Press, 1990, pp. 9–21

Binder RL: Are the mentally ill dangerous? J Am Acad Psychiatry Law 27:189–201, 1999

Dix GE: Clinical evaluation of the "dangerous" or "normal" criminal defendants. Va Law Rev 66:523, 1980

Eth S: The sexually active, HIV-infected patient: confidentiality versus the duty to protect. Psychiatr Ann 18:571–576, 1988

Felthous AR: Personal violence, in American Psychiatric Publishing Textbook of Forensic Psychiatry. Edited by Simon RI, Gold LH. Washington, DC, American Psychiatric Publishing, 2004, pp 471–500

Leong GB, Eth S, Silva JA: The psychotherapist as witness for the prosecution: the criminalization of Tarasoff. Am J Psychiatry 149:1011–1015, 1992

Levin RB, Hill EH: Recent trends in psychiatric liability, in American Psychiatric Press Review of Clinical Psychiatry and the Law, Vol 3. Edited by Simon RI. Washington, DC, American Psychiatric Press, 1992, pp 129–150

Lewis DO, Pincus JHJ, Bard B, et al: Neuropsychiatric, psychoeducational, and family characteristics of 14 juveniles condemned to death in the United States. Am J Psychiatry 145:584–589, 1988

Link BG, Stueve A: Psychotic symptoms and the violent/illegal behaviors of mental patients compared to community controls, in Violence and Mental Disorder: Developments in Risk Assessment. Edited by Monahan J, Steadman HJ. Chicago, IL, University of Chicago Press, 1994, pp 137–159

Monahan J: The Clinical Prediction of Violent Behavior. Rockville, MD, National Institute of Mental Health, 1981, pp 63–90

Monahan J: The clinical prediction of dangerousness. Currents in Affective Illness 10(June):5–12, 1991

Monahan JP: Mental disorder and violent behavior: perceptions and evidence. Am Psychol 47:511–521, 1992

Monahan J, Steadman HJ: Illegal behavior of mental patients compared to community controls, in Violence and Mental Disorder: Developments in Risk Assessment. Edited by Monahan J, Steadman HJ. Chicago, IL, University of Chicago Press, 1994, pp 137–159

Monahan J, Steadman HJ: Violent storms and violent people: how meteorology can inform risk communication in mental health law. Am J Psychol 51:931–928, 1996

Monahan J, Steadman HJ, Silver E, et al: Rethinking Risk Assessment: The MacArthur Study of Mental Disorder and Violence. New York, Oxford, 2001

Norko MA, Baranoski MV: The state of contemporary risk assessment research. Can J Psychiatry 50:18–26, 2005

Perlin ML: Tarasoff at the millennium: new directions, new defendants, new dangers, new dilemmas. Psychiatric Times, November 1999, pp 20–21

Pettis RW: Tarasoff and the dangerous driver: a look at driving cases. Bull Am Acad Psychiatry Law 20:427–437, 1992

Quattrocchi MR, Schopp RF: Tarasaurus Rex: a standard of care that could not adapt. Psychol Public Policy Law 11:109, 2005

Simon RI: Clinical Psychiatry and the Law, 2nd Edition. Washington, DC, American Psychiatric Press, 1992

Simon RI: Discharging sicker, potentially violent psychiatric inpatients in the managed care era: standard of care and risk management. Psychiatr Ann 27:726–733, 1997

Simon RI: Psychiatrists' duties in discharging sicker and potentially violent inpatients in the managed care era. Psychiatr Serv 49:62–67, 1998

Simon RI: The myth of "imminent" violence in psychiatry and the law. Univ Cincinnati Law Rev, in press

Steadman HJ, Mulvey EP, Monahan J, et al: Violence by people discharged from acute psychiatric inpatient facilities and by others in the same neighborhoods. Arch Gen Psychiatry 55:393–401, 1998

Stone AA: Law, Psychiatry, and Morality. Washington, DC, American Psychiatric Press, 1984, pp 161–190

Swanson JW, Holzer CE, Ganju UK, et al: Violence and psychiatric disorder in the community: evidence from the Epidemiologic Catchment Area surveys. Hosp Community Psychiatry 41:761–770, 1990

Tardiff K: A model for the short-term prediction of violence potential, in Current Approaches to the Prediction of Violence. Edited by Brizer DA, Crowner ML. Washington, DC, American Psychiatric Press, 1988, pp 1–12

Tardiff K: Violence by psychiatric patients, in American Psychiatric Press Review of Clinical Psychiatry and the Law, Vol 2. Edited by Simon RI. Washington, DC, American Psychiatric Press, 1991, pp 175–236

Tardiff K: The past as prologue: assessment of future violence in individuals with a history of past violence, in Retrospective Assessment of Mental States in Litigation: Predicting the Past. Edited by Simon RI, Shuman DW. Washington, DC, American Psychiatric Publishing, 2002, pp 181–207

Widiger TA, Trull TJ: Personality disorders and violence, in Violence and Mental Disorder: Developments in Risk Assessment. Edited by Monahan J, Steadman HJ. Chicago, IL, University of Chicago Press, 1994, pp 203–226

Zeldow PB, Taub HA: Evaluating psychiatric discharge and aftercare in a VA medical center. Hosp Community Psychiatry 32:57–58, 1981

Legal References

Barefoot v Estelle, 463 U.S. 880 (1983)

Brady v Hopper, 751 F.2d 329 (10th Cir., 1984)

Estate of Heltsley v Votteler, 327 N.W.2d 759 (Iowa, 1982)

Evans v United States, 883 F.Supp. 124 (S.D. Miss., 1995)

Garamella v New York Medical College, 23 F.Supp. 2d 167 (D. Conn., 1998)

Green v Ross, 691 So.2d 542 (Fla. 2d D.C.A., 1997)

Jablonski v United States, 712 F.2d 391 (9th Cir., 1983) overruled, In re: complaint of McLinn 739 F.2d 1395 (9th Cir., 1984)

Jaffee v Redmond, 518 U.S. 1, 116 S.Ct. 1923, 135 L.Ed.2d 337 (1996)

J.S. v R.T.H., 714 A.2d 924 (N.J., 1998)

Kaiser v. Suburban Transp. Sys., 65 Wn.2d 461, 398 P.2d 14, 401 P.2d 350 (1965)

Lester v Hall, 970 P.2d 590 (N.M., 1998)

Lipari v Sears, Roebuck and Co, 497 F.Supp. 185 (D. Neb., 1980)

Naidu v Laird, 539 A.2d 1064 (Del. Supr., 1987)

Popple v Rose, 573 N.W.2d 765 (Neb., 1998)

Schuster v Altenberg, 424 N.W.2d 159 (Wis. 1988)

Tarasoff v Regents of the University of California, 529 P.2d 553 (Cal. 1974)

Tarasoff v Regents of the University of California, 17 Cal.3d 425; 551 P.2d 334 (Cal. Rptr. 14, 1976)

Thapar v Zezulka, 994 S.W.2d 635 (Tex., 1999)

Thompson v County of Alameda, 614 P.2d 728 (Cal., 1980)

Touchette v Ganal, 922 P.2d 347 (Haw., 1996)

White v United States, 780 F.2d 97 (D.C. Cir., 1986)

Laws

Cal. Civ. Code § 43.92 (2006)
Colo. Rev. Stat. Ann. § 13-21-117 (2006)
Or. Rev. Stat. § 807.710 (2006)
Restatement (Second) of Torts §315(a) (1965)

10

Maintaining
Treatment Boundaries

Clinical and Legal Issues

Psychiatry has long understood the role of patient trust in the success of therapy and the importance of appropriate treatment boundaries in establishing and maintaining that trust. Accepted practice standards recognize that maintenance of these boundaries is a therapist's professional duty. Courts have also come to understand the central role that patient trust plays in the psychiatrist–patient relationship and the harm caused by its breach:

> There is a public policy to protect a patient from the deliberate and malicious abuse of power and breach of trust by a psychiatrist when that patient entrusts to him her body and mind in the hope that he will use his best efforts to affect a cure. That right is protected by permitting the victim to pursue civil remedies, not only to vindicate a wrong against her but to vindicate the public interest as well. (Roy v. Hartogs 1975)

When a psychiatrist breaches a patient's trust for the psychiatrist's benefit (rather than to benefit the patient, as in hospitalizing a suicidal patient or responding to important public concerns [e.g., Tarasoff v. Regents of the University of California 1976]), the law recognizes various civil, criminal, and administrative remedies for that abuse of power. It is common to think of these breaches of trust only in the realm of sexual relations between psychiatrist and patient, but this view is too narrow. Other personal (Figueiredo-Torres v. Nickel 1991: stated claim for medical malpractice was the allegation that the psychiatrist had a sexual relationship with the patient's wife) and business (United States v. Willis 1990: psychiatrist was found liable for insider trading based on use of confidential information from patient-spouse of corporate insider) relations that risk an abuse of power and breach of patient trust by a psychiatrist are also prohibited. The discussions about boundary violations in this chapter are limited to sexual relations, however, because the legal and professional positions on this issue are more evolved.

Overview of the Law

Civil Liability

The law reflects the professional consensus that sexual relationships between psychiatrists and their patients can cause substantial harm to the patient, who is uniquely vulnerable to and dependent upon the psychiatrist. Given this vulnerability and dependence, it is assumed that sexual relations between a psychiatrist and a patient can never be consensual and are always exploitive. Psychiatrists who sexually exploit their patients are subject to civil claims and criminal prosecution as well as professional disciplinary proceedings. Most civil claims are brought as medical malpractice actions grounded in negligence to avoid the intentional act exclusion found in most professional liability policies. As noted in previous chapters, to prevail in a claim grounded in negligence, the plaintiff must persuade the fact finder by a preponderance of the evidence that the defendant breached a duty of care, proximately causing harm. The existence of a duty owed by the psychiatrist-defendant to the patient-plaintiff is addressed by proof of a physician–patient relationship. Whether sexual relations between psychiatrist and patient (or former patient) are a breach of that duty is an issue of professional standards on which courts require expert testimony. Whether the sexual relationship actually occurred is a question of fact that can be answered with cards and letters, pictures, or hotel receipts as well as testimony from others who claim to have been sexually abused by the psychiatrist. Proof that the plaintiff experienced psychological harm because of the relationship is generally an issue that demands expert testimony (see Hare v. Wendler 1997).

Beyond this judge-made, common law tort response, states have responded to the issue of sex between patients and their psychotherapists in three ways (Appelbaum 1990): reporting statutes, civil remedies, and criminalization. Reporting statutes require disclosure to state authorities by a therapist who learns of any past or current therapist–patient sex (see Minn. Stat. § 148A.03 [2005]; Wis. Stat. § 940.22 [2006]). A number of states have enacted civil statutes proscribing sexual misconduct and providing a tort remedy (Cal. Civ. Code § 43.93 [2006]; Fla. Stat. § 458.329 [2005]; Minn. Stat. § 148A.02 [2005]; Tex. Civ. Prac. & Rem. Code § 81.002 [2005]; Wis. Stat. § 895.70 [2006]). Civil statutes articulating a standard of care that proscribes therapist–patient sex make malpractice lawsuits easier to pursue by taking the reasonableness of the therapist's behavior and the issue of consent off the table, leaving only the question of whether the conduct occurred and the harm it caused as issues for the fact finder. For example, legislation in Minnesota provides a cause of action against psychiatrists and other psychotherapists for injury caused by sexual contact with a patient (Minn. Stat. Ann. § 148A.02 West Supp. [2005]). Some of these statutes also restrict unfettered discovery of the plaintiff's past sexual history.

Criminal sanctions may be the only remedy against exploitative therapists who have no malpractice insurance, are unlicensed, or do not belong to professional organizations. Some states have made therapist sexual misconduct a crime (Bisbing et al. 1995). Others prosecute sexual exploitation under their existing rape or sexual assault laws (see Ohio's O.R.C. Ann. § 2305.111 [2006]). Some states have made sexual activity both civilly and criminally actionable:

> A cause of action against a psychotherapist for sexual exploitation exists for a patient or former patient for injury caused by sexual contact with the psychotherapist if the sexual contact occurred: 1) during the period the patient was receiving psychotherapy...if a) the former patient was emotionally dependent

on the psychotherapist; or b) the sexual contact occurred by means of therapeutic deception. (Minn. Stat. Ann. § 148A.02 West Supp. [2005])

A person who engages in sexual penetration with another person is guilty of criminal sexual conduct in the third degree if any of the following circumstances exists:

> [T]he actor is a psychotherapist and the complainant is a patient of the psychotherapist and the sexual penetration occurred: (i) during the psychotherapy session; or (ii) outside the psychotherapy session if an ongoing psychotherapist–patient relationship exists. Consent by the complainant is not a defense. (Minn. Stat. Ann. § 609.344 [2005])

Defenses

The obvious place to begin thinking about defenses to sexual contact is with consent, which ordinarily is important to distinguish appropriate and inappropriate sexual contact. Where the cause of action is statutorily grounded, defendants will find that legislatures have assumed, as a matter of law, that patients are incapable of making competent choices about sex with their psychotherapists. When the sexual exploitation claim rests on common-law tort concepts, courts have also been unwilling to permit the defenses of consent, contributory negligence, or assumption of the risk.

With respect to defenses addressing the standard of care, there is no "respected minority" in the mental health profession that claims that sexual relations with patients is therapeutic. This position had a few adherents at one time but is no longer publicly or privately advocated by mental health professionals. The question that remains regarding the standard of care is whether it is permissible to have a sexual relationship with a former patient. To see evidence of the differences on this issue, contrast the Minnesota civil and criminal provisions quoted earlier. The civil provision proscribes sexual contact while a patient is in treatment and thereafter for as long as the former patient is emotionally dependent on the therapist. In contrast, the criminal statute proscribes only sexual relations with a patient currently in treatment.

Unless the defendant denies that the contact occurred or claims that it occurred long after therapy ended, the most important issues for the defense may be causation and damages. The plaintiff bears the burden of proving that but for the defendant's wrongful conduct he or she would not have suffered the harm for which he or she is entitled to compensation. Sorting out which of the patient's problems existed before therapy and which were caused by therapist–patient sex is not an exact science.

Criminal Sanctions

Even without specialized laws criminalizing therapist–patient sex, sexual exploitation of a patient may be considered rape or sexual assault punishable under the laws of the state where it occurred. The practitioner's means of inducement and the age of the victim often play a significant role in analyzing whether a prosecution can be brought for sexual exploitation under general rape and sexual assault laws. For example, sex with a current patient that was coerced through the use of medication, threats, or force may be criminally actionable under sexual assault statutes (Schoener et al. 1989). Claims of "psychological coercion" via the manipulation of the transference phenomenon have not been successful in establishing the coercion necessary for a criminal case under traditional rape or sexual assault laws. In cases involving a minor patient, the issue of consent or coercion is irrelevant, because minors and incompetent individuals (including adults) are unable to provide valid consent. Thus there is no issue of consent in a case alleging sex with a child or an incompetent individual.

A number of states have enacted laws making sexual relations between a therapist and a patient a criminal offense (Bisbing et al. 1995). What distinguishes these specialized provisions from general rape or sexual assault laws is that there is no need under the specialized provisions to prove deception or coercion, and the defense of consent is removed. For example, a Wisconsin statute provides that any person who is or who holds himself or herself out to be a therapist and who intentionally has sexual contact with a patient or client during any ongoing therapist–patient or therapist–client relationship, regardless of whether it occurs during any treatment, consultation, interview, or examination, is guilty of a class F felony (Wis. Stat. § 940.22 [2006]). Consent is not an issue in an action under this subsection (Gartrell et al. 1986).

Professional Disciplinary Action

State licensing boards are authorized to adjudicate allegations of professional misconduct and to impose discipline, including suspension or revocation of a professional license. There is no fee for a citizen to make an allegation of professional misconduct or a need to employ counsel to do so. Thus it should come as no surprise that many patients who claim to be victims of sexual exploitation by their therapist file complaints with the relevant licensing board. A review of published reports of sexual misconduct adjudicated before licensing boards revealed that in the vast majority of cases in which the evidence was reasonably sufficient to substantiate a claim of exploitation, the professional's license was revoked or suspended for varying lengths of time, including permanently (see Cal. Bus. & Prof. Code § 2960.1 [2006]; Minn. Stat. § 147.091, 147.141 [2005]; Va. Code § 54.1-2915[19] [2006]).

Clinical Management of Legal Issues

Incidence of Therapist–Patient Sexual Contact

In a nationwide survey regarding psychiatrist–patient sex, 7.1% of male and 3.1% of female respondents acknowledged having relationships with their patients (Gartrell et al. 1986). Of the sexual contacts that occurred, 88% were between male psychiatrists and female patients, 7.6% were between male psychiatrists and male patients, 3.5% were between female psychiatrists and male patients, and 1.4% were between female psychiatrists and female patients. Whereas 38.4% of the male psychiatrists were recidivists, none of the female therapists had repeated sexual contacts. Interestingly, 40.7% of the offending psychiatrists sought consultation because of their sexual involvement. Of the psychiatrists responding to the survey, 98% believed that sexual relationships with patients were inappropriate and usually harmful. However, 29% reported that a sexual relationship after termination might sometimes be acceptable.

Of the psychiatrists who responded to the survey, 65% reported treating patients who had been sexually abused by previous therapists: 48% of the previous therapists were psychiatrists, 27% psychologists, 9% clergymen, 7% social workers, and 6% lay therapists. Subsequent treating psychiatrists assessed that 87% of these patients were harmed. Only 8% of these psychiatrists reported the abuse to a professional association or legal authority. These figures are undoubtedly conservative estimates. The problem is likely to be much more pervasive, involving other professionals besides psychiatrists.

The percentage of therapists admitting sexual contact with patients has steadily declined. In 1989, a survey of 4,800 psychiatrists showed a rate of therapist–patient sex of 0.9% for male therapists and 0.2% for female therapists (Borys and Pope 1989). Although no clear reasons for this decline can be given, the conclusion that actual therapist–patient sex has declined by almost 10% since 1980 appears overly optimistic. Even though respondents remain anonymous, the threat of litigation may have caused offending therapists to forgo responding, further skewing the notoriously unreliable data derived from surveys in the direction of underreporting therapist–patient sex.

Ethics and Malpractice

Apart from the role of ethical rules in professional discipline, these rules play an important role in shaping the professional norms that guide negligence determinations. Thus psychiatric ethics are examined as a vehicle to ascertain the standard of care in malpractice litigation. For psychiatrists, the ethical standard is clear. *The Principles of Medical Ethics With Annotations Especially Applicable to Psychiatry* (American Psychiatric Association 2001) unequivocally prohibits psychiatrists from engaging in sexual activity with current or former patients:

> The requirement that the physician conduct himself/herself with propriety in his/her profession and in all the actions of his/her life is especially important in the case of the psychiatrist because the patient tends to model his/her behavior after that of his/her psychiatrist by identification. Further, the necessary intensity of the treatment relationship may tend to activate sexual and other needs and fantasies on the part of both patient and psychiatrist, while weakening the objectivity necessary for control. Additionally, the inherent inequality in the doctor–patient relationship may lead to exploitation of the patient. Sexual activity with a current or former patient is unethical. (p. 5, Section 2, Annotation 1)

This ethical position has a venerable history. One version of the Hippocratic Oath that dates back at least 2,500 years sets the following standard: "In every house where I come, I will enter only for the good of my patients, keeping myself far from all intentional ill-doing and all seduction and especially from the pleasures of love of women and men."

Relying on this articulation of the ethical duties of a psychiatrist, sexual activity between a psychiatrist and a current or former patient requires no nuanced analysis—it is never ethical to have sex with a current or former patient. There is no patient strong enough, no therapeutic pause long enough, and no true love great enough to justify compromising this boundary. Numerous states influenced by this ethical standard recognize that therapist–patient sex is negligent and cannot be excused or justified (Cal. Civ. Code § 43.93 [2006]; Minn. Stat. §148A.02 [2005]; Wis. Stat. §895.70 [2006]). To prevail under these provisions, the plaintiff need only prove that sexual contact occurred and that it caused harm.

Evaluation, Consultation, and Group Therapy

In an evaluation or in consultation, a traditional doctor–patient relationship, with all the correlative rights and duties, does not exist. Thus, particularly where the evaluation or consultation is at the behest of a third party, the patient's right to bring a malpractice claim for sexual misconduct with an evaluator or consultant is a more difficult question. The ethical issue, however, remains unchanged. Often, the sickest patients are seen primarily for medication appointments rather than for psychotherapy. Nevertheless, because of the extent of regression, powerful transference phenomena can occur. The psychiatrist is at a disadvantage in not having an ongoing therapy situation that permits assessment of transference developments. Not surprisingly, some therapists who see patients infrequently espouse theoretical orientations that place little emphasis on or reject outright the importance of recognizing or managing transference phenomena. Group therapy situations are rife with intense transference reactions that may become focused on the therapist but without the benefit of the closer scrutiny of transference that a one-to-one therapy can allow. Regardless of the practitioner's theoretical orientation, the emergence of transference and countertransference issues in the therapeutic relationship requires recognition and management.

Supervisors and Trainees

Supervisors are subject to civil liability for harm caused by the wrongful conduct of their trainees if negligent supervision was a proximate cause of the patient's harm or if the harm arose in the context of an employer–employee relationship between supervisor and trainee. Ethical rules may play an important role here in judging the reasonableness of the supervisor's and trainee's behavior. Trainee therapists must abide by the same ethical principles as fully trained therapists. Supervisors may not be aware of sexual issues between the trainee and a patient under the trainee's supervision. Failure to recognize an emerging sexual relationship raises the specter of disciplinary and civil action against both the trainee and the supervisor. The presence and management of sexual feelings in both the trainee and the patient need to be openly discussed. E-mail between the trainee and patient should be placed in the patient's record as a matter of policy. Ethical principles should be an integral part of every training program.

Sexual relations between supervisors and trainees have recently received close ethical scrutiny. The resulting ethical guidance may shape professional norms relevant in actions between the trainee and supervisor. *The Principles of Medical Ethics With Annotations Especially Applicable to Psychiatry* (American Psychiatric Association 2001) states the following:

> Sexual involvement between a faculty member or supervisor and a trainee or student, in those situations in which an abuse of power can occur, often takes advantage of inequalities in the working relationship and may be unethical because: (a) any treatment of a patient being supervised may be deleteriously affected; (b) it may damage the trust relationship between teacher and student; and (c) teachers are important professional role models for their trainees and affect their trainees' future professional behavior. (p. 9, Section 4, Annotation 14)

The "Natural History" of Therapist–Patient Sex

In psychotherapy, the potential for exploitation of psychologically needy, often regressed patients is always present. Sexual exploitation has a "natural history" or progressive scenario of personal involvement between therapist and patient that is remarkably similar from case to case (Simon 1995; Table 10–1).

Boundary violations leading up to sex with the patient occur gradually and incrementally. Thus the therapist has time to prevent this development (Simon 1989), as does a supervisor who may face a negligence claim for failing to recognize or act on these natural history markers. Sharing personal information with a patient, such as current personal problems experienced by the therapist, is highly correlated with eventual therapist–patient sex. Particularly noxious are therapist disclosures about relationship problems, sexual frustration, sexual dreams and fantasies about the patient, and loneliness (Simon 1991). Self-disclosures not only waste therapy time but also may induce a caretaking role in the patient (Pope 1994). Boundary violations occur in the treatment of patients when the therapist abandons a position of relative neu-

Table 10–1.   The slippery slope to therapist–patient sex

- Incipient boundary violations "between the chair and the door"
- Therapist's position of neutrality is gradually eroded
- Therapist and patient address each other by first names
- Therapy sessions become less clinical and more social
- Patient is treated as "special" (i.e., as confidant)
- Therapist self-disclosures occur, usually relating to current personal problems and sexual fantasies about the patient
- Therapist sits closer to patient
- Therapist begins touching patient, progressing to hugs, embraces, and kisses
- Therapist gains control over patient, usually by manipulating the transference and by negligent prescribing of medications
- Therapy sessions are rescheduled for the end of the day
- Therapy sessions become extended in time
- Therapist stops billing the patient
- Contacts occur outside of therapy
- Therapist and patient have drinks or dinner after sessions; dating begins
- Therapist–patient sex occurs

trality. Sexual misconduct rarely occurs in isolation; rather, it is usually a part of an overall pattern of negligent treatment (Simon 1994a).

Patients with borderline, dependent, masochistic, and histrionic personality disorders appear to be especially vulnerable to sexual exploitation because these patients commonly develop intense dependent, erotic transferences (see Table 10–2). Victims of incest are vulnerable to therapist–patient sexual exploitation. In one study, 23% of previously abused patients who sought psychotherapy were sexually abused by their therapist (The College of Physicians and Surgeons of Ontario 1991). An additional 23% suffered other forms of abuse by their therapist. Less than 30% of the patients received any help from the first therapist they saw. The average incest patient saw a total of 3.5 therapists.

Table 10–2. Some characteristics of vulnerable patients

- Previously well-functioning patients with current depression and loss of an important relationship
- Dependent and other-directed personalities
- Patients sexually and physically abused as children
- Patients with previous hospitalizations, major psychiatric illnesses, suicide attempts, and alcohol and drug abuse
- Patients with borderline, dependent, masochistic, and histrionic personality disorders
- "Attractive" patients with low self-esteem

Maintaining Treatment Boundaries

Treatment boundaries are established by therapists to define and secure a professional relationship with the patient for the purpose of promoting a trusting, working alliance. Considerable disagreement exists among psychiatrists concerning treatment boundary violations. The therapy techniques of one therapist may be unacceptable to another therapist who considers such practices as boundary violations. The variability in defining treatment boundaries appears to be a function of the nature of the patient and therapist, their interaction, the therapist's theoretical orientation, and the status of the therapeutic alliance. For example, exceptions to defining treatment boundaries occur in alcohol and drug abuse programs, in inpatient settings, and with certain cognitive-behaviorally based therapies. Every therapist, however, must maintain appropriate treatment boundaries with all patients. When boundary exceptions occur, they must be made for the benefit of the patient. Boundary crossings that are recognized and rectified can provide important insights into conflictual issues for both the therapist and patient (Gutheil and Simon 2002). The danger to treatment arises when boundary crossings become boundary violations that progress in frequency and severity over time.

Because boundary guidelines maintain the integrity of therapy and safeguard both the therapist and the patient, proponents of therapies that breach generally accepted boundary guidelines risk harming the patient and suffering the legal consequences. Psychiatry is receptive to innovative treatments that offer the hope of helping the mentally ill. The maintenance of basic treatment boundaries, by itself, should not be an impediment to therapeutic innovations. On the contrary, conducting innovative therapies in general accord within accepted treatment boundaries should provide added credibility (Simon 1993). Psychiatrists practicing in small communities and rural settings may have to make unavoidable adjustments in treatment boundaries to avoid disruption of the integrity of the doctor–patient relationship (Simon and Williams 1999).

The identification of early treatment boundary violations is an essential therapist competency. Basic boundary guidelines exist that, with certain exceptions, are generally endorsed by therapists from a wide spectrum of orientations (see Table 10–3; Simon 1991). The basic clinical, ethical, and legal principles that underlie boundary guidelines are listed in Table 10–4.

Seasoned therapists as well as marginally competent or poorly trained therapists can benefit from learning how to identify early boundary violations. Therapists who naively attempt to "reparent" their patients invariably cross treatment boundaries as they become overly involved in their patients' lives. Other therapists masochistically surrender to the endless demands of some patients. They are unable to extricate themselves over the course of progressive boundary violations. Deviant treatment boundaries harm patients in a variety of ways but most often by leading to negligent diagnoses and treatments, even if therapist–patient sex does not occur.

It is always the therapist's responsibility to maintain appropriate boundaries, no matter how difficult or boundary testing the patient may be. If unable to do so, the therapist should refer the patient to a competent clinician. The conduct of psychotherapy is an impossible task because there are no perfect therapists and no perfect therapies. Knowing one's boundaries, however, makes the impossible task easier.

Freud enunciated the principle of abstinence, which stated that psychiatrists must refrain from gratifying themselves at the expense of their patients. The rule of abstinence is a fundamental principle underlying boundary guidelines. The therapist's main source of personal pleasure is the professional gratification obtained from the psychotherapeutic process and the satisfaction gained in helping the patient. The fee for professional services is the material satisfaction the therapist is permitted to receive from the patient. The duty of neutrality is a corollary of the rule of abstinence. It dictates that therapists refrain from interfering in the personal lives of their patients, thus preserving patients' autonomy and self-determination. The psychotherapist–patient re-

Table 10–3. Boundary guidelines for psychotherapy

- Maintain relative therapist neutrality
- Foster psychological separateness of patient
- Protect confidentiality
- Obtain informed consent for treatments and procedures
- Interact verbally with patients
- Ensure no previous, current, or future personal relationship with the patient
- Minimize physical contact
- Preserve relative anonymity of therapist
- Establish a stable fee policy
- Provide consistent, private, and professional setting
- Define time and length of session

Source. Reprinted from Simon RI: "Treatment Boundary Violations: Clinical, Ethical, and Legal Considerations." *Bulletin of the American Academy of Psychiatry and the Law* 20:269–288, 1992. Used with permission.

lationship is fiducial in nature, requiring the therapist to act in the best interests of his or her patients. Respect for human dignity underlies all boundary guidelines.

A quick spot check can help a therapist identify whether boundary violations have been committed. The first question therapists should ask themselves is whether a treatment intervention is for the benefit of the therapist or for the sake of the patient's therapy. If it appears to be for the therapist's benefit, then a second question arises whether the "treatment intervention" may be part of a series of progressive boundary violations. If the answer to either of these questions is yes, the therapist is alerted to desist immediately and take corrective action.

Epstein and Simon (1990) devised an Exploitation Index that can be used by therapists as an early warning indicator of treatment boundary violations. In a survey of 532 psychiatrists who completed the Exploitation Index, 43% reported that one or more of the questions had alerted them to boundary violations, and 29% made specific changes in their treatment practices (Epstein et al. 1992). Gutheil and Simon (1995) postulated that the first boundary vi-

Table 10–4. Principles underlying boundary guidelines

- Rule of abstinence
- Duty to neutrality
- Patient autonomy and self-determination
- Fiduciary relationship
- Respect for human dignity

olations occur at the end of the session "between the chair and the door." Both the patient and the therapist may feel tempted to cast off their respective difficult roles and launch into the ease of an ordinary social relationship. This "transition space" should be carefully scrutinized for incipient boundary violations. As a rule, the therapy session ends *after* the patient leaves, not before.

Managing Transference and Countertransference in Therapy

Patients who seek psychiatric treatment are experiencing mental and emotional suffering. As a consequence, their decision-making capacity and judgment may be impaired. Moreover, the therapist is perceived as a source of healing and hope. Under these circumstances, a transference involving the expectation of beneficent care and treatment evolves that is highly influenced by early, powerful wishes for nurture and care. The therapist is frequently idealized as the all-good, all-giving parent.

In combination with the fear of losing the newly acquired idealized parental figure, the beneficent transference leaves the patient vulnerable to exploitation by the therapist (Simon 1994b, 1994c). The beneficent transference is a common psychological reaction experienced to varying degrees by practically all patients. It should be distinguished from intense transference reactions that develop in some patients undergoing intensive psychodynamic psychotherapy or psychoanalysis.

Transferences often are not what they appear to be. Transferences, like dreams, have both a manifest and a latent content. Freud emphasized that "transference love" must be understood as a specific treatment phenomenon that is not identical to the experience of falling in love as it occurs outside of therapy. Freud (1914/1968) stated that the clinician "must recognize that the patient's falling in love is induced by the analytic situation and is not to be attributed to the charms of his own person; so that he has no grounds whatever for being proud of such a 'conquest,' as it would be called outside analysis" (pp. 160–161). Many patients have felt deprived of nurture and affection in their important relationships. Feelings of rage and revenge can lurk behind powerful yearnings for "love."

When sex between therapist and patient occurs, emotional conflicts pervade the relationship. Patients are almost universally dissatisfied with their sexual relationships with therapists because, in part, transference expectations are so conflicted and unrealistic. Patients who are sexually exploited usually are seeking a warm, nurturing relationship. Sex, both in and out of therapy, merely becomes a vehicle for these strong yearnings. Therapists usually experience poor sexual performance because of their own countertransference problems and because of other personal conflicts. Psychoanalyst Frieda Fromm-Reichman reportedly remarked (perhaps facetiously), "Don't have sex with your patients; you will only disappoint them."

Although it is unethical for any physician to engage in sex with his or her patient, mental health professionals hold a special position of responsibility. Unlike the general physician, who works intuitively within the ambit of a positive transference that provides hope and support to the patient, the therapist often works directly with transference phenomena as a therapeutic tool. As a treatment strategy, the therapist may encourage development of the transference, but he or she is expected to keep any countertransference feelings in check for the benefit of the patient's therapy. The very act of intently listening and caring is itself a seductive process for both the patient and the therapist.

Unfortunately, countertransference feelings, particularly those of the erotic variety, have become associated by some therapists with mismanagement of the patients' treatment and are viewed with shame and embarrassment. The works of Winnicott (1949), Heimann (1950), and Little (1951) stimulated a significant literature focused on the principle that countertransference, when properly managed, can be used as a valuable therapeutic tool. The psychiatric literature on this subject emphasizes that ignorance of the therapist's countertransference may harm the therapeutic process and the patient. The concept of transference and countertransference is not a creation of "believers" or clinicians who practice psychodynamic psychotherapy. Boundary violations and patient exploitation are frequently the result of mismanaging the patient's transference and the clinician's countertransference, which suggests that countertransference responses occur in predictable, coherent patterns. Clinicians of all persuasions should identify and appropriately manage countertransference (Betain et al. 2005).

Pope et al. (1986) surveyed 575 psychotherapists and found that 87% (95% men, 76% women) felt sexually attracted to their clients, but only 9.4% of men and 2.5% of women acted out such feelings; 63% felt guilty, anxious, or confused about the attraction. Tower (1956), who termed these feelings *countertransference anxieties,* believed that virtually all therapists experience erotic feelings and impulses toward their patients. The vast majority of respondents (82%) in the study by Pope and colleagues never seriously considered sexual involvement with patients. Reasons given for noninvolvement included that therapist–patient sex was unethical, that it would be countertherapeutic and exploitative, that it was unprofessional, that it was against the therapist's values because of present commitment to a relationship, and that censure and loss of reputation might ensue. This study supports the axiom that "bad men do what good men dream" (Simon 1996).

The issue of patient transference and competency to consent to a sexual relationship with the therapist arises in civil claims and criminal prosecution of therapists (Simon 1994b, 1994c). Although a patient's transference toward the therapist does not prevent the patient from *understanding* that a sexual relationship is taking place with the therapist, transference reactions may impair the patient's ability to *appreciate* that severe psychic injury will likely result from therapist–patient sex. The presence or absence of patient consent, however, is not the issue. It is the breach of fiduciary trust by the therapist that is the appropriate focus of wrongdoing.

A significant number of sexual misconduct cases are not the result of the mishandling of transference or countertransference. Psychotherapists with character disorders manifesting severe narcissistic, borderline, antisocial, or deviant character traits sexually exploit patients (see Tables 10–5). Analogously, patients with severe character disorders may attempt to seduce therapists into having a sexual relationship. Patients who have been abused in the past will likely test treatment boundaries. Nevertheless, the therapist is expected to maintain treatment boundaries with these difficult patients. Patients who are victims of sexual exploitation are not to blame for their therapists' sexual misconduct.

Table 10–5. Personality profile of a typical sexually involved therapist

Age	40s to 50s
Sex	Male
Family constellation	Teenage children, troubled marriage
Medical symptoms	Chronic, not life-threatening
Psychological symptoms	Depression, sleep disturbances, alcohol and drug abuse
Professional practice	"Burned out," ungratifying
Nature of patient	Recent loss, dependent, prior sexual/physical abuse

Sexual Relationships With Patients Whose Therapy Has Been Terminated

The tenet "once a patient, always a patient" describes a prudent approach to relationships with former patients. When patients terminate therapy, a continuing positive transference may help sustain their psychological stability for a lifetime. A posttreatment relationship with the therapist, even a social relationship, may inflame old conflicts that can destabilize the patient. Furthermore, in a crisis, patients may need additional treatment. Therapists should consider adopting a "closed-door policy" that recognizes that once a patient walks through the therapist's door, it is closed forever to a personal relationship.

A number of states impose civil (but not criminal) liability on psychotherapists who engage in sex with former patients (Bisbing et al. 1995). Some recognize a limited cooling-off period after treatment ends (usually 1 or 2 years) during which time sexual relations between the therapist and former patient relations are barred. Because approximately 98% of sexual involvements with patients occur within a year of clinical contact, this prohibitionary period will likely encompass most instances of posttermination sex (Gartrell et al. 1986). Other states provide no bright line for permissible relationships and instead rely on functional, albeit elusive, criteria such as whether the patient remains emotionally dependent on the psychotherapist, and still other states recognize a lifetime prohibition.

Although it may not be illegal for the psychotherapist to have sex with a former patient after expiration of a prohibition period, it still may be unethical. For example, the patient may not have had a therapeutic termination, but rather an interrupted therapy. Ethical violations involving sex with former patients often signal the likely presence of other deviations in care that may have harmed the patient while in treatment. There is no statute of limitations for filing ethical complaints by former patients.

Appelbaum and Jorgenson (1991) proposed a 1-year waiting period after termination that "should minimize problems and allow former patients and therapists to enter into intimate relationships." If adopted, this policy would likely disrupt treatment boundaries from the outset. What deviations in treatment boundaries would occur if the therapist, from the very beginning of treatment, views the patient as a potential sexual partner? Would the therapy become a courtship? Would the course of therapy be prematurely shortened in order to get to the sexual relationship? Even if therapist–patient sex does not take place, maintaining the option of having sex with the patient would likely lead to boundary violations that could harm the patient. Clinically, it is untenable for a therapist to think that he or she can maintain appropriate treatment boundaries while, at the same time, holding out the possibility of having sex with the patient in the future. From the very beginning of treatment, the most credible therapist position remains "once a patient, always a patient."

Management of the Sexually Exploited Patient

Reporting Sexual Misconduct

Reporting the alleged sexual misconduct of other therapists based on the statements of patients is fraught with complex clinical, ethical, and professional dilemmas. Requiring mandatory reporting creates role conflicts for therapists that can undermine treatment interventions with an exploited patient. Some states have mandatory reporting requirements (Bisbing et al. 1995), but in most of these states reporting may not proceed without the patient's consent. Clinical flexibility is required in the treatment and management of sexually exploited patients. When the patient is a therapist who reports that he or she is exploiting patients, does a *Tarasoff* duty arise to warn and protect the therapist's other patients? The conflicting ethical issues surrounding breaching confidentiality as well as potential *Tarasoff* duties arising from the discovery of an offending therapist's *continuing* sexual exploitation are discussed elsewhere (Simon 1992a).

Ethics

The Principles of Medical Ethics With Annotations Especially Applicable to Psychiatry (American Psychiatric Association 2001) advises psychiatrists to "strive to expose those physicians deficient in character or competence" (p. 5, Section 2). In addition, reporting laws that exist in some states require physicians to report impaired colleagues. The burden of reporting information about impaired physicians is most often placed on health care institutions. A number of states, however, place the duty directly on the physician, although this duty varies widely (Petty 1984). The psychiatrist is placed in a potentially conflicting position because he or she is also obligated to maintain patient confidentiality.

This role conflict is heightened if a requirement to report sexual abuse by a therapist collides with a patient's desire that no such disclosure be made. Most reporting statutes require the patient's consent before a report is made to the authorities. Reporting statutes may not contain immunity provisions protecting the reporting therapist against a lawsuit. Forensic and legal consultations may be necessary in these difficult situations.

Discovery of Sexual Misconduct

The initial revelation by a patient of prior therapist–patient sex usually occurs in the course of therapy with a new therapist. Much less commonly, patient sexual exploitation may be reported by the offending therapist who enters treatment either because of sexual involvement with a patient or for other reasons. In the past, such reports from patients were considered to be either transference distortions or outright psychotic transferences. Patients were not only disbelieved but also blamed when they became sexually involved with therapists. Today, professional concern and awareness of the problem of sexual misconduct is very high. In fact, the pendulum has swung so far in the other direction that even the denials of an innocent therapist accused of sexual misconduct tend to be disbelieved. Untruthful protestations of innocence by an offending therapist may be belied by evidence of involvement, such as numerous boundary violations combined with letters, pictures, and telephone and hotel records.

The Patient's Critical Need for Therapy

Some clinicians recommend that the psychiatrist who hears about patient–therapist sex take a strong position as an advocate for the sexually abused patient. Nevertheless, a strong clinical argument can be made for therapist neutrality (Simon 1992b). This position does not suggest an avoidance of professional responsibility or invalidation of the patient's claim. The patient has concluded a relationship with a therapist in which both the therapist and the patient sexually acted out their problems together. The patient is usually harmed and is now in even greater need of treatment.

The new focus with the subsequent therapist must be on the reestablishment of trust and the development of a therapeutic alliance; otherwise, no treatment can take place. The patient needs to understand the psychological significance of the sexual involvement with the previous therapist. When psychiatrists become advocates for their patients, they again engage these patients through action. If treatment is to succeed, the patient needs less action and more time to think, feel, and reflect. Litigation can be just another way of acting out for both patient and therapist. For example, the patient may initiate litigation as a way of maintaining contact with the previous therapist. A therapist's personal agenda usually drives his or her recommendation that the patient pursue litigation.

Avoiding Role Conflicts

Whether the patient should take action against the former therapist should be first addressed as a treatment issue. Therapist neutrality should not be misconstrued as a professional conspiracy to maintain silence. The patient may justifiably fear endangering his or her marriage, profession, or children by reporting therapist sexual misconduct. The patient must eventually decide whether he or she is ready to face the emotional burdens of an ethical complaint procedure or litigation. The law is a blunt instrument with its adversarial tone, financial strain, invalidation, and delays. The patient, at least initially, may not want to seek redress for a variety of reasons, including a sense of guilt or shame as well as continuing feelings of love and yearning for the previous therapist.

Role conflict arises when the patient is burdened with an adversarial procedure because of the therapist's need to vent personal outrage or to advocate the profession's need to police its own ranks. Moreover, a patient may be unable to express hostile feelings toward the new therapist when the latter has taken on an advocacy role for the patient. Accordingly, therapy should be kept as free as possible from role conflict by the new therapist. It is the patient who has been victimized, not the therapist. Therefore, the therapist needs to acknowledge and control his or her personal feelings about the previous therapist's alleged transgressions so as not to interfere with the patient's treatment. Abused patients are revictimized by subsequent therapists who attempt to "rescue" the patient and undo the trauma caused by the initial sexual exploitation. The therapist may bend treatment boundaries to prove his or her trustworthiness to the patient. As a consequence, serious, damaging boundary violations occur.

Guilty or Innocent?

The therapist who acts as an advocate for the patient also needs to ponder other critical issues. Psychiatrists who abandon a position of neutrality when given information about therapist sexual misconduct may find themselves less credible to a judge or jury (Shuman and Greenberg 2003). Clinical experience demonstrates that some patients develop powerful, eroticized, psychotic transferences that contain the delusion (erotomanic type) of sexual involvement with their therapist. Reports of false claims of sexual misconduct against mental health professionals are rare but are expected to increase (Schoener et al. 1989). Presumably, clinical judgment will differentiate fact from fiction, but is this always possible? There are also vindictive, antisocial persons who may wish to malign a therapist with charges of sexual involvement because of actual or perceived slights or grievances.

Forensic Consultation

Stone (1984) provided a useful recommendation for the new therapist faced with a patient alleging sexual exploitation by a former therapist. He advised using a forensic consultant familiar with legal and ethical issues. Such a referral may help patients who cannot resolve their difficulties solely within the therapy. Also, some patients may not be able to tolerate therapist neutrality, perceiving such a stance as condemnatory or rejecting. The consultant may wish to take a more active advocacy position if this is acceptable to the patient. The extent to which a consultant may facilitate or even hinder the patient's therapeutic progress remains problematic. If reporting requirements exist, the forensic consultant may be able to fulfill this duty, thus sparing the therapist from becoming involved in a role conflict with the patient.

Therapy or Litigation?

Will the patient be burdened or benefited by litigation? Do the litigation risks of secondary victimization and secondary gain/malingering outweigh the potential litigation benefits of empowering the patient-litigant or securing funds to continue his or her treatment (Schafran 1996)? Does the patient have realistic expectations about adversary proceedings? Is the patient psychologically stable enough to withstand the demands of litigation? What is the potential impact of the litigation on therapy, including loss of confidentiality, potential of conflicting roles for the therapist, and patient time demands? These are important questions to address in therapy on a case-by-case basis because there is no one right answer.

Malpractice Insurance

Most professional liability insurance carriers seek to exclude civil claims for sexual misconduct under policy language that denies coverage for an intentional tort or criminal behavior. Seeking to include only the risk pool of careless professional mistakes, the insurers maintain that sex is not professional practice and therefore cannot be medical malpractice. The American Psychiatric Association's position of discouraging sexual misconduct has led to dropping coverage for sexual misconduct cases from its member malpractice insurance plan. Often, the liability insurance company will defend the sexual exploitation claim under a reservation of rights and then institute a second action seeking a judicial declaration that the primary action does not fall within the scope of the policy.

Prevention

A number of prevention options are available to the therapist who is becoming personally involved with a patient.

- Recognize the beginning of boundary violations. This may occur when the therapist starts to think that the patient's sexual feelings are directed toward him or her personally rather than created by the role of the therapist. Get consultation or personal therapy.
- Recognize early boundary violations through application of the principle of abstinence. The therapist's gratifications should primarily derive from the enjoyment of the therapeutic process and the psychological growth of the patient rather than obtained directly from the patient.

- If sexual feelings are impairing the therapist's ability to properly treat the patient, or if sexual feelings threaten to be acted out, a consultation should be obtained or the patient should be referred immediately.
- Therapist involvement with a patient usually occurs gradually rather than suddenly. There is usually sufficient time to obtain help. If progressive boundary violations are occurring that cannot be therapeutically rectified, the patient must be immediately referred.
- A trusted colleague should be consulted who, perhaps acting as a mentor, can restore perspective.
- Psychiatric evaluation and psychotherapy should be seriously considered when personal involvement with the patient threatens.
- Therapist humility is essential. Some patients may present special difficulties and personal problems for the therapist. Limitations of the therapist's ability to treat certain patients should be forthrightly acknowledged. It is a strength rather than a weakness to admit that one has personal and psychotherapeutic limitations. These patients should be referred.
- If the therapist is stricken by the physical beauty or attractive personal qualities of a new patient, serious consideration should be given to not undertaking the patient's treatment. The initial "Where have you been all my life?" reaction to a patient is a certain sign of future trouble. Psychotherapy is difficult enough without such burdensome feelings.
- Mishandling of the transference is an occupational hazard for all psychotherapists. Be alert.
- Countertransference-driven parental roles with patients are doomed to fail. Attempts at reparenting patients do not cure; they merely cast a spell. The task of therapy is not to create an illusion of well-being but to help patients mourn their losses and move on with their lives (Simon 1994b, 1994c). Omar Khayyam's powerful passage from *The Rubaiyat* (Khayyam 2003) reminds us that we cannot rewrite our histories:

> The Moving Finger writes; and having writ
> Moves on: nor all your Piety nor Wit
> Shall lure it back to cancel half a Line,
> Nor all your Tears wash out a Word of it.
> (stanza 71)

- When a therapist attempts to parent the patient, a variety of boundary violations often occur that usually damage treatment. Patient exploitation may be an unintended consequence of the therapist's reparenting role as she or he becomes hopelessly enmeshed in the patient's life.
- Exploitation of patients is not limited to sex. Exploitation of patients occurs as frequently for money, "insider information," social contacts, personal services, and friendship, to list just a few.

The practice of psychiatry can be a lonely, difficult, isolated specialty. Solo practitioners may have infrequent contact with colleagues. A full life acts as a buffer against temptations to exploit patients by providing the therapist with personal gratifications outside of therapy. Love relationships, friends, hobbies, recreation, and physical activities may help vulnerable therapists resist the tendency to live for or with their patients.

References

American Psychiatric Association: The Principles of Medical Ethics With Annotations Especially Applicable to Psychiatry. Washington, DC, American Psychiatric Association, 2001

Appelbaum PS: Statutes regulating patient–therapist sex. Hosp Community Psychiatry 41:15–16, 1990

Appelbaum PS, Jorgenson L: Psychotherapist–patient sexual contact after termination of treatment: an analysis and a proposal. Am J Psychiatry 148:1466–1473, 1991

Betain E, Heim AK, Conklin CA, et al: Countertransference phenomena and personality pathology in clinical practice: an empirical investigation. Am J Psychiatry 162:890–898, 2005

Bisbing SB, Jorgenson LM, Sutherland PK: Sexual Abuse by Professionals: A Legal Guide. Charlottesville, VA, Michie, 1995

Borys DS, Pope KS: Dual relationships between therapist and client: a national study of psychologists, psychiatrists, and social workers. Prof Psychol Res Pr 20:283–293, 1989

Epstein RS, Simon RI: The Exploitation Index: an early warning indicator of boundary violations in psychotherapy. Bull Menninger Clin 54:450–465, 1990

Epstein RS, Simon RI, Kay GG: Assessing boundary violations in psychotherapy: survey results with the Exploitation Index. Bull Menninger Clin 56:1–17, 1992

Freud S: Observations on transference-love (1914), in The Standard Edition of the Complete Psychological Works of Sigmund Freud, Vol 12. Translated and edited by Strachey J. London, Hogarth, 1968, pp 159–171

Gartrell N, Herman J, Olarte S, et al: Psychiatrist–patient sexual contact. Results of a national survey, I: prevalence. Am J Psychiatry 143:1126–1131, 1986

Gutheil TG, Simon RI: Between the chair and the door: boundary issues in the therapeutic "transition zone." Harv Rev Psychiatry 2:336–340, 1995

Gutheil TG, Simon RI: Non-sexual boundary crossings and boundary violations: the ethical dimension. Psychiatr Clin North Am 25:585–592, 2002

Heimann P: On countertransference. Int J Psychoanal 31:81–84, 1950

Khayyam O: The rubaiyat, in Poetry for the Spirit: An Original Anthology of Insightful Poems. Translated by Fitzgerald E. NY, Barnes and Noble Books, 2003, pp 73–74

Little M: Countertransference and the patient's response to it. Int J Psychoanal 32:32–40, 1951

Petty S: The impaired physician: a failed healer. Leg Aspects Med Pract 12:5–8, 1984

Pope KS: Sexual Involvement With Therapists: Patient Assessment, Subsequent Therapy, Forensics. Washington, DC, American Psychological Association, 1994, pp 152–153

Pope KS, Keith-Spiegel P, Tabachnick BG: Sexual attraction to clients. Am Psychol 41:147–158, 1986

Schafran LH: Sexual harassment cases in the courts, or therapy goes to war: supporting a sexual harassment victim during litigation, in Sexual Harassment in the Workplace and Academia. Edited by Shrier DK. Washington, DC, American Psychiatric Press, 1996, pp 133–152

Schoener GR, Milgrom JH, Gonsiorek JC, et al: Psychotherapists' Sexual Involvement With Clients: Intervention and Prevention. Minneapolis, MN, Walk-In Counseling Center, 1989, pp 147–155

Shuman DW, Greenberg SA: The expert witness, the adversary system, and the voice of reason: reconciling impartiality and advocacy. Prof Psychol 34:219–224, 2003

Simon RI: Sexual exploitation of patients: how it begins before it happens. Psychiatr Ann 19:104–112, 1989

Simon RI: Psychological injury caused by boundary violation precursors to therapist–patient sex. Psychiatr Ann 21:614–619, 1991

Simon RI: Clinical Psychiatry and the Law, 2nd Edition. Washington, DC, American Psychiatric Press, 1992a

Simon RI: Treatment boundary violations: clinical, ethical, and legal considerations. Bull Am Acad Psychiatry Law 20:269–288, 1992b

Simon RI: Innovative psychiatric therapies and legal uncertainty: a survival guide for clinicians. Psychiatr Ann 23:473-49, 1993

Simon RI: Sexual misconduct in the therapist–patient relationship, in Forensic Psychiatry: A Comprehensive Textbook. Edited by Rosner R. New York, Chapman and Hall, 1994a, pp 154–161

Simon RI: Transference in therapist–patient sex: the illusion of patient improvement and consent, part 1. Psychiatr Ann 24:509–515, 1994b

Simon RI: Transference in therapist–patient sex: the illusion of patient improvement and consent, part 2. Psychiatr Ann 24:561–565, 1994c

Simon RI: The natural history of therapist sexual misconduct: identification and prevention. Psychiatr Ann 25:90–94, 1995

Simon RI: Bad Men Do What Good Men Dream: A Forensic Psychiatrist Illuminates the Darker Side of Human Behavior. Washington DC, American Psychiatric Press, 1996

Simon RI, Williams I: Maintaining treatment boundaries in small communities and rural areas. Psychiatr Serv 50:1440–1446, 1999

Stone AA: Law, Psychiatry, and Morality. Washington, DC, American Psychiatric Press, 1984, pp 191–216

The College of Physicians and Surgeons of Ontario: The Final Report of the Task Force on Sexual Abuse of Patients: An Independent Task Force Commissioned by The College of Physicians and Surgeons of Ontario. Ontario, Canada, The College of Physicians and Surgeons of Ontario, 1991

Tower LE: Countertransference. J Am Psychoanal Assoc 4:224–255, 1956

Winnicott D: Hate in the countertransference. Int J Psychoanal 30:69–75, 1949

Legal References

Figueiredo-Torres v. Nickel, 321 Md. 642, 584 A.2d 69 (Md., 1990)

Hare v Wendler, 263 Kan. 434, 949 P.2d 1141 (Kan., 1997)

Roy v Hartogs, 81 Misc.2d 350, 366 N.Y.S.2d 297 (N.Y. City Civ.Ct., 1975), aff'd. 381 N.Y.S.2d 587 (1976)

Tarasoff v Regents of the University of California, 17 Cal.3d 425; 551 P.2d 334 (Cal. Rptr. 14, 1976)

United States v. Willis, 737 F.Supp. 269 (S.D.N.Y. 1990)

Laws

Cal. Bus. & Prof. Code § 2960.1 (2006)

Cal Civ. Code § 43.93 (2006)

Fla. Stat. §458.329 (2005)

Minn. Stat. § 147.091, 147.141 (2005)
Minn. Stat. §148A.02 (2005)
Minn. Stat. § 148A.03 (2005)
Minn Stat. Ann. § 148A.02 West Supp. (2005)
Minn. Stat. Ann. § 609.344 (2005)
Ohio O.R.C. Ann. § 2305.111 (2006) § 2305.11 of the Revised Code
Tex. Civ. Prac. & Rem. Code § 81.002 (2005)
Va. Code § 54.1-2915(19) (2006)
Wis. Stat. § 895.70 (2006)
Wis. Stat. § 940.22 (2006)

Appendix A

Suggested Readings

American Psychiatric Association: The Principles of Medical Ethics With Annotations Especially Applicable to Psychiatry. Washington, DC, American Psychiatric Association, 2001

Appelbaum PS, Gutheil TG: Clinical Handbook of Psychiatry and the Law, 3rd Edition. Baltimore, MD, Williams & Wilkins, 2000

Grisso T: Evaluating Competencies: Forensic Assessments and Instruments, 2nd Edition. New York, Kluwer Academic/Plenum Publishers, 2003

Lifson LE, Simon RI (eds): The Mental Health Professional and the Law: A Comprehensive Handbook. Cambridge, MA, Harvard University Press, 1998

Melton GB, Petrila J, Poythress NG, et al: Psychological Evaluation for the Courts, 2nd Edition. New York, Guilford, 1997

Monahan J, Steadman HJ, Silver E, et al: Rethinking Risk Assessment: The MacArthur Study of Mental Disorder and Violence. New York, Oxford, 2001

Morris R, Sales BD, Shuman DW: Doing Legal Research: A Guide for Social Scientists and Mental Health Professionals. Thousand Oaks, CA, Sage, 1996

Perlin M: The Hidden Prejudice: Mental Disability on Trial. Washington, DC, American Psychological Association, 2000

Poythress NG Jr, Bonnie RJ, Monahan J, et al (eds): Adjudicative Competence: The MacArthur Studies (Perspectives in Law & Psychology, Vol 15). New York, Kluwer Academic/Plenum Publishers, 2002

Quinsey VL, Harris GT, Rice ME, et al: Violent Offenders: Appraising and Managing Risk. Washington, DC, American Psychological Association, 1998

Rogers R, Shuman DW: Fundamentals of Forensic Practice: Mental Health and Criminal Law. New York, Springer, 2005

Sales BD, Shuman DW: Experts in Court: Accommodating Law, Science and Expert Knowledge. Washington, DC, American Psychological Association, 2005

Schoener GR, Milgrom JH, Gonsiorek JC, et al: Psychotherapists' Sexual Involvement With Clients: Intervention and Prevention. Minneapolis, MN, Walk-In Counseling Center, 1989

Shuman DW: Psychiatric and Psychological Evidence, 3rd Edition. Cleveland, OH, Thomson/West, 2005

Simon RI: Assessing and Managing Suicide Risk: Guidelines for Clinically Based Risk Management. Washington, DC, American Psychiatric Publishing, 2004

Simon RI, Gold LH (eds): American Psychiatric Publishing Textbook of Forensic Psychiatry. Washington, DC, American Psychiatric Publishing, 2004

Simon RI, Hales RE (eds): American Psychiatric Publishing Textbook of Suicide Assessment and Management. Washington, DC, American Psychiatric Publishing, 2006

Simon RI, Shuman DW: Predicting the Past: The Retrospective Psychiatric Assessment of Mental States in Litigation. Washington, DC, American Psychiatric Publishing, 2002

Slobogin C: Minding Justice: Laws That Deprive People With Mental Disability of Life and Liberty. Cambridge, MA, Harvard University, 2006

Slovenko R: Psychotherapy and Confidentiality: Testimonial Privileged Communication, Breach of Confidentiality, and Reporting Duties. Springfield, IL, Charles C. Thomas, 1998

Slovenko R: Psychiatry in Law. Law in Psychiatry. New York, Brunner-Routledge, 2002

Stefan S: Emergency Department Treatment of the Psychiatric Patient: Policy Issues and Legal Requirements. New York, Oxford University Press, 2006

Glossary of Legal Terms

Action   See civil action.

Adjudication   The formal pronouncement of a judgment or decree in a cause of action.

Assault   Any willful attempt or threat to inflict injury.

Battery   Intentional and wrongful physical contact with an individual without consent that causes some injury or offensive touching.

Beyond a reasonable doubt   The level of proof required to convict a person in a criminal trial. This is the highest level of proof required (90%–95% range of certainty).

Breach of contract   A violation of or failure to perform any or all of the terms of an agreement.

Brief   A written statement prepared by legal counsel arguing a case.

Burden of proof   The legal obligation to prove affirmatively a disputed fact (or facts) related to an issue that is raised by the parties in a case.

Capacity   The status or attributes necessary for a person so that his or her acts may be legally and responsibly acknowledged and recognized.

Case law   The aggregate of reported cases as forming a body of law on a particular subject.

Cause of action   The grounds of an action—that is, those facts that, if alleged and proved in a suit, would enable the plaintiff to attain a judgment.

Cause in fact   Refers to the requirement of fact that without the defendant's wrongful conduct, the harm to the plaintiff would not have occurred.

Civil action   A lawsuit brought by a private individual or group to recover money or property, to enforce or protect a civil right, or to prevent or redress a civil wrong.

Civil law   As contrasted with criminal law, refers to a system for enforcement of private rights arising from sources such as torts and contracts.

Clear and convincing   Proof that results in reasonable certainty of the truth of an ultimate fact in controversy (75% range of certainty). For example, the minimum level of evidence necessary to involuntarily hospitalize a patient.

Common law   A system of law based on customs, traditional usage, and prior case law rather than codified written laws (statutes).

Compensatory damages   Damages awarded to a person as compensation, indemnity, or restitution for harm sustained.

Competency   Having the mental capacity to understand the nature of an act.

Consent decree   Agreement by a defendant to cease activities asserted as illegal by the government.

Consortium   The right of a husband or wife to the care, affection, company, and cooperation of the other spouse in every aspect of the marital relationship.

Contract   A legally enforceable agreement between two or more parties to do or not do a particular thing upon sufficient consideration.

Criminal law   The branch of the law that defines crimes and provides for their punishment. Unlike civil law, penalties include imprisonment.

Damages   A sum of money awarded to a person injured by the unlawful act or negligence of another.

Defendant   A person or legal entity against whom a claim or charge is brought.

Due process (of law)   The constitutional guarantee protecting individuals from arbitrary and unreasonable actions by the government that would deprive them of their basic rights to life, liberty, or property.

Duress   Compulsion or constraint, as by force or threat, exercised to make a person do or say something against his or her will.

Duty   Legal obligation that one person owes another. Whenever one person has a right, another person has a corresponding duty to preserve or not interfere with that right.

False imprisonment   The unlawful restraint or detention of one person by another.

Fiduciary   A person who acts for another in a capacity that involves a confidence or trust.

Forensic psychiatry   A subspecialty of psychiatry in which scientific and clinical expertise is applied to legal issues in legal contexts embracing civil, criminal, correctional, or legislative matters.

Fraud   Any act of trickery, deceit, or misrepresentation designed to deprive someone of property or to do harm.

Guardianship   A legal arrangement wherein one individual (the guardian) possesses the legal right and duty to care for another individual (the ward) and his or her property.

Hold harmless   An agreement to protect a party from damages.

Immunity   Freedom from duty or penalty.

Incompetence   A lack of ability or fitness for some legal qualification necessary for the performance of an act (e.g., being a minor, or mental incompetence).

Informed consent   A competent person's voluntary agreement to allow something to happen that is based upon full disclosure of facts needed to make a knowing decision.

Intentional tort   A tort in which the actor is expressly or implicitly judged to have possessed an intent or purpose to cause injury.

Judgment   The final determination or adjudication by a court of the claims of parties in an action.

Jurisdiction   Widely used to denote the legal right by which courts or judicial officers exercise their authority.

Malpractice   Any professional misconduct or unreasonable lack of skill in professional or fiduciary duties.

Miranda warning   Refers to the *Miranda v. Arizona* decision that requires a four-part warning to be given prior to any custodial interrogation.

Negligence   The failure to exercise the standard of care that would be expected of a normally reasonable and prudent person in a particular set of circumstances.

Nominal damages   Generally, damages of a small monetary amount indicating a violation of a legal right without any important loss or damage to the plaintiff.

Parens patriae   The authority of the state to exercise sovereignty and guardianship of a person of legal disability so as to act on his or her behalf in protecting health, comfort, and welfare interests.

Plaintiff   The complaining party in an action; person who brings a cause of action.

Police power   The power of government to make and enforce all laws and regulations necessary for the welfare of the state and its citizens.

Power of attorney   A document giving someone authority to act on behalf of grantor.

Preponderance of evidence   Superiority in the weight of evidence presented by one side over that of the other (51% range of certainty). The level of certainty required in order to prevail in civil trials.

Privileged communication   Those statements made by certain persons within a protected relationship (e.g., doctor–patient) that the law protects from forced disclosure.

Proximate cause   The direct, immediate cause to which an injury or loss can be attributed and without which the injury or loss would not have occurred.

Proxy   A person empowered by another to represent, act, or vote for him or her.

Punitive damages   Damages awarded over and above those to which the plaintiff is entitled, generally given to punish or make an example of the defendant.

Respondeat superior   The doctrine whereby the master (i.e., employer) is strictly liable in certain cases for the wrongful acts of his or her servants (i.e., employees).

Right   A power, privilege, demand, or claim possessed by a particular person by virtue of law. Every legal right that one person possesses imposes corresponding legal duties on other persons.

Sovereign immunity   The immunity of a government from being sued in court except with its consent.

Standard of care (negligence law)   In the law of negligence, that degree of care which a reasonably prudent person should exercise under the same or similar circumstances.

Stare decisis   To adhere to precedents and not to unsettle principles of law that are established.

Statute   An act of the legislature declaring, commanding, or prohibiting something.

Subpoena   A writ commanding a person to appear in court.

Subpoena ad testificandum   A writ commanding a person to appear in court to give testimony.

Subpoena duces tecum   A writ commanding a person to appear in court with particular documents or other evidence.

Tort   Any private or civil wrong by act or omission, not including breach of contract.

United States Code (U.S.C.)   The compilation of laws derived from federal legislation.

Vicarious liability   (See *respondeat superior*.)

Index

Page numbers printed in **boldface** type refer to tables or figures.